PLAYING OUR GAME

EDWARD S. STEINFELD

PLAYING OUR GAME

*Why China's Economic Rise Doesn't
Threaten the West*

OXFORD
UNIVERSITY PRESS

2010

OXFORD
UNIVERSITY PRESS

Oxford University Press, Inc., publishes works that further
Oxford University's objective of excellence
in research, scholarship, and education.

Oxford   New York
Auckland   Cape Town   Dar es Salaam   Hong Kong   Karachi
Kuala Lumpur   Madrid   Melbourne   Mexico City   Nairobi
New Delhi   Shanghai   Taipei   Toronto

With offices in
Argentina   Austria   Brazil   Chile   Czech Republic   France   Greece
Guatemala   Hungary   Italy   Japan   Poland   Portugal   Singapore
South Korea   Switzerland   Thailand   Turkey   Ukraine   Vietnam

Copyright © 2010 by Edward S. Steinfeld

Published by Oxford University Press, Inc.
198 Madison Avenue, New York, NY 10016

www.oup.com

Oxford is a registered trademark of Oxford University Press

Library of Congress Cataloging-in-Publication Data
Steinfeld, Edward S. (Edward Saul), 1966–
Playing our game : why China's rise doesn't threaten the west / Edward S. Steinfeld.
p.   cm.
Includes bibliographical references and index.
ISBN 978-0-19-539065-0
1. China—Economic conditions—21st century.
2. China—Foreign economic relations—United States.
3. United States—Foreign economic relations—China.
I. Title.
HC427.95.S74 2010
330.951—dc22   2009052386

1 3 5 7 9 8 6 4 2

Printed in the United States of America
on acid-free paper

TO MY PARENTS,
BARBARA AND LEONARD STEINFELD

Contents

Acknowledgments

TWO THINGS TRUE of all books: They never get written as fast as the author would like, and they always depend on more help than could ever be adequately acknowledged. This book is no different. For me, being an academic is all about being the ultimate student, a person continually graced by the unstinting generosity of all manner of teachers. Some of those individuals have been my "official" teachers, my professional mentors and colleagues. Others have been unofficial teachers, people who, frequently through their participation in field interviews, have helped me to understand the world through their own privileged lenses. Still others have been my own students, budding scholars who through their brilliance, their questions, and their fresh perspectives have profoundly influenced my views. I cannot mention each and every one of those teachers here, both because the list of names would be endless, and because some of those individuals, for reasons political or otherwise, prefer to remain anonymous. Nonetheless, I am grateful to all of them. They have provided generously, and never asked for anything in return. This book could never have been written without them.

I would like to take the opportunity, though, to thank a few of my teachers by name. Through the course of this project, the MIT Department of Political Science and the MIT Industrial Performance Center have served as intellectual homes. At those venues I have had the honor of learning from a wonderful set of colleagues, particularly Suzanne Berger, Richard Lester, Richard Locke, Michael Piore, Richard Samuels, Barry Posen, Stephen VanEvera, Charles Sodini, Tayo Akinwande, and Timothy Sturgeon. At MIT I have also had the good fortune to be surrounded by an extraordinary team of fellow China specialists: Yasheng Huang, Lily Tsai, Taylor Fravel, and the late—and incomparable—Lucian Pye. Several of my current and former students at MIT—co-researchers, really—have deeply influenced the ideas presented in this book. I particularly want to thank Edward Cunningham, George Gilboy, Douglas Fuller, Danny Breznitz, Jonas Nahm, Kyoung Shin, Gao Xudong, and Greg Distelhorst.

Moving slightly farther afield geographically, through the course of this project I continued to benefit immeasurably from the mentorship of my teachers at Harvard: Roderick MacFarquhar, Dwight Perkins, Ezra Vogel, and Tony Saich. And still farther away, but no less crucial, I have benefited tremendously from extensive interactions—and often extended stays—at Peking University's China Center for Economic Research (where I would particularly like to thank Professors Justin Yifu Lin, Yi Gang, Hai Wen, Yao Yang, and Hu Dayuan), Tsinghua University's School of Economics and Management (where I particularly benefited from the guidance of former dean Zhao Chunjun), and Tsinghua's School of Public Policy and Management (where I would like to thank Professor Xue Lan).

A number of other scholars, policy makers, and business practitioners have been unfailingly generous in sharing their wisdom. I would like to mention in particular Ambassador Chas. Freeman, Ambassador Erwin Schurtenberger, Douglas Steinfeld, Professor Peter Nolan (University of Cambridge), Professor Ashutosh Varshney (Brown University), the late Professor Ellis Joffe (Hebrew University), and Dr. Mark Qiu.

This project could never have been completed without financial support of a number of organizations and agencies. Crucial portions of the research were supported by grants from the following: the MIT Sloan School of Management China Program (where I am especially grateful for the steadfast support of Senior Associate Dean Alan White), the MIT Industrial Performance Center's Project on Globalization, the MIT Study on the Future of Coal, and the Essonne Development Agency of the Government of France (where I would particularly like to thank Mr. Thierry Mandon).

The book itself would never have come to fruition without the guidance and advice of Lynn Franklin. At Oxford University Press, I am indebted to David McBride, Keith Faivre, and all their staffers who worked tirelessly in speeding the manuscript through the publication process.

My teachers are spread across the world. Some of the most important ones, however, are those nearest at hand, my family. My wife, Zhuqing, a scholar with plenty of professional responsibilities of her own (all while being a fully engaged mom), has been an unfailingly generous intellectual companion, sounding board, and cheerleader. So too have my sons, Daniel and William, who have never stopped asking questions and coming up with interpretations as they've traveled the world through the course of this project. My great hope is to be to them the kind of teacher that my own parents, Barbara and Leonard Steinfeld, have been to me. It is to them—my first teachers, of course— that I dedicate this book.

PLAYING OUR GAME

ONE

The Quiet Revolution

1989 to 2009: Two Decades, One Quantum Leap

In the summer of 1989, I arrived in China for a one-year stay as a visiting faculty member at a major Chinese university. Two decades have passed since then, a blink of the eye in the grand sweep of things. Yet, the China of twenty years ago is so far removed from the present as to feel like a distant dream, a sort of alternate universe to what we witness today. Had you in 1989 predicted that China twenty years down the road would look the way it does today, you would have been laughed from the room and with good reason. The things we take for granted in present-day rising China—the phenomenal growth rates, the high levels of exports, the vast foreign exchange reserves, and the sheer robustness of the system even in the face of serious worldwide recession—extraordinary though they may be, are the least of it. These are but surface manifestations of far deeper changes in China's social, political, and economic core. Chinese society in its most fundamental relationships—that between citizen and state, citizen and economy, and citizen and fellow citizen—has undergone a profound revolution. That revolution, China's capitalist embrace, is the subject of this book.

The Waning Days of Totalitarianism

As I try to make sense of the contemporary scene, I often find myself thinking back to the summer of 1989. In June of that year, the Chinese government had violently and decisively quelled a popular uprising, a movement that for all its jumbled causes and motivations unquestionably pitted itself against the ruling party-state. Although the violent suppression was confined primarily to the capital, the political crackdown, like the popular uprising it targeted, extended across the nation. In its wake—figuratively if not literally—was left the smoking ruins of a deeply wounded society. Engulfed in the inescapable pall of governmental crackdown, China's urban citizens, almost all of whom had been caught up in the carnival-like protests of the previous spring, were left emotionally drained and spiritually defeated. By the late summer of 1989, the prevailing feeling was one less of terror than profound demoralization. The nation appeared dead in the water.

For all its uncertainties, life that autumn took on an apathetic, enervated quality. People kept their heads down and returned to normal work routines. They minded their own business as they waited nervously for the next shoe to drop in the deepening crackdown. Guarded in their conversations with one another, they were left mostly on their own to ponder questions of both personal and national import. "How far will the crackdown go?" "Will it make it to my door?" "What price am I going to pay for all I said and did months earlier?" Given how widespread the protests had been, virtually everyone was implicated and everyone was culpable. Even those who had done nothing felt they had done something.

For many people at the time, watching the seven P.M. nationwide television news broadcast became a sort of daily ritual. Night after night, benumbed citizens would tune in to see their premier, Li Peng, stridently upholding the banner of socialism, pledging to cede no ground to malign forces of liberalization, and vowing to apprehend those who had sought to sow disorder. Following such speeches would often be a broadcast of the most wanted list, an airing of official identification photographs—grainy portraits extracted from students IDs, citizen registration forms, and workplace IDs—for those being hunted down as leaders of the counterrevolutionary movement.

In the waning months of 1989, so much seemed to be moving forward elsewhere in the world. Truly wild things were happening: the dismantling of the Berlin Wall, the disintegration of the Iron Curtain, and the birth of democracies across Eastern Europe. All this followed closely on the heels of democratization in the Philippines and South Korea. In China, though, the only movement seemed to be in reverse. While the rest of the world hurtled forward with giddy enthusiasm, Chinese citizens were offered little more than televised manhunts for teenage college students and a defiantly backward-looking ideology of no's: no liberalization, no spiritual pollution, no peaceful evolution from socialism, no capitalism, and on and on. To its domestic audience in 1989, the state offered a clenched fist and wagging finger. To those abroad, Beijing turned its back, vowing that although reform might be for others—Gorbachev's Soviet Union, the countries of Eastern Europe, and anybody else foolhardy enough to tempt the forces of dissolution—the Chinese government would hold the line. And as Eastern Europe captured the world's imagination with its heady revolution, the world turned its attention away from China. The future so clearly lay elsewhere.

The predicament for Chinese society at that time, though, went deeper than just the crackdown. Officially by this point, the policy of "reform and opening" (*gaige kaifang*) had already been under way for ten years. Yet, for the ordinary urban citizen, so much seemed not to have changed. The whole country felt mired down, incorrigibly stuck. Visitors to China twenty years ago could not help noticing a singular feature of Chinese cities: their darkness. Urban centers at the time had very limited public lighting, logically enough, for there was precious little activity worth illuminating. A scant few stores existed, and almost all shut down early. Service establishments—restaurants, noodle shops, teahouses—were virtually nonexistent. The opening of a private dumpling shop, no matter how ramshackle, was cause for great curiosity in late 1980s urban China. A place to go out to eat! Something to do! Something new to try!

Stores, such as they were, were state owned and idiosyncratically stocked. Of the smaller shops that existed, most were just streetfront experiments in retail set up by the state factories and industrial establishments occupying the underlying premises. Their primary mission, which was taken up less than enthusiastically by the unfortunates assigned to work there, appeared to involve peddling their parent factory's surplus output. A few consumer knickknacks would also usually find their way onto the shelves. As a result, one would find these establishments selling the oddest combinations of merchandise: ballpoint pens and lathes, badminton birdies and sewer piping, eating utensils and engine lubricants.

Although perhaps trivial, such combinations pointed to a pervasive reality. This system was never intended to foster the kinds of transactions we take for granted in modern life. Nowhere to be found were the sort of relationships upon which modern-day markets, communities, and social networks are built. Indeed, urban Chinese society at the time was expressly structured to *impede* entrepreneurship, enterprise, civic interaction, and even the movement of people more broadly. It was a society thoroughly confined within a state-determined institutional hierarchy, a chain of command that extended from the heights of the party-state bureaucracy to the depths of the ordinary citizen's place of employment.

Contrary to the freewheeling world of the marketplace, this was a realm of verticality and control, a society structured at its most elemental level by the state-controlled work unit (*danwei*).[1] Citizens were assigned to these units, these places of employment, by the state. Even the privileged—college students, for example, on the verge of graduation—were assigned to units from a list handed down through the state allocation system. This assignment (*fenpei*), carried out in the case of college students by the department in which they majored, was fraught with import. It determined everything: one's job, one's city of residence, one's social circle, one's career prospects, and one's entire life trajectory more or less. It was a sentence as much as an assignment. Once assigned to an employer—generally, a state-owned factory, school, or governmental administrative organ—the citizen remained under that employer's jurisdiction, with only a few exceptions, for life. He or she was housed by that employer, cared for medically by that employer, and politically monitored by that employer. Almost anything the citizen might hope to do—marry, buy a ticket for travel to another city, apply for a passport, move from a dormitory into an apartment, and so on—was contingent upon receiving the employer's official approval.

Life under such circumstances was not about acquiring things in the marketplace or navigating through horizontal networks of acquaintances. It was about struggling from the bottom up against a maddeningly inflexible, utterly indifferent, and totally overtaxed state hierarchy.

This was more than just a political hierarchy, though. It was also an economic hierarchy inextricably linked with the logic of socialist command planning. The work unit, with all its restrictions and responsibilities, integrally supported the entire system of state-determined prices, state-controlled allocation of material goods, state-enforced scarcities, and state-determined goals of forced-draft industrialization.[2] The unit, then, was not only the place in which the citizen's life was lived and his or her social circle was confined. It was also the end of the chain, the grassroots manifestation of the intertwined political and economic hierarchies defining Chinese socialism.

For the individual citizen, existence within one of these units amounted to a sort of cellular life, "cellular" not in terms of the omnipresent mobile phones so characteristic of present-day Chinese life but rather in terms of the physical walls that characterized so much of China through even the 1990s. Work units—whether schools, factories, or hospitals—were surrounded by high-perimeter walls (*weiqiang*). Contained within these walls were not just production facilities but also housing blocs, dormitories, canteens, clinics, and stores. The physical walls of the workplace defined the community within which one's life unfolded. It was from within those walls that you likely found your spouse, made your friends (and enemies), raised your children, got into and out of trouble, and negotiated your way through the political campaigns your employer administered as an arm of the state.

This system was about more than suppressed wealth or stifled opportunity. It was about more than the absence of stuff to buy, things to do, or places to go. Fundamentally, it was about a kind of enforced subordination, a kind of one-sided social contract between citizen and state that for all its tedium and blandness supplanted so many of the social relationships we view as intrinsic to modern life. In their residences, for example, people did not generally have telephones because telephones were allocated by the unit in only exceptional circumstances and always on the basis of status. But then again, people did not have the kind of extended circle of friends—whether in different jobs, different professions, or different neighborhoods, let alone distant cities—to whom a call might conceivably be directed. One's community was defined not by one's own preferences or interests but instead by a state-determined, employment-centered boundary.

Under such circumstances, the social contract, if it can be termed that, was straightforward. The state ruled, and the citizen obeyed. The state reached into the citizen's life and meted out basic daily necessities, and the citizen coped, often by competing against peers for the few crumbs of opportunity that made their way downward through the system. And finally, by locking citizens into walled-off, state-controlled workplace communities, the state ensured that daily life would remain subject to the mandates of a political hierarchy. The social and the economic, in essence, would always remain subordinate to the political.

By the late 1980s, the era of the heated, Maoist-style mass campaign was already dead and buried. The era of enforced obedience, however, was decidedly not. For the ordinary citizen in the summer of 1989, then, how despairing it was in the aftermath of Tiananmen to hear the powers that be offer nothing but paeans to past socialist glories and threats against present-day doubters. The leadership vowed defiance against the forces of liberalization. The citizenry, meanwhile, confined at the bottom of a massive state apparatus, had no out, no exit option.

Beyond the Revolution:
Post-totalitarian China

Now, jump forward twenty years. What a different world we find in Chinese cities. Bursting at the seams with new skyscrapers, new public transportation systems, and new public facilities, they look nothing like they did just years ago. Streets abound with stores and restaurants. Commerce can be found virtually everywhere and at any time. The physical remake, though, is the least of it. China's cities, even in the present economic downturn, vibrate with activity. That they do—that yesterday's grinding torpor has been replaced by today's frenetic buzz—is possible only because fundamental social change has taken place. Somehow, forces of liberalization have managed to run rampant. What that means, though, goes well beyond new attitudes or new degrees of permissiveness. The very structure of society itself, at its most elemental level, has become completely transformed.

At the heart of these changes is the disappearance of the socialist work unit. That which twenty years ago so shaped Chinese socialism—that which defined neighborhoods, social networks, and political life—is now thoroughly extinct. One day it seemed to determine everything. The next day it was gone. Revolution had occurred with nary a shot fired, a barricade mounted, or a manifesto proclaimed.

Employment figures, while not explaining how or why this happened, give a sense of what was involved. In 1978, roughly 80 percent of China's urban residents were employed in state firms—basically, traditional work units. The rest, often living in the traditional state units that employed other members of their immediate family, worked in collectives, smaller scale firms owned by local government. Private firms were nonexistent. By 1990, the figures had not changed all that much: 60 percent of urban residents were still employed in state units, 20 percent in collectives, and a smattering in nascent private firms. The state unit still shaped the core of urban life. By 2007, however, a different world had come into being. A wide variety of employer types had burgeoned forth: private firms, limited liability firms, sole proprietorships, foreign-invested firms, wholly foreign-owned firms, and new state firms, among others. Only about a quarter of residents by this point were still working in state-owned or collective enterprises, but even these relatively traditional employers had shed the work-unit functions of yore.[3] The key point is that in today's China, the vast preponderance of urban citizens are employed outside the state sector.

Think, for a moment, what this means. For a private or foreign-owed firm to come into being, it has to hire workers. For even something as simple as that to happen, though, workers have to be mobile. They somehow have to be separated from long-standing practices of involuntary job assignment and lifetime attachment to the (state-owned) firm. In essence, a labor market has to develop. At the same time, workers being redeployed by these labor markets still have to be housed. Housing, then, rather than being monopolized by a handful of state-owned firms, has to be made available through another set of markets. Of course, for such housing markets to grow, they have to be supported by additional institutions like ownership rights, financing mechanisms for buyers, and rules for property transfer. Along similar lines, newly mobile workers still need health care, so health care must be detached from the state-owned firm and allocated on some other basis. As happened in China's case, markets would develop here too, with health care in today's ostensibly socialist China provided mostly on a fee-for-service basis and with very limited availability of insurance.[4]

Many economists argue that new enterprise starts, the number of new businesses created, are not just an indicator of economic robustness but really a key precondition for growth, especially in developing countries.[5] China over the past twenty years has realized extraordinary gains in this area. But for that to have happened, a whole series of markets had to cascade into place. Moreover, they had to *replace* mechanisms of allocation that, at least for the citizen, tightly linked socialist-style material provision with extensive political and social control. In essence, economic change meant political and social change as well.

From Maoism to...Reaganism

For many Chinese, these changes were at once liberating and unsettling. What is so interesting is that the changes, and the populace's response to them, bear a certain resemblance to phenomena that have unfolded in the United States in recent decades. China, of course, as a nation still undergoing basic industrialization and urbanization is in a very different situation from the United States, not to mention being somewhere between eight and sixteen times poorer than the United States in per capita terms, depending on how the exact calculation is done.[6] Nonetheless, populations in both countries in recent decades have experienced a roughly comparable series of work-life changes: the disappearance of traditional jobs in manufacturing, the replacement of lifetime employment by flexible employment, the decline of employer-provided benefits, the rise of home ownership, and the rise of self-financing for health care.[7] Looking only at what happened on the ground, one could be forgiven for believing that the Reagan or Thatcherite revolution found its truest adherents in socialist China.

Workplace change in China unfolded quickly and in many ways brutally for the dispossessed. Labor market development in the late 1990s translated into job losses for millions of state enterprise employees, layoffs that took place in the absence of a meaningful social safety net.[8] In the process, the whole structure of employment was changing. Employment in manufacturing peaked in 1995 and then fell steadily through the early 2000s.[9] Meanwhile, the working-age population was ballooning in cities as people seeking better lives flooded in from the countryside. In 1980, just over 80 percent of the Chinese population lived in the countryside, and just under 70 percent of the Chinese labor force was employed in agriculture.[10] By 2005, less than 60 percent of the population was still classified as rural, and less than 45 percent of the workforce still worked the land. In any given year by the 2000s, some 140 million people constituted the "floating population" of temporary rural migrants into China's cities.[11] Whether for permanent urban dwellers laid off from traditional manufacturing jobs or these new migrants seeking to leave farming, the new jobs would come primarily in construction, transportation, low-end services, and retail—sectors associated with flexible and often quite unreliable employment.

Housing markets throughout this period have translated into unprecedented levels of individual home ownership for Chinese citizens much as they have for Americans. Also as in the United States, though, such markets in China for some have translated into no housing, substandard housing, or the previously unheard of situation of being priced out of housing entirely. Chinese feel many of the same pressures that Americans do on this front, but unlike Americans, they tend to have much less access to mortgage financing. Hence, the individual Chinese citizen's exposure to phenomena like the American subprime mortgage debacle is somewhat minimized.

In a way much more reminiscent of the United States, Chinese health-care provision has been largely marketized, often in a manner more extreme than what Americans experience. For many Chinese citizens, markets for health care now often mean minimal insurance coverage, medical services available only on a cash-on-the-barrel basis, and wildly escalating costs for individuals and families.[12] For the vast majority of ordinary citizens, a major illness—something requiring surgery, a blood transfusion, or a round of chemotherapy—can lead to the impoverishment of not just a single person but several generations of an extended family. Many Chinese hospitals now offer state-of-the-art procedures and world-class medicines but only to those who can pay and pay up front in cash. For everybody else, including those showing up at an emergency room in desperate need of care, it is tough luck.

Whether for jobs, housing, or health care, the old system guaranteed provision, albeit at an extremely low level of quality and with no possibility of choice for the individual. The new system, replete with markets, offers almost the opposite: no guarantees, a tremendous range of quality standards—mirrored, of course, in a fee structure—and lots of choice. Needless to say, stark inequality has become an ever-present reality.

Political Life: The Transformation from Subject to Citizen

Harsh or not, the new markets of the present era have profoundly affected people's interactions with one another and the state. Consider, for a moment, what the end of the work-unit system has meant. Citizens now live not where they were assigned, and not necessarily among those with whom they work, but instead wherever they want or, more accurately, wherever they can afford to buy or rent. Their social networks have become exponentially more varied and diverse. Those relationships, in fact, have become completely different in character. No longer are they inward-looking relations of comradeship and competition within the physical confines and rigid hierarchies of the state work unit. Now, they are of types far more familiar to us: local relationships with neighbors; more geographically dispersed relationships with people who might share a common interest, hobby, or religion; and still other dispersed relationships with professional peers or fellow workers. This is the kind of outwardly directed pattern of social interaction that fuels commerce, fills stores with customers, packs restaurants with patrons, and crowds streets with window shoppers. It is a pattern that, whether blissful or banal, most of us would recognize as normal civil society, something China's revolutionary leadership had effectively wiped out from the 1950s all the way through the early 1990s. The pattern today is also now supercharged by the incredibly rapid proliferation of communication technology: cell phones, text messaging, e-mailing, Internet browsing, and richly diverse electronic media.

Of course, state strictures affect each of these modes to the extent they touch politically sensitive issues. Yet, even in their most mundane, apolitical uses—socializing with friends, connecting with wider social circles, accessing stories about the wider world—these new modes transform the citizen's self-awareness and his or her access to a variety of new, organically created social constituencies. In essence, the citizen has been cut loose and cast into a social environment rich with choice, opportunity, risk, and pressure.

At one level, what this means politically is that people enjoy a freedom they had lacked for decades, the freedom simply to be left alone. This may not sound like much, but it has major implications for the kind of control the state can and cannot exert against the individual citizen. In the not-so-distant days of the work unit, the citizen existed in a position of economic dependence vis-à-vis the state. Things like job advancement, permission to marry, housing upgrades, and health-care access could all be used as conditioning devices, extended to reward compliance and withdrawn to punish insubordination. In those days, everything in life was political. Today, almost nothing is. Indeed, now, rather than enveloping the citizen in politics, the state strives to keep the citizens out entirely. Politics has gone from being all pervasive to being essentially off limits, an exclusive domain one enters at one's own risk but which one need not enter to live most aspects of daily life.

Thus, authoritarianism continues in China, but it continues on a wholly different footing and in a wholly different social context from the past. The social contract has been utterly transformed in ways that are still evolving today. No longer is the implicit principle "we the state rule by politicizing all aspects of your life, and you the citizen obey." No longer can it be that way given the marketization of so many aspects of life. Instead, the principle seems to have become "we the state rule the political domain, you the citizen are restricted from that domain, but all else is yours to do with as you want." Instead of civic life being subsumed within a political hierarchy—the totalitarian approach, in effect—the state now shuts the citizen out, drawing a series of red lines (i.e., the organization of an independent political party, the staging of a political movement, the calling publicly for the end of the Communist Party) that the citizen is forbidden from transgressing. As important as those red lines may be for political expression, what is so interesting is that virtually everything else, including much behavior that we as outsiders might consider political in nature, is now fair game for the Chinese citizen.

Equally interesting, while the state can and does squash the few souls who, whether wittingly or not, cross the proverbial red lines, it faces a much bigger challenge with regard to the rest of the citizenry. It now needs these generally apolitical citizens to pay taxes, observe the laws, show up to work, and do all the other mundane but absolutely essential things necessary for stable social and economic development. But these positive behaviors, these positive forms of participation, can no longer be dictated through intimidation. The citizenry, after all, no longer constitutes a captive audience living day to day under the economic thumb of the state. Daily life is now governed by markets, not state hierarchy. What the government must do, therefore, is persuade ordinary, apolitical citizens that it rules in their interests and thus deserves their loyalty. It must, in essence, earn the voluntary compliance of its citizenry. Getting this appeal right—whether it involves the delivery of concrete material benefits or the proclamation of more abstract aspirational goals—represents no mean feat and is arguably far more challenging than harassing malcontents or arresting activists, which the Chinese state unquestionably also does on a regular basis.

The effort leads to some extraordinary situations today. We may routinely tell ourselves that the Chinese government's legitimacy rests on its ability to achieve national economic growth, a tall order in its own right. Official pronouncements by Chinese senior leaders, however, suggest that legitimacy rests increasingly on goals far more expansive and challenging even than that.[13] We now routinely witness China's leaders committing themselves publicly to aspirational goals like rule of law, equitable distribution of wealth, affordable health care, and a clean environment, just to name a few. The repeated avowals of Marxism-Leninism-Mao Thought are long gone. So too are many of the references to socialism. In their stead have come pledges to achieve not just national economic growth but also a kind of growth that brings measurable benefits and a particular quality of existence for individual citizens. This is not only about growth for the nation. It is about a kind of growth that benefits and serves the individual citizen. Oft-repeated official pledges to build a "middle class" (*xiaokang*) or "harmonious" (*hexie*) society may appear vague and propagandistic. To some in the West, they seem comically so. In China's increasingly pluralistic society, though, they are anything but comical. Their vagueness, in fact, provides space for increasing numbers of constituencies—some within the state, some beyond, and many somewhere in between—to scramble in and fill in the blanks. Hence, even in mainstream media channels and regular public statements by government technocrats, the term "middle-class society" has come to include everything from clean air, safe products, and material wealth to access to education, a law-based system, and leisure time to pursue spiritual enrichment.

Whether and to what degree these things have been delivered is open to debate. That the government has now publicly tied its legitimacy to them, however, is beyond dispute. Whether such proclamations have been made with cynical intent is, frankly, immaterial, for as the commitments have been repeated over time, the state has become a prisoner of its own discourse. An ever-expanding rhetoric now drives an ever-expanding agenda of the sort that in any country requires dauntingly complicated policies and vast amounts of expertise to address. After all, we are talking about achieving outcomes amid complicated interactions among policies, bureaucracies, commercial actors, markets, different strata within society, and differing preferences among individual citizens. That is what governance in marketized environments is all about. Few governments anywhere, even in the richest, most advanced nations, have the capacity to negotiate their way through all of this effectively. In one way or another, most rely on civil society for help.

And here too, ironically, we witness the Chinese state drawing closer and closer to established Western norms in ways that underscore how rapidly the social contract in China is evolving. The state with one voice still warns citizens off politics, crudely swatting down those who venture into the ambiguously defined no-go zones of anti-state activism. Yet, with another voice, perhaps out of desperation, it now encourages civic actors to jump into an important piece of politics, governance. The state, having now publicly proclaimed itself accountable to the citizenry, and accountable along a wildly expanding array of dimensions—most of which it has limited capacity to address—requires the public's help.

It needs this help in at least two ways. First, it seeks the public's assistance in policing lower levels of state officialdom, levels that to the extent they veer off into egregiously corrupt and abusive conduct undermine the legitimacy of the political order. Hence, it arms citizens with new legal rights and public information campaigns to ensure an understanding of those rights.[14] As a result, it often ends up triggering localized social movements and protests against local governmental malfeasance.[15] Sometimes, for reasons still poorly understood, it embraces such movements and extols them in the national press. At other times, for reasons equally unclear, it crushes them. In almost all cases, members of the state establishment—officials, academics, journalists—get involved on all sides, thus making it difficult to ascertain what the state's position is and whether the state should even be viewed as a coherent, rational whole.

Indeed, while many of us are inclined to view politics in oppositional terms (i.e., state vs. society), we might be better off adopting a more organic, evolutionary model of change to understand what is happening in China. Some of the most interesting forms of political activism in China today seem to involve overlapping efforts among ordinary citizens, muckraking journalists in the state media, and publicly minded gadflies in the state bureaucracy. Viewing their actions as patriotic and system supporting, these individuals coalesce loosely to fight what often amount to specific injustices: substandard construction of schools, excessive taxation of peasants, environmental violations by large companies, or corrupt real estate development.

Second, in areas for which the state has no capacity to deliver public goods at all, it tolerates and even encourages efforts by civic groups to step in and fill the void, particularly in local endeavors like building schools or mending roads.[16] Of course, such encouragement, whether of legal rights or civic groups, is often tentative and ambivalent. Civic actors who step too far forward under the current situation run the risk of crossing some unknown red line. Not surprisingly, aspects of rule of law and civic association are intensely threatening to the state. Hence, it is interesting that, in the current climate, they have at the same time become instrumentally important to the state, critical for maintaining effective governance, and arguably, critical for ensuring regime survival. The very things that in the past were absolutely forbidden precisely because they were so politically threatening have now become relatively commonplace. They have become so because under the new social order, threatening though they may be, they have become central to governmental survival. Ironically enough, the sources of stability and instability have become one in the same.

Exactly where this is heading is anybody's guess. It is already the case today, though, that one can witness head-spinning change, even at the highest reaches of the political system. The Central Party

School of the Chinese Communist Party provides a good example. This Beijing-based institution is the premier training academy for high-level officials. Its curriculum almost by definition must embody and reflect the official line, the official policy direction of the party-state. Not so long ago, the curriculum was firmly anchored in Marxist theory and ideological indoctrination. Today, such indoctrination has yielded to technical courses in public administration, public finance, environmental administration, and a variety of other functional specialties. Most interesting of all, in its political dimensions, the curriculum now includes courses on comparative democratic systems and the role of civil society in effective governmental performance.

In recent years, scholars within the school have issued public reports carefully outlining multistage plans for China's political development that, while mirroring the official discourse on scientific development and harmonious society, also specify representative democracy as the ultimate endpoint some decades down the road.[17] Authoritarianism, while by no means condemned, is presented as a transitional stage toward what the authors treat as the ultimate developmental endpoint, vibrant civil society and democratic governance. Given that these ruminations are emanating from the Central Party School and are being published in the open, they are taken by the public to signify at least some aspect of official thinking at the party's core. Interpret all this as you may, but how ironic that the greatest threat to the state in 1989—democratic governance and civic organization—is held out to officials in training, not to mention the public at large, as instrumentally necessary for making authoritarianism work and normatively appropriate as a long-term developmental goal.

Along equally head-spinning, albeit more down-to-earth, dimensions, we now see a government that, though it possesses the largest foreign exchange reserves in the world, today routinely has to cope with vitriolic public criticism of its handling of those funds. With the collapse of the American mortgage agencies Freddie Mac and Fanny Mae in late 2008 and into 2009, Chinese online bloggers and regular journalists alike began to question the Chinese government's exposure to overseas financial risk. Additionally, the government's official overseas investment arm, the China Investment Corporation, has been pilloried both online and in the Chinese print media for buying overpriced American securities at the peak of the market just prior to the downturn.[18] By spring 2009, Chinese Premier Wen Jiabao began expressing caution about the safety of China's $1-trillion holdings of U.S. Treasury bills.[19] Some outsiders interpreted this as evidence of a more assertive China emboldened by U.S. financial troubles. Numerous Chinese insiders, however, understood these comments as part of an effort to mollify a domestic audience that has become increasingly restive with awareness of how deeply their leadership has tied them to the U.S. economy.

These new circumstances may not be about people rising up en masse against a regime. They may not fit easily with concepts like contestation, state versus society, or officials versus dissenters. Yet, these new circumstances are about rapidly changing terms of participation by citizens and public officials alike. They are about all sorts of new social fissures and coalitions that rarely match up neatly against the kinds of divisions we are trained to think about: state versus citizen, public versus private, or government versus dissenter. And they are about a variety of societal players—some within the public sector and many outside it—scrambling to exert some influence over the whirlwind of changes affecting their country. This is not a story for the most part about some people pushing change and others resisting it. Rather, it is about many different kinds of people trying to get their hands on the helm and doing so in ways that the political hierarchy, whether wisely or not, has deemed legitimate. This is about political change that feels so exciting precisely because it involves politics that feels so normal. So much of modern Chinese history involves extraordinary circumstances—upheaval, struggle, mass mobilization, and political excess—erupting so frequently as to become almost routine. In that light, the emergence of true normality in politics, social life, and economics today seems utterly revolutionary.

The Chinese system today is hardly ideal. Pieces of it unquestionably operate with arbitrariness, brutality, and injustice. At the same time, however, the system is remarkably different from what it was two decades ago. It now operates in ways that would have been unimaginable in 1989, but ways that feel increasingly familiar to people who witnessed liberalization in the late stages of South Korean and Taiwanese authoritarianism. Somehow in the course of two decades, China has been transformed from a worn-out totalitarian throwback, a quirky and depressing historical outlier, to something far more recognizable, an authoritarian liberalizer in the East Asian developmental tradition. The Chinese state, not unlike the authoritarian regimes that existed in South Korea and Taiwan, may be wholeheartedly committed to preserving its own rule. In the current environment, however, the very steps it is taking to secure its rule are fundamentally transforming—indeed, have already transformed—the nature of that rule.

Making Sense of Change

This book seeks to make sense of the epic changes that have swept over China. It argues that those changes have been far deeper and broader than has generally been acknowledged. Indeed, the outcomes that garner the most attention today—China's phenomenal growth record, its massive accumulation of foreign reserves, its expanding global economic reach—are but reflections of far more profound transformations at the deepest interstices and most fundamental underpinnings of Chinese society. Because most of us either misunderstand or are wholly unaware of these underlying transformations, we misconstrue the surface economic story as well. The story is important because it involves not only China's place in the world but also our own, whether we happen to be Americans, Europeans, Japanese, or citizens of any other advanced industrial locale. How we understand China's story will largely determine how we—again, as citizens of the advanced industrial world—respond to the great challenges of our era: climate change, energy sustainability, geopolitical security, and economic competition. This book seeks to get the story right.

The Chinese government's official position is that the story begins with the December 1978 launching of Deng Xiaoping's policy of "reform and opening" (*gaige kaifang*). This book, however, while acknowledging the importance of that moment, argues that the story really begins over a decade later in the years immediately following the Tiananmen crackdown.[20] That is, Deng Xiaoping's initial reforms, crucial though they were, did not lead in a straightforward linear fashion to what we observe in China today. Instead, something critical happened in between, a major disjuncture that would jolt China off one path and reroute it onto another leading to the present. That disjuncture, that series of changes that took place in the 1990s, marked the point at which China's real revolution began. This revolution, like every other in human history, has involved interlinked political, social, and economic change. Peaceful for the most part and at once dislocating, bewildering, and exhilarating for the citizens swept up in its course (not to mention those of us feeling the effects from afar), it is a transformation whose scope and breadth rivals that of the more traditionally ascribed revolutionary moments in human history: the French Revolution, the Russian Revolution, and even China's own Communist Revolution of 1949. Once the dust has settled and time has passed, we will look back with wonder.

For the present, though, three key points are worth noting about this revolution. First, it has involved the yoking together of economic and political change. It is, unfortunately, often taken as a truism today that China's post-Mao reforms have involved great shifts on the economic front but precious little change on the political. In fact, nothing could be further from the truth. Political and economic change have marched hand in hand across a variety of domains, often with bewildering rapidity. China today is obviously not a liberal democracy. We should not allow that to blind us to other changes that have occurred, though, regardless of whether they do or do not constitute steps on the democratization process. Regardless of what category these changes fall into and where they are ultimately heading, simply recognizing that they have occurred is crucial for correctly interpreting even just the economic changes with which they have been coupled. In short, even if you are just interested in economics, you have to get the political story straight.

Second, this linked political-economic transformation has been driven by globalization. The changes China experienced were driven by the country's linkage to the global economy. Moreover, that linkage took place when the worldwide economy itself was undergoing a profound transition that many of us in the world's richest nations are still struggling to comprehend. China's domestic revolution is intimately linked with—and indeed, driven by—the globalization revolution.

Globalization here does not mean exactly what many people think it means. It is not primarily about the spread of markets, the leveling of the competitive playing field, or the emergence of rising powerhouse economies, though all of those phenomena have occurred to some extent in recent years.[21] Instead, it is about the creation of a new form of production that involves taking all the carefully orchestrated and highly regimented steps that had taken place within the single firm and instead spreading them across multiple firms and multiple national borders. This new worldwide organization of production—a new division of labor, really—entails as much or more hierarchy and control than ever existed before.[22] This is not about a "flat" world but rather one deeply tilted, at least in commercial terms, toward the traditionally powerful.[23] It is to this world that China hitched its fate and experienced an epic domestic transformation as a consequence. The point for anybody trying to make sense of this is that to get China right (and frankly, to get ourselves right), one has to get globalization right.

Third, understanding globalization correctly permits one to see that China's current economic emergence is not about a nation somehow standing up and rewriting the rules of global commerce. This is not a story about a retrograde political outlier harnessing its idiosyncrasies to grow at the rest of the world's expense. It is not about a rising revisionist power remaking the global system in its own image. This is not even about plain old mercantilism, the use of economic statecraft to build national power. Instead, China's current revolution is about a nation that has rescued itself from existential crisis by linking itself to a particular kind of global economic order. This economic order involves, really for the first time in history, a truly global organization of production. The existence of this global division of labor does not by definition force change on every country of the world. It does, however, force change on those who participate deeply. None has chosen to do so in a deeper fashion than China, and none has undergone as dramatic internal change as a result.

The bottom line is that China today is growing not by writing its own rules but instead by internalizing the rules of the advanced industrial West. It has grown not by conjuring up its own unique political-economic institutions but instead by increasingly harmonizing with our own. In essence, China today—a country at the peak of its modernization revolution—is doing something it historically never really did before. It is playing our game.

That China is playing our game—the game of modern capitalism effectively defined by the United States since World War II and practiced, in various forms, by all the nations of the advanced industrial West—should not be understood as signifying the victory of some new kind of American imperialism. China has not somehow thrown up the white flag and placed its fate in the hands of a foreign master. Rather, China has made a societal choice to play and, in so doing, has reshaped its own developmental trajectory, and ours too.

An important point, though, is that by doing so, China is serving not just its own interests but ours as well. The global division of labor that China has fostered by joining is the very same one that has permitted the world's wealthiest nations, particularly the United States, to surge forward in technological innovation and commercial creativity. Chinese specialization in manufacturing assembly has facilitated not only U.S. but also Western European and Japanese specialization in something far more difficult to replicate: knowledge creation and invention. China has done well through this division of labor. The leading market economies of the West, at their much higher levels of wealth, have done equally well or even better.

At the same time, while China has chosen to play our game, we should not allow that fact to make us complacent about the quality of the economic system we have built. We need look only to the recent global financial collapse and the utter bewilderment with which it has left us to be reminded of the deep problems that continue to exist in economic institutions of our own creation. Now, rather than standing outside those institutions, China is very much part of them and, like us, at once vulnerable and beholden to them. What is interesting is that in both the United States and China, significant segments of the public were left behind during the boom years of the 1990s and early 2000s, and those segments have suffered disproportionately in the current downturn. It is important to recognize, however, that many of these outcomes are more the product of social choice and domestic political failure within each of the countries involved than anything inherent in the global division of labor. The toughest social problems are driven from within and must be solved from within. There is nothing to be gained by either the United States or China in blaming each other or globalization more generally.

Unfortunately, at the very time we most need to get this story right, we have frequently been getting it wrong. In the coming months and years, Americans and their counterparts in Western Europe and Japan will be making choices about not just our own problems but also those of broader global significance. Some, such as the global economic downturn, are upon us right now. Others—climate change, for example—are longer term in nature but no less urgent. Each in its own right is monumental. That we face them all simultaneously is breathtaking. The reality is that every one of these problems and every one of the potential solutions in one way or the other now involve China. Any course of action we take—cooperation, conflict, going it alone—will be based on assumptions we make about China, conclusions we draw about what China fundamentally is, where it is headed, and what it is likely to do. We need to get those assumptions right. In part, they are about understanding China and its place in the world. In part, they are about understanding ourselves and our own place. This book represents an effort to do both.

TWO

Toward a New Framework
Institutional Outsourcing

C HINA'S POLICY OF "reform and opening" (*gaige kaifang*), by official accounts, began at the end of 1978. The most dramatic changes, however, occurred not in the late 1970s or 1980s, but rather in the early 1990s. Since then, both economic *and* political change has been far wider and deeper than most people recognize. The one-party authoritarian state persists, but virtually everything else about China, including the nature of its single-party regime, has undergone epic change. It is not simply that authoritarianism has flexed slightly on the margins so as to solidify its iron grip on the core. Something much more interesting and open ended is under way. An authoritarian system, scrambling to keep pace with tempests of change unleashed by its own policies, is now recasting itself in ways that fundamentally challenge the basis of its rule. Policy shifts initiated in the 1990s have effectively brought revolution to China.

This revolution emanated from a particular response the Chinese government adopted in the face of a paralyzing existential crisis. That crisis—really a series of crises that unfolded one after another in the late 1980s and early 1990s—nearly devastated the nation one decade into its post-Mao reforms.[1] The response, intended partly to revive a flagging economy and partly to salvage a tattered political system, involved aggressive engagement with the global economy. However, engagement took place at a time when the global economy itself was in the midst of revolutionary transformation. Understanding the global system's transformation, therefore, becomes as important as understanding China's own. The two are inextricably linked. A revolution in China has effectively marched hand in hand with a revolution in global production. This chapter provides a basic sense of what each is about and how they interact.

Understanding Globalization

In wealthy nations like the United States, globalization is usually taken to mean an almost explosive expansion of trade and competition, a spread of markets that has moved faster than our capacity to fully understand or regulate. Our current financial crisis, replete with its vocabulary of international capital flows, exotic investment instruments, and daisy chains of financial risk, is part and parcel of this. For many people in an even broader sense, globalization has come to signify a sort of unfettering, a replacement of old rules and constraints by a new pattern of unbridled worldwide exchange and interaction. These changes are enabled presumably by new technologies (i.e., the Internet, e-mail, cell phones, inexpensive long-distance telephony, etc.), new markets (i.e., China, India, Brazil, Russia, Eastern Europe, etc.), and new ideologies of deregulation. Globalization, then, becomes many of the things we used to do in the past—trade, compete, invest, buy, sell—but now pumped up to steroidal dimensions and blown out to the farthest reaches of the world, often beyond the reach of national regulatory control.

For many people, the quintessential image is that of Thomas Friedman's "flat" world.[2] Technology and deregulation, in this view, become massive, worldwide levelers that create unprecedented opportunity for those who previously had nothing. Jobs, companies, and even whole industries are envisioned as picking up from where they had long been rooted and sliding over to where they had never been before. For advanced industrial nations, then, globalization becomes the "giant sucking sound," the massive outsourcing of their core productive activities to the world's newest rising economies.

For all its emphasis on newness, this view of globalization posits a fairly traditional view of national and corporate boundaries. Its world is one in which rising and declining national economies, each with their respective portfolios of stand-alone national industries, compete in the global marketplace. This is a world in which it makes perfect sense to think about the American automobile industry competing against the Japanese automobile industry or the software industry moving from the United States to India. Moreover, this is a world in which nation-to-nation trade becomes a major focus of attention, and trade imbalances are a major source of concern.

This overall image undoubtedly captures a piece of the reality that is out there. Trade obviously does flow from one country to another, and various kinds of surpluses and deficits show up on the books as a result. Jobs, too, sometimes flow from one place to another, occasionally across international boundaries.

What the overall perspective does not capture, however, is what is truly novel about globalization. Phenomena like trade, international competition, and flatness have in many respects been around for ages. What has not, though—and indeed, what is truly new about our current era—is the ability across so many different kinds of industries to organize production on a worldwide basis. Globalization is not really about different parts of the world trading at arm's length and competing head to head. Quite to the contrary, it is about the world, including places once considered the farthest frontiers, getting pulled into complex production hierarchies that once existed only within the firm.

In recent years, technology and deregulation have clearly facilitated increased competition, trade, and financial flows. What they have done even more profoundly, though, is to allow processes that traditionally could happen only within the confines of a single company to be split apart and spread across multiple firms and geographies. That which previously, due to technological limitations, had to happen under one corporate roof and under one clear corporate chain of command—all the carefully orchestrated steps that go into designing, engineering, and manufacturing a product—now ends up dispersed across constellations of interdependent commercial organizations.

With this dispersal of activity, hierarchy and control do not disappear. They intensify. The world does not flatten. It becomes even more steeply tilted. Entire industries do not pick up like giant self-contained silos and move to the cheapest places available. Instead, those industries are pulled apart and disaggregated in ways that technologically and organizationally would have been impossible before. A new division of labor emerges with new forms of specialization and new deployments of productive assets. Some of the newly separable pieces of the production process remain firmly rooted in their traditional corporate and geographical homes. Others migrate to new organizations and sometimes get performed in new distant locales.

As in any division of labor, though, all the production steps, to the extent they are going to lead to a usable finished product, ultimately need to fit together. From the simplest to the most complicated, they all have to come together in the right way, at the right time, and in the right place over and over without fail. This can happen only with extensive coordination, control, and monitoring. Globalization has led to the fragmentation of the production process. In traditional ownership terms, it has led to the deverticalization of that process. Yet, for this new multifirm production process to function, it has to be coordinated and controlled through decidedly vertical relations of authority. Now, though, those relations of authority have to be made to work beyond the boundaries of a single company and instead across a network.

In the globalized world, then, activities disperse, but power does not. That is, the world may appear flat in that some production activities can get hived off and relocated to new places. The world is anything but flat, however, in that these dispersed activities, to the extent they successfully lead to a coherent product, are still ordered through a hierarchy. Thus, in the networked world of global production, there inevitably arise lead firms and follower firms, rule makers and rule takers. This can be seen in industries as far ranging as aerospace, automobiles, telecommunications, and beverages.[3] In each of these sectors, a select few lead firms crack the whip, and the rest hang on to the other end. All must stay in sync, lest those complicated "made in China" products that we now rely on every day (i.e., Apple iPhones, Dell laptops, HP printers, etc.)—gadgets that are designed and assembled by Taiwanese contract manufacturers operating in China, that incorporate high-tech subcomponents produced in Japan and Korea, that use semiconductors designed by "fabless" design houses in Silicon Valley, and that use software written in Seattle and debugged in Bangalore—would neither make it into our hands nor reliably come to life when our fingers hit the on button.

This is the global system to which China tied itself in the early 1990s. China did not do so through a carefully crafted long-term vision or a clearly articulated ambition to build industries and unseat global competitors. Almost the opposite was true. China joined out of desperation, an urgent need to stimulate growth and create jobs as rapidly as possible. The immediate solution did not involve an elegant handshake with the international community of nations. This was not about a textbook approach in which farsighted government officials first establish all the right institutions—private property rights, commercial legal codes, minimal tariff barriers, mechanisms for currency exchange—and then let global markets magically grow the country.[4] Instead, this was about something far more ad hoc, far messier, and far more difficult to interpret at the time.

China, prior to getting the institutions right—indeed, when institutional reform had ground to a virtual halt—simply went ahead and threw itself open to global production. More accurately, China threw itself open to the overseas companies organizing global production chains and allowed them to bring into the country whichever production activities they saw fit. Rather than creating a production system of its own, China set itself up to become a cog in an already extant, albeit rapidly changing, global system managed and controlled by others. There is nothing inherently wrong with this. It does not by definition entail selling out or caving in. It does not mean the triumph of any one nation or the capitulation of any other. Indeed, given the growth record China has achieved, particularly compared to that of many other developing nations during the same period, it may very well constitute an optimal strategy. Nonetheless, in pulling off this strategy, no developing nation, not even one as large as China, ends up in a position to call the shots. Instead, it must accommodate the shots as called by the lead commercial firms of the various production chains involved.

The textbook approach would have had China first getting its house in order and then joining the global economy. In reality, China first joined the global economy and only subsequently scrambled to get its house cleaned up. A kind of order would ultimately be achieved but one as much of the global commercial world's choosing as China's own.

In the broadest sense, then, Chinese growth has not been about China rewriting the rules of economic development. It has not been about China reshaping the world in its own image. This is not a story about China playing its own game. Instead, it is a story about China playing *our* game, a game created and defined by the world's advanced industrial economies, most notably the United States. By pursuing global integration according to the rules of the advanced industrial West, China's reform architects, whether wittingly or not, unleashed in their nation one of the most extraordinary political and social transformations in modern history.

Institutional Outsourcing

One way to understand this process is through the phenomenon of outsourcing, although not the kind people usually think of with regard to China. The sort of outsourcing that is relevant here is not about the movement of jobs and production activities from places like the United States to China. That sort of movement, of course, happens, but it is not what most directly shapes change in China. Rather, the real driver of change is something else: institutional outsourcing. This kind of flow, moving from China to advanced systems like the United States, involves ceding to a third party the power to define key societal rules that govern and shape social interaction. In this form of outsourcing, it is not jobs or manufacturing activities that flow but rather the power to define key societal institutions. In China's case, global commercial entities have selectively outsourced certain manufacturing activities to China. Yet, they have done so with such alacrity because at a more profound level, China has outsourced the power to define its domestic institutions—and thus, shape its developmental trajectory—to those commercial entities and other outsiders.

As is discussed later, Chinese institutional outsourcing has evolved in stages across time. Especially during the early phases in the 1990s, it operated as a policy device purposively employed by reform architects to ram change through the system.[5] Over time, however, largely because of the domestic changes it unleashed, it took on a life of its own, reshaping social constituencies, reshaping the types of people staffing elite governmental and commercial positions, and in many cases, reshaping the range of options they faced in responding to various challenges. As it would happen, the socioeconomic consequences of early rounds of institutional outsourcing drove demand in subsequent rounds for ever more ambitious, ever more sensitive, and ever more revolutionary forms of outsourcing. Many of these would come to involve the very definition of political legitimacy in China and the very nature of the citizen's relationship to the state. This interplay between institutional outsourcing as a policy instrument and institutional outsourcing as a transformative force unto itself is evident to varying degrees in each of the four examples of institutional outsourcing discussed in the following sections.

Outsourcing Domestic Industrial Restructuring to Foreign Companies

In this variant of outsourcing—really the opening shot in what would prove to be an escalating historical process—the Chinese government pursued national development by having foreign firms fit China into the newly globalized international division of labor. The country was thrown open to global supply-chain organizers, allowing them to relocate to China whichever pieces of the manufacturing process they believed feasible and appropriate. In the process, these foreign firms selectively upgraded Chinese domestic industry and reshaped it to meet specific global needs. The task of domestic industrial restructuring, a monumental one given the lingering effects of socialist command planning, was effectively outsourced to foreign commercial entities. The result was a dramatically improved domestic industrial base with far more efficient firms, far more advanced technology, and far more sophisticated managerial techniques. At the same time, this ceased to be a soup-to-nuts, stand-alone, autonomous national industrial system. Instead, it was a set of firms organized primarily by outsiders to contribute one piece, or a small set of pieces, to a much broader global puzzle.

In the earliest phases, the pattern manifested itself in industries like shoes, textiles, and apparel—not coincidentally, the first industries worldwide to experience truly globalized production.[6] In a fairly typical export-processing model, inputs would be brought in from abroad, assembly would be done in China-based firms, and then the finished products would be sold on foreign markets. The pattern, though, has proliferated and deepened in more complex industries like advanced electronics manufacturing and information technology (IT), which involve state-of-the-art design and engineering, tremendous amounts of componentry, and rapid product cycles. Today, we increasingly see the pattern not only in manufacturing but also in research and development (R&D), particularly as R&D itself in industries like pharmaceuticals, software, and IT now is performed on a global basis with tasks divvyed up across many different locales in an extended network. Precisely because of institutional outsourcing, China-based firms now perform key roles across all of these global industries. At the same time, one cannot meaningfully say that China—or perhaps anyplace else—has a stand-alone apparel, electronics, or IT industry. China has grown by letting others thoroughly remake it in a way that can fit into a global division of production tasks.

The point here is not to judge whether this is good or bad for long-term development or whether it amounts to selling out Chinese citizens (as foreigners are accorded extraordinary influence over China's developmental path) or selling out American workers (as production activities once performed in the United States are now performed in China).[7] The point is more straightforward. Restructuring domestic industry so as to have it mesh seamlessly into global production is an exceedingly challenging task involving the development of highly specialized capabilities both at the level of the firm and the economic system as a whole. This is not about simply importing a bunch of components, slapping them together in a sweatshop, and then dumping them as a finished product onto an overseas market. Rather, this is often about highly sophisticated, highly design- and quality-intensive production, a process involving coordination across many players. That China-based firms have been able to step into these roles, often edging out competitors in other developing or developed country locales, says a great deal about what this system has achieved. At the same time, building these kinds of capabilities means that other kinds of capabilities, for better or worse, are neglected. That is, institutional outsourcing—having foreign players reshape industry to tie it into global production—has major consequences for how domestic industry and its collective skill set develop over time. They develop to complement rather than supplant leading incumbent firms. Nonetheless, as these capabilities are built, pressures for change bear down across various pieces of the surrounding social context: the structure of the workplace, the operation of labor markets, the manner by which citizens and companies interact, and the manner by which they all interact with the state.

As noted in the previous chapter, in encouraging, or least allowing, all of this to happen, China diverged from the standard textbook sequencing of reform. Rather than getting the institutions right to stimulate economic activity, China in a way did the opposite. That is, Chinese reformers left in place a bunch of institutions that were wrong but plowed ahead and opened the country up to foreign investment anyway. The investors that showed up, global supply-chain integrators, were precisely those that had a history of working in dodgy, poorly institutionalized countries. The idea on the part of reformers seemed to be to let those firms bring in whichever activities they saw fit. Let them create whatever jobs they could. Let them determine which pieces of domestic industry were worth investing in and upgrading. Let them take on the responsibility of managing domestic firms so as to make them productive. If productive meant "productive in terms of meshing with somebody else's global supply chain," then so be it. In the absence of decent domestic institutions, foreign firms, through direct investment and management, selectively upgraded wide swaths of Chinese industry and effectively carved out from China's dying industrial base a separate, stand-alone, globally integrated industrial subsector.

At least two things happened as a result. First, as this subsector took off, its very existence pushed ad hoc, microlevel institutional change. At the national level, domains like property or contract law may have remained a mess, but on the ground, as producers got hooked into global supply chains, very real changes occurred. In fact, change had to occur for the production system to get off the ground. Labor markets, housing markets, modes of health-care delivery, and systems for training and education all had to change to meet the new demands of global production. While this did not have to happen all at once and at the national level, change had to happen at least at the firm level simply to make globally linked production feasible.

Second, over time, as the globally oriented portion of Chinese industry both grew in complexity and grew in its contribution to overall Chinese economic output, it drove demand for national-level change. That is, it drove demand for the sorts of macrolevel institutions necessary for its further development (and necessary for preventing its migration to other countries): clearer regulation, regulation more consistent with overseas standards, better intellectual property rights enforcement, greater labor flexibility, and so forth. Moreover, by involving and enriching so many different parts of Chinese society, it galvanized broad social constituencies that would support such change. In the process, it created a situation in which senior government officials came to view delivery of these institutions not as a threat to their power, as they arguably once had, but instead as a vital source of legitimacy.

Outsourcing the Formal Rules for Cross-Border Transactions

Once China was brought into the global division of labor on the commercial side—that is, once export processing took off—pressure rose on the Chinese state to modernize and standardize the rules by which the Chinese system connected with the global economy. Here, we are not talking about high-end institutions: elaborate corporate legal codes, intellectual property protection, minority shareholder rights, sophisticated channels of finance, and so on. Much of that would have to wait until later. Instead, we are referring to the more rudimentary institutions needed to allow export processing to grow: reduced barriers to trade, reliably low tariffs, and basic mechanisms for converting currency. Export processors could cope with what at times seemed like almost lawless conditions within China. However, they needed reliable rules for China's connection to the outside world. Assembly operations within China were tightly linked in production terms to upstream and downstream operations abroad. They had to respond on short notice to new orders from New York, new designs from Taipei, new components from Southeast Asia, and so on. For those linkages to be sustainable, at a minimum, material goods and currency would have to transit China's borders smoothly. And for that to happen, something would have to replace the cumbersome regulatory mechanisms inherited from socialist command planning whose express purpose had been to inhibit such flows.[8]

In each of these areas, the Chinese government scrambled to deliver, and in each, the government looked outward to define the rules. In some cases, namely, with respect to trade matters, the state bound itself explicitly to rules set by external agencies. By joining the World Trade Organization (WTO), for example, the Chinese government outsourced key aspects of trade regulation to an international body. According to the terms of its 2001 WTO accession agreement, China committed itself to significant reductions in statutory tariffs and the elimination of trade licenses that had previously restricted cross-border business to only a few favored firms.[9] In addition, China agreed to adopt within its own borders international standards for intellectual property rights protection and global norms for national treatment of all businesses operating in the domestic economy. The latter effectively meant that foreign-owned and locally owned firms would be treated equally under the law.

The overarching point is that in moving from an outdated trading regime to something new, China chose not to pursue a unique institutional design of its own, an idiosyncratic third way between plan and market. Rather, it defined its new system through worldwide standards handed down, through negotiation, by the WTO. At the same time, the premier at the time, Zhu Rongji, used the WTO accession agreement as a lever to downsize the state bureaucracy and drive out ministerial resistance to reform.[10] Tying China to external rules served the production needs of export processors. It also served the political needs of a reformist premier.

In terms of currency and foreign exchange management, the shifting of authority to outsiders was subtler but no less potent. As the Chinese economy became increasingly reliant on export processing and foreign-owned supply-chain integrators, the state could no longer feasibly hang on to its traditional mechanism for currency control, the socialist "double airlock" system of trade and foreign exchange licenses.[11] That system may have been wonderful for ensuring near absolute government control. It was not so wonderful, however, for facilitating the operation of cross-border supply chains. For such production systems to work, not only goods but also payment for those goods must flow seamlessly back and forth across borders. There was simply no way these conditions could be compatible with a system in which the state set exchange rates by fiat and then enforced those arbitrary rates by allowing only those firms anointed with a state license to access foreign currency.

By the early 1990s, it became clear that China would have to develop a more flexible, more modern, and inevitably more complicated system of market-based currency management, something roughly akin to what exists in advanced capitalist systems like Hong Kong, Japan, or the United States. These involve open-market operations by central bankers, seamless convertibility for at least commercial players (if not ordinary households), and stable exchange rates for everybody involved. In such systems, exchange rates are determined not by fiat but instead by market forces of supply and demand. Should a government choose to peg its exchange rate to a single external currency—as famously pro-free-market Hong Kong has long done with respect to the U.S. dollar—it maintains that rate not by diktat (and accompanying access restrictions to dollars) but instead by stepping in as a market actor in its own right, buying or selling dollars in a great enough quantity to shift the price, in dollar terms, of its home currency. This is essentially what China did with the renminbi (RMB) from 1997 through 2005. A government may employ similar mechanisms to manage its exchange rate in reference to a broader basket of global currencies as China has done since 2005.[12]

Americans today may object to the particular value, in dollar terms, at which the Chinese government maintains the RMB. Whether rightly or wrongly, we attribute China's large trade surpluses with the United States to what we feel are purposive efforts on the part of the Chinese state to undervalue its currency. Be that as it may, what we tend not to recognize is that the mode by which the Chinese government now manages its exchange rate, regardless of whether that rate is too high or low, has undergone epic change in the past twenty years. China has moved from a thoroughly alien, socialist mode of currency management to a system that roughly imitates our own. In terms of Chinese foreign exchange valuation, we may not like the current price, but we should recognize that the mechanisms now used to manage that price fall solidly within the spectrum of standard capitalist practice. Whether such price management is optimal from a policy perspective can and should be debated. Interestingly, numerous Chinese academics and officials, particularly within the government's central bank (The People's Bank of China), argue that it is not and should be viewed only as a stepping-stone to full currency liberalization. Nonetheless, that currency pegs have at various times in recent history been considered legitimate—and even at certain moments, laudable—modes of market governance is indisputable.

The more important issue is that for China, getting to this point involved replacing a simple system that Chinese bureaucrats knew well with an intensely complex system that they barely understood at all. That, then, drove demand for new kinds of bureaucrats—not traditional party loyalists but highly trained specialists. By the early to mid-1990s, it became clear that many of these technocrats would have to be drawn from the ranks of Chinese who had gone abroad for education and training and were now thoroughly conversant in the monetary and exchange management techniques of modern market systems.[13] Participating in overseas, cross-border production networks meant incorporating overseas currency exchange rules. Indigenizing overseas rules, in turn, meant absorbing into the central bureaucracy people who had been educated, trained, and socialized in the overseas way of doing things. When they left China years earlier, most of these individuals saw little likelihood of ever returning. The system, in turn, for years treated them as turncoats, throwing up obstacles to their return in any sort of professional capacity. Institutional outsourcing would change all that. Now, these former turncoats, these insider-outsiders, would be critical for managing the new practices China was scrambling to adopt. The system, rather than holding them out, would now have to find ways to lure them back in.

Outsourcing of industrial restructuring led to outsourcing of institutional design over trade and exchange rate regimes. Outsourcing of design over these key governmental functions then led to the outsourcing of training and supply for skilled technocrats. In a pattern that would spread across government, academia, and industry, the senior management team, so to speak, would increasingly be drawn from people who had been trained abroad, often in the United States. These individuals not only spoke English, but they spoke and fully absorbed the language of modern market systems. They valued such systems, realized professional status from prior experience in those systems, and saw as their personal mission the fostering of China's modernization through adoption of those systems. Thus, in perhaps the profoundest form of outsourcing of all, one that wends it way through all the others, China has turned outside—to us, essentially—to answer the question "who will lead?"[14]

Outsourcing Governance over "National Champion" Companies

Outsourcing of domestic industrial restructuring (to foreign companies) permitted the creation of a new export-processing sector. Harmonization of China's trade and foreign exchange regime with international standards then permitted that sector to thrive. Arguably, though, these forms of outsourcing did not directly affect what some consider the core of the Chinese economy: state-owned national champion firms. Nonetheless, such core firms—usually found in state-dominated pillar industries like banking, energy, automobiles, and steel—proved hardly immune from the institutional outsourcing phenomenon. Indeed, the kind of outsourcing to which they were exposed had more dramatic political ramifications than the variants previously discussed.

In the late 1990s, China's political leadership, most notably then-Premier Zhu Rongji, embarked on a bold effort to revitalize core state-owned enterprises (SOEs) by exposing them to foreign governance strictures. The program's emphasis was not on taking foreign-style corporate governance rules and re-creating them in China, though some of that was done. Rather, the approach involved taking the Chinese companies themselves and delivering them—figuratively, if not literally—to the regulatory strictures of the world's leading market economies. This was done by publicly listing Chinese national champion firms on overseas stock exchanges, most notably New York and Hong Kong but also London.

At least at first, these moves seemed hardly to constitute real reform. After all, even after public listing, ownership over these firms barely changed. Elaborate efforts were taken on the Chinese side to ensure that the state remained not only the majority owner but the majority owner by huge margins. Prior to listing, firms were generally divided in two, with viable commercial assets moved over to what would become the publicly listed company and money-losing operations left in the original 100 percent state-owned company. This unlisted organization would serve as a holding company, controlling upwards of 75 percent of the shares of the newly listed spin-off.[15] More conservative officials could persuade themselves that with the parent company remaining fully state owned and the listed company remaining firmly in the hands of the parent, state control over the economy's commanding heights was being preserved. Any hint of Russian-style privatization could be avoided. Similarly, skeptical observers, including this author at the beginning of the process, argued that the program amounted to little more than an effort to dress up state-owned industrial dinosaurs so as to pull in foreign investment while avoiding any real reform.[16]

Over time, though, surprising things began to happen in the listed companies. Although ownership did not change much, ownership, as would become apparent, is not where the action is in terms of the transformative power of overseas listing. Instead, the action lies at the intersection between the firm's managerial practices—its expansion efforts, its financing mechanisms, its technology acquisition efforts, its cross-border deal making—and the regulatory strictures of the stock market on which it is listed. With the passage of time after overseas listing, the firms changed dramatically in terms of how they operated, who populated their senior management teams, what kinds of external stakeholders they were becoming reliant on, and what types of broader networks they became immersed in.

Even as majority state ownership remained unchanged, a revolution was taking place on the operations and management front. In fact, state owners were in many ways cut out of the loop. Although the firms to this day remain at least nominally state owned, they are no longer playing the socialist game. Having launched out on strategies of their own and their commercial partners' design, they are in many cases not even playing a state-dominated mercantilist game. Instead, immersed in international networks, advised by international bankers and lawyers, partnered with leading global companies in their respective sectors, and subject to the regulatory strictures of foreign governments, they are in many respects behaving as standard commercial entities.

Overseas listing has driven these changes in several ways. Simply to prepare for listing abroad, state firms—whose senior managers entered the process with virtually no knowledge or experience in these matters—had to do at least two things. They needed to turn outside to develop deep relationships with the global investment banking firms and international lawyers who would shepherd them through the regulatory maze of underwriting and initial public offers. They also needed to turn outside to pull onto their management teams Chinese citizens who understood what management, particularly financial management, in a publicly listed global company was all about. In a manner akin to what the government had to do with regard to foreign exchange management, these firms needed to persuade overseas-trained Chinese citizens—the kind of successful business professionals who would never previously have considered working for a state-owned behemoth—to join the team.

This infusion of new players and new thinking was then further encouraged by the listing requirements of the major global exchanges, whether in New York, Hong Kong, or London. Listed firms were required to set up boards of directors with at least a handful of independent nonexecutive directors. So, although these boards may have been dominated by people ostensibly representing the state owners, the boards were also populated by outsiders—the independent nonexecutive directors—deemed necessary for guiding the company in its new surroundings. Leading global businesspeople, industry experts, economists, and retired foreign diplomats, among others, entered the fray, pulling up a seat, so to speak, at the governance table. Although loyal to the company, they also had to meet their directorial obligations as defined by the laws of the country of listing. Indeed, their reputations were staked upon doing so. Hence, they may not have had overwhelming voting power, but they would at the very least need to be informed of decisions and guaranteed that proper procedures were followed before affixing their signature to any filings required by the host exchange (and that exchange's home country regulatory authorities). More important, because these individuals generally had a deep understanding of international business, they could engage the management team at a level of sophistication that more distant state bureaucrats could not.

The point is that while formal ownership still remained in the hands of the state, a variety of new players began to enter the picture not on the peripheries but dead center in the boardroom. At first, these new players entered because of the technical or regulatory requirements of the listing itself. Yet, over time, these players began to exert increasing influence on the commercial strategies of the firms themselves.

It is worth remembering, after all, that it was in these listed companies that the viable commercial assets of the original pillar state firms were concentrated. In an oil and gas firm like the China National Offshore Oil Corporation (CNOOC), for example, it was the critical exploration and production business that ended up in the listed company. Moreover, by virtue of its listing charter, only the listed arm rather than its parent state-owned holding company was permitted to participate in this business. Potential investors, after all, would have to be assured that the parent would not compete with the listed child.

Consequently, anything important the company would do commercially would have to be channeled through the listed arm. For exactly that reason, it was also within and around the listed arm that so much new talent and so many new players ended up concentrated. More than a few of these players—the investment bankers, the lawyers, the industry consultants, the nonexecutive directors—were foreign. Whether from China or abroad, none of the players, including the overseas-trained Chinese brought onto the senior management team, had as a primary concern the enhancement of Chinese state power or the carrying out of Chinese governmental directives. It was not that they were subversives or in any way disloyal. Rather, it was that their entire identity and life experience was tied up in global business, not politics. Like ambitious businesspeople anywhere, they sought to do deals, build the firm, and make money. Moreover, they were in a position to do something revolutionary and exciting by bringing in the kinds of deals that a traditional Chinese state-owned firm would never have been exposed to in the past: global acquisitions, overseas partnerships and joint ventures, and cross-border technology partnerships. As they got more involved in such deals, the companies became ever more reliant on external advisers—particularly investment bankers—and the overseas-trained members of their management team. The cycle of internationalization and delinking from the state grew deeper and deeper.

But all this time, who was governing the firm? As listed firms' operations became increasingly sophisticated and global in nature, China's state bureaucracy had no means to exert effective monitoring. Any bureaucrats with the skill and knowledge to make sense of such deals had in all likelihood already shifted career paths and entered the managerial ranks of the firms themselves. After all, that is where all the money and excitement, not to mention power, could be found. In climbing the steep learning curve to becoming truly global and truly world class, managers in key listed companies outpaced the ability of the Chinese system to exert either the top-down control of a state bureaucracy or the more market-oriented oversight of a majority owner.

There was, however, something that still remained to bind these firms: the regulatory strictures of the stock markets on which they were listed. Ironically enough in some cases, managers of Chinese pillar industry state-owned firms ended up more accountable to the U.S. Securities and Exchange Commission than to the Chinese central government.

Institutional outsourcing, while perhaps targeted at economics, over time chipped away at the political foundations of Chinese socialism. The single-party, authoritarian state obviously survives. However, the nature of that state, its relationship to its citizenry, and its sources of legitimacy have all been fundamentally altered.

Most tangibly, the state lost its institutional mechanisms for controlling the citizen's day-to-day existence. The remolding of domestic industry to fit global production destroyed the traditional, state-controlled workplace. With it went the complete array of systems by which the party-state for decades had determined the citizen's fate. Coercive police powers—many of them seemingly arbitrary and unjust—would still be wielded against overt dissenters and trouble makers.[17] For the average apolitical citizen, on the other hand, the once omnipresent party-state ceased to be much of a presence at all.

All the while under the surface, societal constituencies were shifting, including those that interpenetrated the elite ranks of the party-state. Whole categories of citizens deemed in the 1980s to be politically suspect were by the 1990s and 2000s becoming critical to the system's very survival. Technocratic intellectuals capable of navigating the intricacies of global commerce—whether in government or industry—gained unprecedented access and leverage. So too did entrepreneurs and private businesspeople, for they were the ones creating jobs, generating growth, and fueling the export economy. Overseas-trained PhDs began to move into key teaching and administrative positions in Chinese academia. Long excluded from the inner sanctums of political power, or even from the Communist Party more generally, all these individuals had risen for the most part by relying on their own devices. Although perhaps not hostile to the party, they had an identity separate from it and no outstanding debt to it. As their importance rose, the party leadership would move to embrace them. In some cases—whether out of instrumentality or patriotism—they would embrace back. Almost by definition, however, they would always enjoy a professional exit option. While at any given moment the connections afforded by party membership might prove useful, for most of these individuals, their livelihoods and future life chances were determined less by politics than by their own personal achievements—their level of educational attainment, their professional expertise, their overseas experience, or their business acumen. Once excluded from the establishment, these people now became the establishment.

These very same individuals, in large part because of their ties to the global economy, were also making common cause with a variety of overseas players. Previously clear distinctions between Chinese and foreigner, insider and outsider, state-owned and private all became increasingly blurry, even at the highest echelons of the system. Complicated coalitions of interests formed, virtually all of which were absorbed by the existing political order in ways that would have been unimaginable years earlier. Once inside, the individuals involved—simply by virtue of their education, training, social networks, and life experiences—would inevitably change that order, whether intentionally or not.[18]

So much began to happen at once by the late 1990s and early 2000s. On the surface, the party-state adhered steadfastly to its communist brand. Beneath the surface, it had forsaken key instruments of social control and opened itself up to new constituencies. Meanwhile, in the country at large, it faced growing threats not just to its own survival but to the maintenance of social order more generally.

Institutional outsourcing saved China by unleashing extraordinary economic dynamism. That dynamism, however, created needs that Chinese society had not in recent memory had to meet. Laws were desperately needed to govern increasingly complex business transactions. New regulations and enforcement mechanisms were desperately needed to address the by-products of torrid growth: pollution, corruption, labor unrest, disease, consumer product safety, and crime, among others.[19] In quite tangible ways, the party-state began facing urgent pressures to deliver more stuff—more regulatory goods, public services, infrastructure, and monitoring.

Such demands were coming from a population not totally satisfied with the fruits of economic growth.[20] In the abstract, citizens could take pride in their country's economic achievements. More concretely, though, the country's outwardly directed growth model obliterated the old social contract. For large swaths of the urban populace, everything from guaranteed lifetime employment to free housing and health care had in short order been completely erased. What was left were conditions that to some extent mirrored conditions in the United States, albeit in China's case at just a tiny fraction of America's level of per capita wealth. Like Americans, ordinary urban Chinese knew that their country was growing rapidly. But they also saw in their own lives that employment was available on only a flexible basis, health care was available only through individual choice (with health-care costs skyrocketing), and housing was available only on the basis of ability to pay.

Wages seemed to lag overall national growth, and disparities across society were becoming glaringly apparent.

Thus, the evolving situation was demanding more than just stuff from government. It was demanding some kind of vision, some kind of overarching logic that could make sense of where things currently were and where they were ultimately heading. It was demanding a story that could keep citizens onboard and collectively operating on the same page.

Rather than steadfastly holding the line—or even worse, retreating—China's leadership did something else. It did not choose to do what North Korea and Cuba have since done: resist almost all reform as a matter of national principle and ruling party identity. It did not even stick with the brief phase of retrenchment, the crackdown on private enterprise, and the reintroduction of industrial planning and price controls that it pursued in the year immediately following the Tiananmen crackdown. Retrenchment would be laid to rest with Deng Xiaoping's "southern tour" (*nanxun*), the former leader's now famous 1992 trip to Guangdong when he extolled the virtues of stock markets and systemwide economic transformation. From this point on, the succession of individuals holding the highest positions in the Chinese system—people like Jiang Zemin, Zhu Rongji, Hu Jintao, and Wen Jiabao—though perhaps not liberal in our sense of the term, were certainly liberal in the Chinese sense.[21] Their careers had been built in one way or another on the pursuit of, rather than resistance to, reform.

Thus, when facing rising popular aspirations for something more than just aggregate economic growth, their primary reaction was neither to deny nor to squash. Instead, they effectively upped the ante by adopting the political rhetoric of the West.[22] That is, they once again turned abroad, effectively allowing outsiders to define the terms by which China's domestic political transformation would unfold. In one sense, the leadership justified economic hardship as a necessary element of China's coming of age, its "getting on the global track" (*shang guoji guidao*)[23] and joining the community of advanced nations (which were, of course, all bastions of market capitalism). In another sense, the leadership committed itself to addressing these hardships through concepts drawn from the Western political tradition: the building of a law-based society; the pursuit of growth models measured not by their achievements in the aggregate but rather by the degree to which they benefit individual citizens; the encouragement of civil society; the building of formal institutional mechanisms for government accountability to the citizenry; the achievement for each citizen of a middle class or moderately prosperous (*xiaokang*) existence; the encouragement of a long-term path toward democratization; and the protection of citizens' individual rights.[24] The overarching terms may have been vague—a scientific outlook on development, a rule of law society, a moderately prosperous society, a harmonious society (*hexie shehui*)—but as the leadership time and again repeated them in official pronouncements, the message became obvious. For China to be modern—and by extension, for its government to be legitimate—society would have to be governed in a certain way that sounded a lot more like contemporary Western democracy than traditional Chinese socialism.

Harmonious society could mean many things. One thing it clearly did not mean, however, was class struggle. The party would stick with its brand, communism, but it would have to look outside for an utterly new way to govern.

There are many reasons to be skeptical about the earnestness with which this vision has been laid out. In some ways, though, intentionality has become irrelevant. With this last form of institutional outsourcing—the outsourcing of society's political ideals—a particular kind of discourse with an accompanying array of expectations has been launched into the public domain. As it hits a society already so altered by other forms of institutional outsourcing, it takes on a powerful life of its own.

What Kind of China Is This?

It is fairly self-evident that no two countries look or behave exactly alike, and no single country, even among the most advanced, has somehow reached the end point of its development. Everybody, to some extent, is in a continual state of transition. China will never look exactly like the United States any more than France or the United Kingdom will. However, as we try to make sense of our world, we can and do think in terms of groupings and categories. We speak meaningfully of nations like Germany, France, the United Kingdom, the United States, and even Japan as being similar enough politically and economically to constitute a category: the West. We also speak meaningfully about a select few nations—South Korea and Taiwan, for example—that have developed politically and economically in ways that now make them recent entrants into that group. What the institutional outsourcing perspective says is that China, too—for its own unique reasons and along its own unique pathway—is traveling along exactly that trajectory.

It should be acknowledged that this perspective departs in important ways from much that has been written about China in recent years. Of course, to say that a conventional wisdom exists about China is an overstatement. In recent years, scholars and other observers have articulated a rich diversity of views about China. Many of these perspectives derive from extensive and innovative on-the-ground research. Few can be dismissed simply as conventional or commonplace. At the same time, many of these views share an overall approach, an overall way of framing things, that sets them apart from the institutional outsourcing perspective.

The institutional outsourcing view argues that Chinese politics and economics are undergoing rapid development and doing so in sync. That is, they are developing organically—and swiftly—in an interlinked process. Engagement with global production is then treated as an important driver. Many other works, however, begin with the assumption that in China, politics and economics are out of sync. The task for these works, then, becomes to explain what the consequences of such a disconnect ultimately might be. In essence, China gets portrayed as a nation that has undergone substantial economic change but minimal political transformation—at least minimal transformation of the kind that observers treat as normal in economic development. Normal here is usually understood to involve a connection between marketization on the economic front and liberalization—some combination of democratization, establishment of rule of law, deregulation, and diminished state intervention—on the political. China, then, gets treated as a departure from the normal processes of political-economic change that ostensibly happen in other countries.

The point is not that this kind of framing somehow guarantees a particular analytical conclusion about China. Indeed, works that adopt it express highly divergent opinions about what the country is and where it is heading. Rather, the point is that the common framing shapes the nature of the questions being asked and, in so doing, circumscribes the range of answers that are provided. The answers end up diverse, but they misconstrue the real nature of the change that is actually going on.

A brief taxonomy of at least part of the existing literature might help clarify the point. The works mentioned are sophisticated and provocative, and all are well worth reading in their entirety. Describing them in a sentence or two hardly does them justice. Nonetheless, they can be placed into categories based on the different ways they present China as experiencing an abnormal disconnect between politics and economics.

First, there are scholars who are committed to the idea that late development—the developmental challenge faced by poor nations today—requires a departure from normal political-economic solutions. These scholars believe that to realize growth, poor nations today cannot simply open up markets, push deregulation, and downsize the state. Instead, they must do the opposite and aggressively jump in and have the state purposively manage markets.[25] The market in this view may be necessary for development, but at least for poor countries, it is not sufficient. Hence, China's departure from normal development—its coupling of marketization with a strong, highly present state—explains why the country has grown so successfully.[26] Politics remains retrograde, so to speak, so that economic growth can occur. The key image to emerge from this perspective, then, becomes "China as developmental state."

A more controversial variation on the theme embraces not just an interventionist state but an explicitly authoritarian one. This perspective argues that Chinese growth has been enabled not only by the maintenance of a strong, interventionist state but more particularly by the postponement of democratization.[27] Although understandably offensive to twenty-first-century sensibilities, the equating of "rule of the many" with profligacy and expropriation has roots in Western thought ranging from Aristotle to the American *Federalist Papers*.[28] In any case, the prevailing image here becomes one of China as "antiliberal alternative" to the West.

Next is a category of scholars who interpret China's politics-economics disconnect not as a necessary condition for growth but rather as a departure from globally prevailing rules of fair play. That is, they do not assume a strong state like China's is necessary for growth. Growth, for these scholars, presumably happens naturally through marketization and state retreat. Their argument, however, is that the kind of hypergrowth China is now experiencing (or that Japan experienced in the 1980s) is possible only if the state unfairly manipulates markets at other countries' expense. Thus, in this view, an unreformed, illiberal regime is using economic statecraft to harness markets to the overarching goal of national empowerment. China is not just growing, but it is rising (relative to the world's most powerful nations, particularly the United States), and rising on the basis of an alien political-economic system. This perspective leaves us with a series of images: "China, Inc.,"[29] "China as rising threat,"[30] and "China as modern mercantilist."[31]

The images do not stop there, though. Belief in the abnormality of China's political-economic situation can lead to a very different set of conclusions that emphasize China's weaknesses and failings. Many of the observers writing from this perspective tend to take a neoclassical approach to growth. They believe, in other words, that growth, even in developing countries, requires basic market fundamentals: decent property rights; privatization; independent courts; and a state that provides basic regulation and social welfare but avoids excessive interference in markets and direct ownership over productive assets. These scholars acknowledge that growth has occurred in China, but they also recognize that the authoritarian state fails to resemble the minimalist market ideal. This leads them then to question how sustainable China's growth model will prove in the future. That is, they assert that the government's steadfast determination to avoid any challenges to one-party rule prevents it from supplying the kinds of institutions necessary for sustainable market development.[32] After all, things like independent courts or legal restrictions on the state's ability to expropriate amount ipso facto to threats against the regime. Hence, these scholars argue that growth has occurred *despite* bad policy, that better growth could have been realized under more optimal political conditions, and that whatever growth that has been achieved is ultimately vulnerable because of the state's failings and inhibitions. In other words, China has done well so far, but it could have done far better, and unless it changes politically, it will soon do far worse. The image that emerges here is one of "China as recalcitrant socialist," "China as halfway reformer," and "China as caught between plan and market."

A variation on this theme involves a slightly different tack, an argument that whether or not politics limits economics, it certainly lags economics. Scholars holding this view argue that rapid growth in any country generates tremendous societal dislocation, tension, and potential conflict. For society to avoid completely collapsing into disorder, the argument goes, such challenges must be resolved by a political system that is at once impartial, fair, and responsive, all qualities that are said to elude the current Chinese system.[33] We are thus left with the image of a China in "trapped transition," a nation immobilized by its own political failings.

Noteworthy is that all of these images—China as East Asian developmental state, China as antiliberal alternative, China as rising mercantilist, China as blinkered socialist reformer, China as failing market system, and China as looming societal meltdown—are compatible with a flat world view of globalization, a view that emphasizes trade over production. The images assume a world in which countries are unique, self-contained institutional constructs. These countries within their own borders can establish whatever rules they like and pursue any practices they choose. Thus, China can look one way, Japan another, and America still another. That they end up structured so differently, though, does not prevent them from trading with one another. After all, trade is but an exchange requiring little coordination. It simply happens in response to the most elemental signal of all: price. As long as the price is right and the parties to the transaction show up, the goods can effectively be tossed over the wall from seller to buyer, and vice versa. In this sort of setting, a country like China, then, whether to its benefit or detriment, can reasonably be described as maintaining an abnormal arrangement between its economic and political spheres, even as it becomes a major global trader.

Things look very different, however, if the world is viewed through the lens of production. Here, the primary form of interaction is not uncoordinated arm's-length exchange but rather highly regimented and orchestrated joint production. This is less about the horizontality of the freewheeling market than the hierarchy of the multicompany production chain, the "external" firm.[34] To become deeply integrated in this kind of system, a developing nation must make its domestic economic institutions compatible with those of supply-chain leaders. Institutional harmonization need not happen across the board, and it need not necessarily be formal, but it has to happen in practice in key areas involving production.[35] Most of those areas cross the boundaries between economics and politics. This is the kind of world that globalization has created. China could never have become such an integral global player—such a hub for global manufacturing—had it not undergone extraordinary economic *and* political change. In short, the production view says the entire notion of a politics-economics disconnect is inaccurate.

What happens then if we adopt a more accurate production-oriented view of globalization? What if we discard the notion of a uniquely Chinese politics-economics disconnect and instead argue that politics and economics in China today are evolving in an interlinked, organic fashion? What images of China emerge then?

The answer involves a sequence of images unfolding over time. First, there is the "globalist converger," a China that in response to an existential societal crisis in the 1990s regrounded itself through participation in a newly emerging global production system. "Getting on the global track" became not just a political slogan but a broadly shared societal mission. It was something that bolstered the citizen's sense of self-worth, made sense of the tempest of change sweeping across day-to-day life, and gave society as a whole a unifying purpose.[36]

Second, there is the "capitalist facilitator," a China that rather than following the standard advice given to developing countries to get their institutions correct beforehand, simply in its barely reformed condition plunged ahead and opened itself up to supply-chain integrators, foreign firms who would do on the ground what was needed to link China into global production. By default, it became these firms' responsibility to restructure Chinese industry from the bottom up. Of course, restructuring then would be conditioned around the needs of those foreign firms and the kinds of decisions they were making about which pieces of production to base in China. Hence, we would get a China purposively built to fit into a global division of labor, hardly the image of a self-contained rising giant.

Third, there is the "institutional outsourcer," a China that once ensconced in global production, followed the logic of its commercial needs, and step by step attached itself to externally defined rules. In some cases (i.e., WTO accession, the overseas listing of pillar industry firms, etc.), it directly tied itself to foreign rules and foreign rule-making authorities. In other cases (i.e., currency management, enterprise law, employment law, environmental regulation, etc.), it internalized practices borrowed from abroad. In all cases, it had to pull into the establishment entirely new kinds of people with new kinds of training, often garnered overseas, to navigate these new institutional settings.

Fourth, there is the "double-down state," a China—a Chinese government, more precisely—that when confronted by the political blowback of institutional outsourcing, threw the dice and tried to incorporate those new forces into the existing political order. The point is not that this is a gentle system. It has over the past twenty years repeatedly crushed overt dissent, often through means directly contravening Chinese law. Nonetheless, this is also a system that has repeatedly drawn political red lines one day only to embrace changes that obviously cross those lines the next. In the Maoist and early reform era, law was seen as a weapon of capitalist exploitation. Now, it is a basis for governmental legitimacy. Private entrepreneurs were seen as counterrevolutionaries. Now, they are welcomed into the Communist Party. Civil society and civic organization were by definition viewed as political threats. Now, they are heralded as sources of governmental accountability. Overseas-trained scholars and professionals were seen as a potential fifth column to be treated with suspicion. Now, they are courted by commercial firms and government alike. Indeed, the Ministry of Education recently mandated that national key universities meet or exceed minimum quotas for numbers of foreign-trained personnel in their professorial ranks.

The Chinese party-state is by no means a liberal regime. Yet, at key moments in the growth process over the past two decades, it has faced decision points at which it could either hold the line politically or press forward. Push a rule of law agenda or resist it? Formally recognize private ownership or force it to remain underground? Expose key state-owned firms and banks to foreign influence or keep them firmly under governmental control? Tolerate civic organizations or crush them? Populate the establishment with apolitical or even overtly liberal professionals or keep them out? In each of these cases, the leadership has found its way to the side of progress. Perhaps, this was done out of the belief that such incorporation would always mean co-optation and that anything the party-state embraced could ultimately be controlled. What is beyond doubt is that the pattern involved repeated gambles—repeated throws of the dice and repeated doubling down of the bets.[37]

In one respect, the gambles have paid off. The party-state remains. In other respects, however, the results have been far more ambiguous. Communism as an ideology is dead in China. Claims to legitimacy on the basis of past revolutionary glories are virtually inoperative. The government rules today on the basis of its ability to deliver a version of modernity defined by the advanced industrial democracies of the West. Indeed, regardless of its own prior red lines, the government has increasingly embraced in its official discourse the political elements of that overseas version of modernity, concepts like popular sovereignty, governmental accountability, rule of law, rights, and democracy. Parts of the ruling establishment have undoubtedly done so cynically. Other parts, however, are increasingly populated by people who venerate these concepts as core aspects of China's destiny. These individuals are not revolutionaries. They are not aiming to mount the barricades. Rather, they are working quietly and professionally within the system today so as to make for a very different China tomorrow. Whether in business, government, academia, or any other vital sector, they are most definitely *in* the current system but not *of* that system.

And that leads to a fifth and final metaphor: China as "self-obsolescing authoritarian." Needless to say, China's party-state, much like other authoritarian regimes in history, aims organizationally to stay in power. That governments seek to stay in power and that ruling elites rule in their own interests are truisms.[38] The real issue is what those interests are and how they change over time. The Chinese government and the Chinese Communist Party (CCP) more broadly, perhaps for reasons of pure self-preservation, have drawn into their embrace institutions, concepts, and individuals that in the past would have been anathema. As the historian Benjamin Schwartz said about an earlier era of Chinese reform (that of the Qing Dynasty in the late nineteenth century), it is not just that the outer walls of the fortress have been breached but rather that the inner sanctum has been thrown open.[39] The fortress is still obviously there, but it is no longer clear who is being kept in and who is being held out. To preserve itself, the party-state has pursued growth through institutional harmonization with the West. In so doing, it has shifted the composition and interests of those populating its establishment. More important, by justifying its rule through a commitment to deliver modernity, it has promulgated the logic for its own natural end point.

In this sense, the CCP is traveling a path not so different from that of its historical doppelganger, the now Taiwan-based Kuomintang (known also as the KMT or Nationalist Party). Neither party ever set out to dismantle authoritarian rule. Both, arguably for reasons of survival, came to legitimize themselves through commitments to concrete developmental goals. Achieving those goals necessitated the empowerment and incorporation of previously unwelcome societal players. In each case, the party, in its effort to survive, embraced within its fold all the contradictions of the broader society it was attempting to govern.[40] As a result, the party's relationship with its own elites and with society at large changed irrevocably. Again in each case, commitments to the party's monopoly status remained top on the agenda, but they were joined by so many other items, many of which were pressing and many of which in the minds of the new elite establishment rivaled in importance the sanctity of the party itself.

Developmental authoritarianism reached this point in Taiwan in the 1980s and in mainland China some twenty years later. In Taiwan, of course, the process continued to unfold. Today, the KMT lives on but in the setting of a thoroughly transformed, multiparty democracy. Who won and who lost in that process are impossible to say and probably immaterial. One could argue that the authoritarian party instilled its vision in a set of institutions that ultimately transcended the party itself. Having done that, the party could subject itself to competition, step aside when out of favor, and all the while claim victory for having fixed its legacy in a broader set of national institutions.

Perhaps the most important lesson from Taiwan's experience is that right up to the moment authoritarianism disappeared, *real* political change—that is, regime change—appeared unlikely if not impossible.

In other words, virtually anything the party did—admit outsiders, push new laws, commit itself to new goals—could be dismissed by observers as avoidance of change rather than change itself. Right up to the very end, the KMT was suppressing dissent and throwing political prisoners in jail. And right up to the end, it was insisting that while democratization was a long-term goal, one-party rule was a national necessity for the time being. Even in the final days of authoritarian rule, reasonable, informed observers found ways to argue that real political change had eluded this place. After all, regime change had not occurred. In reality, of course, the official end of authoritarianism—that is, the legalization of an opposition party, the holding of presidential elections, the first changeover of government—came not as a single, bolt-out-of-the-blue, revolutionary break from the past. Instead, it was but the denouement of an extended historical process, an accumulation of changes that each in and of itself would have appeared insignificant. Real change had been under way for years.

In China's case, the final steps in unwinding authoritarianism have obviously not yet come. Nonetheless, many of the preliminary and intermediate steps have, and they have done so in ways comparable to what transpired in other transitions from authoritarianism across the region. Our attention today is better spent trying to understand the changes that have already occurred in China rather than arguing that they constitute no change at all. It is that pattern of change that will be probed in detail in the following chapters.

THREE

The Quest for Modernity

C HINA HAS BEEN deeply transformed by its engagement with global production. Global production, though, does not by definition force change on all countries. Even in the most basic sense, sovereign nations can choose whether to opt in or opt out. And once they are in, they can to some extent control the depth of their participation. China's story of institutional outsourcing is very much about a nation that purposively embraced the international system and did so not just once but repeatedly. The consequences of international engagement may not have always been fully appreciated by those pushing the policies. But time and again, even when confronted by unintended and often uncomfortable consequences, decision makers across society elected to move forward and deepen the global embrace. This chapter seeks to explain why.

The answer involves two related dimensions. First, this globalist embrace coincided with a disjuncture in China's reform process. In the early 1990s, well over a decade into China's officially proclaimed "reform and opening," a break occurred. Prior to that point, reform had been treated as a kind of experimental medicine administered to the ailing patient of socialism. Socialism, an end unto itself, was clearly the thing to be saved, but reform was an acknowledgment that the patient was suffering a serious degenerative illness. Certain innovative treatments could be permitted and attempted, but not those that might challenge the core attributes of socialism itself. The treatment could not be allowed to kill the patient.

Yet, by the 1990s, a switch happened. Reform—the treatment—become an end unto itself, and the patient increasingly became seen as an impediment. In the 1980s, the idea was to use reform to save socialism. By the 1990s, the idea became to dismantle socialism to save not just reform but the political system as a whole. Somehow, socialism—direct state control over the means of production, allocation by plan rather than market, and social organization through the state-controlled workplace—lost its status as an inviolable principle, the paramount definer of the Chinese system. The government would stick with its communist brand but simultaneously retreat—aggressively in many cases—from actual socialism in practice. In socialism's stead would come a new ethic of modernization through globalization or, more precisely, modernization through participation in global capitalism.

Material enrichment has obviously become important in China as in many other nations. Yet, this emphasis on a particular kind of globally focused growth has gone beyond just materialism. It has taken on an almost spiritual quality, a collective national mission. It could do so because it unfolded at a particular historical moment of widespread, almost existential, societal crisis.

But that leads to a second point. While China's globalist—and capitalist—embrace derived from unique historical circumstances in the 1990s, the quality of the reaction—its collectiveness, its spiritual element, and its determination even in the face of substantial societal costs—harkens back to reformist drives that have erupted in China for at least a century. In essence, the globalist embrace fits into China's century-long quest for modernity.[1] Moreover, this is not today, nor has it ever been, about modernity in the abstract. Rather, it is about modernity as defined concretely by the world's wealthiest and mightiest nations, countries that embody all the ostensibly positive qualities that China lacks. China's history over the past century has in many ways revolved around a societal struggle for self-definition, a quest to attain those qualities deemed by outsiders to constitute modernity. The socialist embrace was one manifestation of this. The capitalist embrace that has arisen in its place is another. One need only have witnessed the opening ceremonies of the 2008 Beijing Olympics—its monumental grandeur, its celebration of technology, its emphasis on China's place in the community of advanced nations, and its utter silence with regard to socialism—to get a sense of how much more than just economic growth this whole story is about.

Market Reform: From Experimental Treatment to National Salvation

China's record of economic growth since the early 1980s appears on paper as a smooth, upwardly sloping curve. What that majestic curve hides, however, are the sharp turns—the upheavals, the abrupt policy shifts, and more general institutional changes—that had to happen to keep that curve flowing upward across the decades. We may still have a poor understanding of exactly how different kinds of policies and societal rules lead to different kinds of economic outcomes whether in China or any other place for that matter. What we do understand broadly, however, is that for growth to be sustained over long periods of time, institutions have to evolve and be responsive. They have to meet the changing needs of producers, whether entrepreneurs or assembly-line workers, so as to ensure continued growth. At the same time, they must cope with the social consequences of growth so as to avoid upheaval.

China's efforts along these fronts, even through the present, are frequently described as gradual and tentative. During the first decade of reform in the 1980s, such descriptions would have been accurate. In those years, the focus remained decidedly on socialism and its moral value as the raison d'être of the Chinese nation state. Though perhaps grievously wounded by the worst excesses of Maoism, social-ism held on as the core orthodoxy, the core organizing principle of the Chinese polity, even well after the demise of Mao Zedong himself. Reform in this context—the introduction of economic incentives for producers, the exposure of some prices to the forces of supply and demand, tolerance on the margins of alternatives to state ownership—to the extent it managed to continue moving forward despite consider-able conservative opposition was understood as a treatment, something that could tweak, improve, and ultimately save socialist command planning. Although relatively dramatic change occurred in the rural peripheries, the system's urban industrial core remained firmly rooted in socialism.

All this would change by the mid-1990s. It was not simply that reform accelerated. This was about more than just pace. The very essence of reform shifted. The terms of debate became completely transformed. Whereas in the 1980s, the debates had been about whether to reform, by the 1990s, they were almost exclusively about how. No longer would reform be a treatment to save socialism, something to be meted out parsimoniously only to the extent that socialist fundamentals remained untrammeled. Instead, reform—radical systemic transformation—would become an end unto itself, a core source of legitimacy for the entire political-economic system. To the extent that socialist institutions stood in the way, they would have to be dismantled. Reform had once been intended to save socialism *for* the nation. Now, reform would have to save the nation *from* socialism. China, in essence, embraced global capitalism. It did so, ironically enough, for many of the same reasons it had embraced socialism decades earlier, to reestablish itself on what it understood as the path to modernity.

1989–1999: A Decade of Shocks

China's embrace of capitalism was in many ways revolutionary. It occurred, however, in the absence of revolution. There was no change in political regime. The party remained firmly in control, its monopoly on political power relatively intact. There was no sudden reordering of contending classes and societal interests (though as a result of the embrace, the composition of society and the ruling-party establishment would evolve in new directions). There was not even the rise of a charismatic leader capable of remaking society through sheer force of will. If anything, the break from socialism happened as China's last charismatic leader, Deng Xiaoping, faded from the scene and yielded the stage to a collection of dry technocrats: Jiang Zemin, Zhu Rongji, Hu Jintao, and Wen Jiabao. None of these had the inclination or capability, as Mao Zedong once had, to wage war on society and bend it to his will.

None of the normal ingredients for discontinuous change were present. Yet, such change ensued, and in ways that have proved more profound and lasting than anything wrought previously by Mao. Without the clear firing of a starter's gun, society embarked on a collective effort at transformation. It was an effort that in some sense required the cooperation of all the individuals, households, enterprises, and state agencies now thrust into the market. For all the incidents of individual malfeasance, governmental corruption, and localized protest, the collective endeavor on the whole moved forward with remarkable fluidity. How could this have happened? What was the impetus? What was it that held everything together once the process got under way?

The answer involves a nationwide response to crisis, a shared recognition among many Chinese of their country's peril in a world that had come suddenly unglued. Beginning in 1989 and extending into the 1990s, China was hit by a succession of cataclysmic events that shook the foundations of long-held assumptions and widespread societal beliefs.

The first, of course, was the 1989 Tiananmen movement and its tragically violent denouement. Coming a decade into China's initial reform process, the movement, involving all strata of urban society and extending into the very core of the Communist Party, represented an utter repudiation of the existing order, including that order's tentative reform agenda.[2] During the first ten years of reform, urban residents had experienced few gains. They still lived within the straightjacket of the socialist workplace, opportunities were few in number, and wealth was nowhere on the horizon. For the majority of citizens, getting ahead somehow required an in, permission or access granted by somebody higher up the chain. Indeed, coping with authority seemed to be the essence of the social contract. The government talked vaguely about bringing reform, but it quite explicitly instructed citizens to remain patient, obedient, and quiet. Meanwhile, as the halfway measures of market socialism creaked along, inflation and corruption ran rampant. Those with an in appeared to reap greater ill-gotten gains than ever, and everybody else was left out in the cold with nothing. China appeared to be going nowhere. It was instead Gorbachev's Soviet Union, far off over the horizon and caught up in the promise of *glasnost,* that fired the imagination.

A variety of emotions fueled the Tiananmen spring, the waves of demonstrations that swept across the nation in late April and May of 1989. There was undoubtedly anger, frustration, and boredom but also curiosity and joy. What is abundantly clear, though, is that those protests nearly toppled the Communist Party. The violent June 4 crackdown in Beijing, through sheer force of intimidation, silenced people nationwide. What it also did, however, was to confirm what the very protests themselves suggested—the traditional socialist social contract was moribund.

Teaching in a Chinese university in the months following the crackdown, I witnessed on a daily basis the expressions of hopelessness and despair on the part of my students and colleagues. Some were party members, others not, but virtually all had been on the streets protesting during the preceding spring. Coercion, for at least the time being, forced people to hunker down and often encouraged them to lapse into passivity, lassitude, and indifference. Compliant, in a sense, they were certainly in no mood to stand up again and hit the streets in protest. At no time during that 1989–1990 period, though, would I encounter sensibilities associated with more enduring forms of civic compliance: national pride, a sense that the country was heading in the right direction, a belief that the future would be better than the present, or faith that those in power were reliable custodians of the citizens' interests. For all intents and purposes, socialist China—as a nation, a social order, and a political system—appeared to have breathed its last.

Just months later, in precisely this atmosphere of hopelessness, China would be hit by a second crisis, this time beyond its borders. In what seemed like the blink of an eye, the Berlin Wall came crashing down and the entire Soviet bloc fell asunder. Romanian leader Nicolae Ceausescu, a longtime ally of the Chinese government, was dragged out by his own people and summarily executed. How strange it was for many Chinese during their own winter of discontent to listen in—generally through the static of partially jammed short-wave radio broadcasts—on revolution erupting abroad. The spirit of the Beijing spring was finding its natural outlet not in China but in Eastern Europe. And just as it had been so many times in the past, China was again left in the dust.

And then, the most bewildering thing of all happened. The Soviet Union itself collapsed. At times an embodiment of China's aspirations, at times a bitter ideological foe, the Soviet Union throughout was the mother ship of global socialism, the fount from which everything else sprung. Now, unbelievably, the Soviet Union was gone. Even crazier, this former global giant, this once mighty superpower, was left in utter societal collapse: an imploded economy, a wrecked military, and a dismembered nation. In a brief moment, the Soviet Union plummeted from global superpower to third world disaster area. China alone would be left to bear the banner of socialism, if it were worth bearing at all.

The Soviet collapse reverberated in complicated ways across Chinese society. On one level, it bought time for China's leadership. In its demonstration of the devastating social ills that could be unleashed in the wake of political overthrow, it forced many Chinese to rethink their own behavior in 1989. In 1991 and 1994, as I interviewed acquaintances in Chinese intellectual and bureaucratic circles—people who had all been out on the streets in 1989—I found them expressing newfound doubts about their behavior during the Beijing spring. Whether rightly or wrongly, they looked out at the disaster ensuing in the former Soviet Union and felt that it could just as easily have happened in China had the 1989 protests been permitted to reach their natural end point. As one prominent and very liberal academic noted, "We were so naive that spring, so caught up in the excitement."[3] Rather than necessarily justifying or otherwise condoning the violent crackdown, though, these individuals were primarily looking inward and reconsidering their own judgment years earlier. To the extent it provoked such emotions, the collapse of the Soviet political order may have been the salvation of China's.

On a different level, however, the Soviet collapse clearly was a warning shot, a potent statement of the fragility of the social contract. Traditional socialism was indeed dead. No longer could the government, if it hoped to stay in power, rule solely on the basis of claims anchored in the past. No longer was the fact that the Chinese Communist Party had brought revolution or national liberation or socialism enough. After all, the Soviet Communist Party too had brought those things, took those things with it when it collapsed, and once the dust settled, left nothing of value remaining. The socialist promise, in effect, was hollow. The emperor had no clothes. It was in this context and at this point that Deng Xiaoping definitively declared development as the "hard rule."[4]

The collapse of the Soviet Union, though, was only half the story. The rise of the United States to unrivaled global status was the other. A few months after the Soviet Union's collapse, Chinese citizens in the winter of 1991—with as much amazement as Americans themselves—watched television footage of U.S. bombs being coolly and clinically guided down the smokestacks of Iraqi buildings. Those images represented more than just military might. They signified an awesome, almost incomprehensible, fusion of technology, creativity, know-how, and determination in the one global superpower left standing. In a bitterer vein following America's 1999 bombing of the Chinese embassy in Belgrade, Yugoslavia, a young Chinese acquaintance, liberal in outlook and with several advanced degrees earned in the West, commented, "My mind tells me that this was an accident, but in my heart I feel differently. Just the fact that Americans can fly cruise missiles right into [Yugoslav President] Milosevic's bedroom says to me how incredibly advanced this place is. I see that and I am reminded of all the things America can do that we cannot. It is as if my face is being rubbed in the ground."[5]

American ascendancy extended far beyond the field of battle. For better or worse, intellectual concepts like the "end of history"[6] and policy approaches like the "Washington consensus"[7] gained currency across much of the world. American economic institutions appeared to be the answer for global development, America's financial markets the ultimate fuel for generating wealth, and America's legal code the embodiment of rule of law. America had Silicon Valley, a powerful image in itself of almost uncontainable ingenuity, competition, and creativity. It had globally ascendant companies in the most technologically advanced industries and new entrepreneurial start-ups at almost every turn. It had banks that could finance the extension of these activities anywhere in the world. America had a powerful state, a potent military, well-functioning laws and economic institutions, the best universities, the best companies, and on and on. Nobody else had all these.

Both in the United States and abroad, analysts tried to disaggregate the pieces of the puzzle so as to draw broader theoretical conclusions. All manner of conceptual claims emerged. "Broader [American-style] financial markets are better than narrower [French-style] ones." "Formal [American-style] property rights regimes are more conducive to wealth generation than informal ones." "Entrepreneurship is fundamentally driven by [American-style] mechanisms of venture finance." Still, for many Chinese, the whole was somehow far greater than the sum of its parts. In a manner similar to the way late nineteenth-century Chinese intellectuals looked at the United Kingdom, late twentieth-century Chinese saw the United States—whether they loved it or hated it—as an extraordinary amalgamation of spirited individualism, cooperative civic mindedness, dynamism, and energy. America was about assertiveness, purposiveness, and the "realization of all potentialities."[8] China, still reeling from Tiananmen, was the opposite: stuck, cautious, passive, enervated. China was out of gas, and the United States was exploding with Promethean might.[9]

Just as China's reform architects began kicking into action and responding, their system was hit by yet another crisis: the Asian financial collapse. In late 1997 and into 1998, one after another, China's neighbors—economic dynamos in their own right—experienced economic implosion. Although the Asian financial crisis did not involve China directly, it further pushed China along its radical and purposive break from the socialist past. In essence, it engendered within the nation a reframing of how elites and ordinary citizens understood the political, social, and economic challenges facing their nation.

For many of those in China's neighboring nations who endured the volatility of the late 1990s, the Asian financial crisis served, and still serves today, as a cautionary reminder of the fragility of markets and the ease with which things can go awry. This is, of course, a message that resonates once again, now in the United States itself. In China, however, the lesson at the time was somewhat different. As noted previously, China, from the inception of reform in the late 1970s all the way through the aftermath of Tiananmen in the early 1990s, maintained an essentially planned economy at the nation's industrial core. Reforms happened at the margin, but fundamentally, the socialist equilibrium persisted. Large firms employing large numbers of people still dominated production. Those firms, in part because of their massive employment and social welfare obligations, could not compete commercially with new non-state entrants, let alone the foreign firms that would come later. Unable to compete but essential, as it was believed, for maintaining employment and social stability, those firms were time and again bailed out by the state with loans from state banks.[10] Citizens saved money, and state banks then loaned that money to moribund, albeit politically important enterprises. Nobody in the mid-1990s—and certainly not this author—believed China would shift from the pattern, no matter how destructive the economic ramifications over the long run. Pulling the plug on socialism just seemed too risky politically, basically unimaginable.

Yet, with the Asian financial crisis, an event that coincided with the rise of Zhu Rongji to the Chinese premiership, the tenor of debate inside China changed. It was as if the unexpected collapse of the neighboring economies, countries that had previously stood out as beacons of hope, flipped on a light of recognition within China. The recognition was less about what was happening abroad than about what had long been going on at home. Informed domestic observers understood that circumstances in Thailand, Indonesia, and South Korea differed from China. China had neither the fully liberalized foreign exchange regime nor high levels of foreign-denominated debt that to some extent fueled the collapses across East Asia. However, China did share something deeper with those nations (including Japan, which by this point was mired in stagnation): an economy dominated by politically connected industrial behemoths, a bank-dominated and heavily state-influenced financial system devoted to investing in those behemoths, and high levels of household savings put at risk funding the whole operation. It was not capitalism that suddenly fell into doubt—something that could have been treated as a foreign problem—but instead, the East Asian model of state-led development, something the Chinese unmistakably identified as relating to their own.

As these crises of confidence unfolded—the post-Tiananmen malaise, the collapse of communism in Eastern Europe, the dissolution of the Soviet Union, the burgeoning of American hegemony, and the financial collapse of East Asia—so too did changes in party line, policy, and overall discourse.

Response to Shock: Shifts in Party Line, Policy Content, and Societal Discourse

The shocks of the 1990s reset the entire context within which China's reforms would proceed. The agenda would no longer be so clearly circumscribed by the confines of socialism. Reform would not be about saving socialism. Instead, it would be about saving the nation. National salvation, however, would involve an intermingling of difficult-to-reconcile or even antithetical objectives: radical adoption of modern (advanced industrial nation) market institutions, radical elimination of traditional socialist economic and social structures, rapid development of a modern regulatory state,[11] maintenance of authoritarian rule, preservation of social order, and increasing exposure of the political system to public scrutiny and participation. The objectives were so mixed as to defy neat description. What they clearly signified, however, was political change along three overlapping avenues: overall party line, actual policy content, and broader societal discourse about the nation's developmental destiny.

In terms of party line—the broad, doctrinal statements from the party center about the direction in which upcoming policies will head—the key shifts occurred in 1992 and 1993. At the Fourteenth Party Congress in late 1992, China's senior leadership formally proclaimed the establishment of the "socialist market economy" as the ultimate aim of reform, thus replacing the prior terminology of "market socialism" (*shichang shehuizhuyi*).[12] Mind-numbing though the semantics may be, the switch in terminology was meaningful. In the original formulation, "socialism" was the unquestionable focus—the noun, in effect—and "market" was the tentative modifier. In the new formulation, "market economy" moved strikingly to center stage, while the term "socialist" was relegated to the role of modifier. Even for ordinary Chinese citizens, the semantic shift was noteworthy. A reordering of governmental priorities was clearly under way.

The phrasing became more concrete with the November 1993 "Decisions on Issues Concerning the Establishment of a Socialist Economic Structure" (adopted at the Third Plenum of the Fourteenth Party Congress), which officially called for the establishment of numerous market-supporting institutions, including a standardized federal tax system, standard monetary policy management mechanisms, and a formal social safety net.[13] State-owned enterprises, the heart of the old socialist system, were to be transformed into modern firms that were to enjoy formal governance structures, separation of ownership from management, clear property rights, and scientifically based management. Each of these declared aspirations, although not explicitly stated as such, directly contravened core tenets of traditional socialist political, social, and economic organization. In other words, achieving any of them would require substantial dismantling of what just months or years earlier had been considered sacrosanct aspects of Chinese socialism.

Relatively abstract doctrinal shifts intersected with a second avenue of change: new policies, new international commitments, and new de facto realities on the ground. In 1994, the enterprise reform policy of "grasping the large and releasing the small" (*zhua da fang xiao*) kicked into gear, thus leading to the elimination of some 80,000 firms from the roster of SOEs.[14] Five years later, during a visit to the United States, then-Premier Zhu Rongji announced China's bid to enter the World Trade Organization on stringent terms that Chinese negotiators had previously resisted over thirteen years of bargaining with WTO (and previously the General Agreement on Tariffs and Trade, GATT) member nations. That same year, 1999, would also witness another important semantic change, the Chinese constitution's formal recognition—and thus, legitimation—of private ownership as an important component of the socialist market economy. So too would the constitution be amended that year to emphasize the need for rule of law and the goal of "establishing a socialist, rule of law country."[15] Two years after that, Jiang Zemin, in his capacity as head of state and Communist Party general secretary, would officially welcome private entrepreneurs into the party. Meanwhile, the nation's leading state-owned enterprises were taken public, exposing them to a variety of new conditions as they were listed on stock exchanges both at home and abroad. Simultaneously, official efforts were undertaken to open up positions in leading enterprises and state agencies to Chinese currently residing abroad, particularly those with advanced academic degrees and established careers in global commerce, law, and regulation.

The clustering of these reforms was hardly coincidental. Shutting down huge swaths of the state sector necessitated, if only to maintain public order, the creation of alternative jobs. Alternative jobs would have to come from alternative kinds of firms, namely, private and foreign-invested ones.[16] Moreover, these private entities would need financing, technology, and markets, presumably all things that would have to come from abroad. Hence, the push for unprecedented integration with the global economy.

New firms, set up to engage not in the vertical relations with the state so characteristic of command planning but instead in the horizontal transactions with other producers and consumers so characteristic of markets, would need contract law, property law, and employment law. Even if the new domestic entities would not immediately demand these, the new foreign-invested companies playing an ever-greater role in national industrial production, particularly with China's accession into the WTO, surely would. If foreign firms were to achieve status within China as legal entities, surely domestic private firms would have to as well. Hence, the belated legitimation of private ownership, well after foreign firms operating in China had been granted legal status.

Meanwhile, even traditional state-owned firms in heavy industry would have to prepare for foreign competition. They would have to be infused with new expertise, surrounded by new governance structures (often through listing on domestic and foreign stock markets), and refocused on commercially viable objectives.

Indeed, the system as a whole would have to learn to operate on a new footing. Now devoid of direct ownership over the economy, the state would have to learn to manage through alternative instruments of indirect control: regulation, legislation, fiscal policy, monetary policy, and exchange rate management, to name a few. Of course, each of these areas would require the creation, virtually from whole cloth, of new procedures, new administrative organizations, new mechanisms, and most important, new skills. Whether in the firm or the state, a completely new type of individual, armed with an entirely new set of skills, would be required to make the system work.

In the context of a steadily rising economic growth curve, this cascading series of changes—many of them quite turbulent—unfolded with surprising rapidity. Little evidence exists that the changes unfolded by prearranged plan or careful design. The process was—and still is—messy, confusing, uncertain, and replete with miscues. With each new problem that arose, bitter debates ensued about optimal solutions. Rarely, however, were the debates about what they had been in the 1980s, whether or not to reform, and whether or not to move forward. Instead, they were almost invariably about how best to move forward. Leadership transfers took place, personnel with the party's most elite ranks came and went, but for all its fits and starts, the system continued to move forward toward a clear goal, the market. Embracing capitalism had become the establishment norm.

Perhaps even more remarkably, this embrace, which in so many ways whipsawed the lives of ordinary citizens, managed to move forward with the general forbearance and even outright support of the Chinese populace. Urban citizens in the process lost all their socialist entitlements: lifetime employment, pensions, free housing, and free health care. Life in the vertical hierarchy of the state was exchanged for life in the relative turmoil of markets, be they markets for employment, housing, health care, educational opportunities, or retirement investment. All of these avenues of competition and choice opened up quickly, but none cleanly, predictably, or transparently. At one level, citizens, to the extent they had any say in the matter, traded the predictability—and almost universal poverty—of the state system for the promise of the market. Yet at some deeper level, for all the disruption, pain, and dislocation this change induced, so too did it carry with it a certain spiritual appeal, a certain quality of legitimacy that extended well beyond just economics.[17]

That, then, gets to the third and most revolutionary avenue of change: the shift in overall societal discourse. The shocks of the 1990s unquestionably ushered in new policies and new economic realities on the ground. Even more profoundly, though, they ignited new ways of thinking and talking about the direction in which the nation was heading. These were not just elite discussions among policy experts or the most educated segments of society. Far broader than that, they involved cross-societal conversations about China's future. Most important, as has frequently been the case in modern Chinese history, issues of national identity and individual identity became intermingled. Discussions about what China would ultimately become—and how it would ultimately stand in the world—inevitably spoke to the citizen's understanding of what it means to be Chinese. Between the disasters of Maoism, the disappointments of early reform, and the disillusionment following Tiananmen, that connection between national progress and individual self-worth had been ruptured. The collapse of the Soviet Union just reaffirmed how far off the mark China had strayed in its commitment to socialism.

The revolutionary changes that ensued in many ways represented an effort to repair that rupture between citizen and nation. People, in a manner of speaking, had to be motivated to pull collectively and voluntarily in the same direction, something that new policies alone could never do. Policies had to be surrounded by a new way of thinking, a new way of articulating what the future would be all about. People had to be persuaded that sacrifices today would lead for citizen and nation alike to far better outcomes tomorrow.

The first step in this new discourse came from the top down. Constant reaffirmations of socialism receded into the background and were replaced by the new official imperative to "modernize" (*xiandaihua*) and "get on the global track" (*shang guoji guidao*). Societywide, the mission became to establish disparate pieces of modernity: a "modern enterprise system" (*xiandai qiye zhidu*), a modern system of "rule of law" (*fazhi*), a modern system of public finance, and a modern system of ownership.[18] Over and over again, people were reminded of the need to realize standards: a standard (*biaozhun*) system of intellectual property rights protection, a standard (and scientific) system of enterprise management, a standard system of labor relations, and so on.

Overarching everything was the goal of building a modern, complete market economy. The underlying implication, of course, was that what had come previously was neither complete, nor modern, nor acceptable. Modernity, the holy grail of Chinese nation builders for well over a century, now became unequivocally associated with the market, and not just any market, but rather the specific institutional set-up found across the advanced economies of the West. The market came to signify world-class competition, world-class standards, and world-class status. And all of those became associated with moral qualities such as objectivity, fairness, and even in some sense, justice.

Hence, one could observe in the 1990s a tendency even among those bearing the greatest costs of the market embrace to rationalize away their plight in ways surprisingly devoid of bitterness. Unquestionably, some furloughed SOE workers and pensioners protested and, in some cases, violently. More common, however, were the individuals who simply walked off quietly to face their uncertain futures alone. As Marc Blecher observed in interviews conducted in 1999, even workers who had lost everything—their lifetime jobs, benefits, pensions—continued to associate markets and competition, the very mechanisms that undermined their livelihoods, with progress and fairness.[19] They tended to chalk up their problems to their own bad fate, their own lack of skills, or their own or their employer's incompatibility with the elevated standards of global modernity. In my own interviews with steelworkers during this period, I found that people facing layoffs or entitlement cutbacks would routinely rue their own inadequacies, explaining that they just did not have what it takes to succeed in the modern age of global competition. That China should enter this age, however, was rarely doubted. After all, China's dream—the dream of all its citizens—was to be modern, whatever modern exactly meant.

When resistance did arise, most notably in the countryside, it often embraced rather than eschewed the new discourse. Rural citizens, protesting excessive taxation or land expropriation by local officials, appealed to higher authorities on the basis of specific new administrative statutes and rule of law more generally, the very things the central government was promising to deliver as crucial foundations for the modern market system.[20] Not infrequently, resisters would ally themselves with new members of the mainstream establishment—lawyers, legal academics, and journalists—whose very status was tightly linked to the nation's market embrace. Such individuals had enjoyed little if any prominence during the previous decade. Lawyers barely existed as a professional class through the early 1990s. Yet, with the elevation of the market as a national goal, a societal cause, they came to play increasingly central roles as policy advisers, opinion shapers, and advocates for further change.

With the turn to the market, the state would come to rely on all manner of new professionals. Of course, these included new kinds of central bureaucrats, new kinds of local officials, and new kinds of enterprise managers. But they also included new kinds of lawyers, academics, and journalists—members of the establishment who, perhaps like members of mainstream establishments anywhere, ended up straddling both civil society and the state. All these new professionals, from the new central regulators to the lawyers, not to mention the citizens appealing to them, would now become arbiters of modernity. The official goal of the nation had been established. The exact definition of that goal, however, was thrown open for interpretation.

This, of course, underscores why perspectives emphasizing zero-sum contestation (state vs. society, citizen vs. official, democrat vs. authoritarian) so often fail to capture the depth of change, or even the depth of contestation, that goes on now in China. The battle lines today rarely follow in neat fashion traditional boundaries between citizen and state. Everybody now, whether within the state or beyond it, is—at least ostensibly—pushing forward collectively in the national goal of modernization. Where they frequently differ—and in fact, what they contest over—is the exact definition of modernity. What exactly needs to be in? Law? Democracy? Order? What can be left out? Again, the answers—or more precisely, the various people grouping together to provide answers—frequently cut across the boundaries of state and society, public and private, and even Chinese and foreign. Moreover, the participants in these discussions often do have personal interests at stake, and are trying to exert those interests against those who stand in the way. So, although contestation may not take place in the system's formal political institutions, it does take place in the context of this national discourse on modernization. In scrambling to leave their imprint on how the terms are defined, various groups and individuals are fighting for their interests, often in the name of patriotism. Indeed, for the participants themselves, the lines between self-interest and patriotic selflessness become thoroughly blurred.

It would be a great mistake to believe that this discourse over modernity amounts merely to idle discussion or parlor philosophy. In the contemporary Chinese context, terms like modernity, modern market system, and getting on the global track, while perhaps ill defined, are anything but mere abstractions. Deng Xiaoping famously described reform as "crossing the river by feeling for the stones" (*mouzhe shitou guo he*). Though observers over the years have tended to focus on the metaphor's implications for process—namely, its implied emphasis on gradualism, pragmatism, and caution—the phrase by the 1990s began to signify something more daring and sensitive. It seemed to be saying something about the ultimate destination, the end point of reform. China was indeed crossing a river, but now, the focus shifted from the crossing itself to the bank awaiting on the other side: the market. And it was not only the market in the abstract, but rather the market as represented concretely and tangibly by the world's wealthiest advanced industrial economies.

As the economist Fan Gang pointed out in 2008 on the thirtieth anniversary of Deng's initial reforms, for all the hand-wringing among Chinese elites about the direction of reform, and for all the ambiguity over the years in official pronouncements, things became increasingly clear each and every time a concrete policy problem came up. At each step by the 1990s, the question, even among the most senior leaders, inevitably became: "How did market economies deal with this?" "What is the global standard?" "What did the United States and Western Europe, or Hong Kong, or Singapore do?"[21] China may have been in self-described transition, but whether it was officially acknowledged or not, people in their very framing of the problem and their continual reference to advanced market economies as models to duplicate knew exactly what the ultimate destination was going to be. It was to be neither the obscure, officially described "planned commodity economy" (*jihua jingji yu shangpin yaosu xiang jiehe*) of the 1980s nor some highly stylized textbook definition of a market economy. Instead, it was to be the West.

Development, as Deng Xiaoping clearly and repeatedly asserted by this point, was the "hard rule."[22] But development now meant not just GDP growth. Instead, it came to encompass the establishment of the full set of societal institutions understood as modernity—everything, in effect, that the West possessed and China did not.

Historical Antecedents: Past as Present

Reeling from crisis, China in the early 1990s bound itself to an established international order. That linkage, then, would shape domestic institutional development and define the terms by which social and political contestation would unfold. Perhaps most important, the linkage would come to define the identity—and status—of nation and citizen alike. Hence, political, social, and economic change would all play out in the context of a grand societal mission. Moreover, social contestation, interest articulation, and struggles for political voice and representation would all get channeled through the language of patriotism, national loyalty, and common cause. Radical change would proceed, but would be framed by those fostering it as "within the establishment" or "on behalf of national modernization."

As people familiar with modern Chinese history know, this kind of description of the late twentieth century could just as easily be applied to the late nineteenth. The events of the 1990s, after all, by no means marked the first time in Chinese history that orthodoxy came crashing down in the face of crisis. Nor was it the first time that the search for solutions turned to the West. Indeed, the pattern in many important ways harkens back to the nation's plight of almost exactly a century earlier.

From the late eighteenth century all the way through the end of the nineteenth, China's imperial system absorbed an almost continual series of blows: famine, internal rebellion, stagnating revenues, domination by foreign powers, and increasingly in the wealthiest coastal areas, overt foreign occupation. Still, the imperial system, bound in a self-reinforcing Confucian orthodoxy, stubbornly resisted change. The orthodoxy represented not just a given social order, a prevailing power structure, but a widely inculcated set of moral principles: the privileging of stability over change, the celebration of frugality over enrichment, and the ennobling of subsistence agriculture over industry and commerce, to name a few. As pressure for change grew, even the more reformist elites grasped for only those solutions—new technologies, new tools, new weapons—that would leave orthodox core values untouched. Not entirely unlike the efforts of those attempting to reform socialism in the late 1980s, the elites addressing a comparably decrepit system in the 1880s were determined to maintain the faith. They were committed, in effect, to seeking only those treatments that would rejuvenate rather than reject the Confucian core.[23]

That would all change, however, with China's crushing defeat in the 1894–1895 Sino-Japanese War. This was a defeat, after all, not to the great imperialist powers of the West but instead to Japan, an ostensibly inferior, derivative, and offshoot stepchild of the culturally dominant Middle Kingdom. Furthermore, this was a defeat involving real loss of territory, the ceding to Japan of both Taiwan and Korea. China's elites were thrown back on their heels. The system had been eroding for years, but now, the erosion could be ignored no longer.

As would happen a century later, the terms of debate suddenly shifted. No longer would the focus remain on finding only those pro- grammatic responses that could simultaneously preserve the ideologi- cal core. Now, the overriding imperative would be to build wealth and power, even at the expense of the core. As with socialism in the early 1990s, the Confucian orthodoxy was neither vilified nor even officially abandoned. Rather, it quietly, but absolutely critically, ceased to stand as an end unto itself. What had once been sacrosanct now became part of a question. The imperative became not the preservation of the old but instead the achievement of something new: wealth and power. Once that happened, Confucianism, like socialism a century later, could be judged in terms of its utility for achieving this goal. Even if it were not categorically proclaimed deficient, it could be coupled with system- wide innovations that, in effect, rendered it defunct. And where would those innovations come from? Not from indigenous thinkers or vague abstractions but, instead, from very real external models—namely, the West. National revival, in essence, became an act of translation.

The greatest translators, people like Yan Fu, turned to all manner of writings by Darwin, Spenser, Adam Smith, Marx, Montesquieu, and numerous others. Yet, as Benjamin Schwartz points out, their search, broad as it was in scope, was directed toward one object, some kind of intellectual grasp over the basis of the West's awesome, bewildering power. That the search extended across so many domains—biology, sociology, economics, law—suggests the degree to which the West, particularly the mightiest nation of all, Great Britain, was viewed not just as an alternative collection of institutions but instead as a totally different social universe. Late nineteenth-century Great Britain, in its laws, its markets, its civic-minded citizenry, its strong state, and its breathtakingly potent military, was everything that China was not. More profoundly, the West, especially Great Britain, appeared to have liberated human intellectual energy, the individual spirit, and harnessed it for the betterment and power of the nation as a whole.[24] Hence, we find Chinese intellectuals reading into Darwin, Spenser, and Smith the rejuvenating potential of competition and struggle. We also see those intellectuals fusing individual freedom and struggle with the vitality, wealth, and power of the social organism, the nation-state.[25] Somehow, the West had figured out how to ignite human liberty and creativity, directing it to the fearless exploitation of the boundless resources of the universe.[26] The West had no fear, and Confucian China had only fear. It feared exploitation; it feared that resources were always limited; and it feared the chaos it assumed would ensue if human appetites were truly unleashed.

The West was an interconnected machinery of individualism, industrialism, entrepreneurialism, bureaucracy, corporate organization, and military might—a concatenation of opposites that somehow translated into a rich society and powerful nation. But how, Chinese intellectuals pondered, could China possibly duplicate this? What made nations like Great Britain so mighty? Was it the laws, the free markets, the companies, the bureaucratic machinery, the core social values? Was it any one of these or was it perhaps all of them?

The questions lived on for a century as China experimented with a bewildering panoply of Western-inspired solutions: Marxism, Leninism, fascism, democracy, and so on. By the second half of the century, China had settled on an answer that established a new orthodoxy: socialism. Pummeled by Maoist excesses through the 1950s and 1960s, just as the Confucian orthodoxy had been pummeled by its own set of challenges in the nineteenth century, traditional socialism still hung on desperately in the 1980s. Then, like Confucianism in the face of defeat to Japan, so too would socialism come crashing down, for all intents and purposes, in the face of crisis.[27]

Clearly, similarities exist between the two historical moments: the sudden crisis of faith at home, the searching for answers from abroad, and the willingness to directly import from abroad sweeping institutional fixes that would completely upend prevailing forms of social organization. Pervading all these efforts, then and now, is a sense of national mission, a sense of collective effort to achieve a modernity defined by more powerful societies abroad. Thus, one can understand the confounding of our own liberal sensibilities as we try to grasp what is transpiring in China. Whether rightly or not, we have trouble envisioning concepts like state and market, individual and society, or liberty and obedience as existing in anything other than contention. For many Chinese, at once observing and participating in their nation's purposive quest for modernity, the contrasts—the dichotomies—are less obvious. The nation's quest for status and modernity is, in some sense, the individual's own quest. Obviously, Chinese society, like any other, is replete with contending interest groups and tensions in the prevailing social order. At the same time, however, suffusing everything is a common societal mission, a collective quest. And in this quest, the transformation of the nation-state blends with the individual's own sense of status and identity. The notion of a national mission, after all—even among those who abhor particular policy approaches or social trends at any given moment—enjoys broad societal legitimacy. Hence, even when individuals or groups challenge the prevailing political order, they do so using the rhetoric of rule of law, getting on the global track, or any of the other terms that have come officially to be associated with modernity. Moreover, they do so not just for political cover but because they often genuinely believe it. They may be acting in their individual interests, but they are also furthering the broader societal quest for modernity. Similarly from the other side of the ledger, the government's pursuit of prosperity—"development as the hard rule"—is indisputably about individual livelihoods, but so too is it about the power of the party and nation-state. For state and citizen alike, the embrace of markets or rule of law—things grounded in the primacy of the individual and the rejection of hierarchy—is of course about unleashing human potential and liberty, but so too is it about empowering the nation.

In China's May 4 Movement at the dawn of the twentieth century, intellectuals cast China's plight as one of not just national crisis but also spiritual crisis. The problem was seen to involve not only the state and its institutions but the core values and beliefs of the individual citizen. China's plight was as much about the state's decrepitude as the citizen's "Ah Q" cretinism.[28] Hence, the search for solutions abroad exposed China to some of the West's worst excesses of social engineering: brutal authoritarianism, unbridled Leninism, Marxist class struggle, and forced-draft industrialization.

By the late twentieth century, the worst excesses were perhaps over and done with. Still, when China found itself in crisis again, this time the crisis of socialism, the problem was still understood as one of not just institutions but also societal values. Hence, the turn to the market, the effort to get on the global track, inevitably became as much about new ways of thinking as new ways of running an economy. Addressing one side of the problem inevitably involved addressing the other as well. State and society, rules and faith, and collective interests and individual liberty frequently may have contended, but so too did they intermingle in ways difficult for outsiders to comprehend. It is no wonder, then, that what so many Chinese see as their embrace of markets and their utter eschewal of old forms of state dominance, Americans and many others in the West still view as thoroughly state dominated and obviously mecantilistic. The frames of reference are so utterly different.

Yet, not everything is the same between what happened in China in the early twentieth century and what happened in the early twenty-first. The differences, in fact, may ultimately narrow the gap between the Western and Chinese frames of understanding. In the early twentieth century, Chinese reform was about borrowing external models—selecting them, importing them, and then re-creating them in indigenized form. One might be forgiven for thinking the same thing is going on in the twenty-first century, given the frequency with which terms like *market* are modified in official proclamations by the phrase "with special Chinese characteristics" (*you Zhongguo te se de*). Yet, as will be discussed in subsequent chapters, the underlying circumstances under which institutional borrowing takes place today are markedly different from what existed in the past. Most critically, production—the basic organization of how goods are made—works very differently now from how it did then. By embracing the global economy at the particular moment in the late twentieth-century that it did, China, regardless of its desires, could not set itself up as an autonomous industrial entity, an independent national production silo trading its own finished products with those of other national economies. Rather, global production today proceeds through the extraordinary dispersion of activities across myriad enterprise and national boundaries. To the extent its own growth has become dependent on linkage with the global economy, China, simply to keep its own domestic production system going, must abide by rules made abroad. China has joined the global economy, but so too has the global economy interpenetrated China.

Thus, while China is still on a national mission of modernization, this mission is not just about China any longer. It is certainly not just about Chinese leaders in isolation picking and choosing national models to import. Now it is about linking the nation's fate to a series of external rules controlled, shaped, and periodically changed by powerful actors beyond China's borders. It is also about opening the domestic system to a variety of new players, including a variety of foreign commercial entities whose presence becomes critical to the operation of domestic industry. The needs and demands of those players, then, have to be met in many cases to keep the system chugging along. Moreover, those players blend with domestic constituencies, ally based on common interests, and push for paths of market transition that suit their needs. Even if we accept the problematic assumption that the modern Chinese state seeks growth only to legitimize its monopoly over political power, that which is needed to sustain growth today in a globalized production system fundamentally reshapes the nature of the political monopoly. In the modern context for China, institutional borrowing means integrating with somebody else's system both abroad and at home. That integration on the surface may appear to be only about economics. Its underlying reality, however, is inherently social and political. Though it may have been pursued to preserve one political order, integration has developed a dynamic that is leading to—and indeed, has already created—a different order entirely.

FOUR

Taking Industry Global

China as Rising Industrial Powerhouse Versus China as Capitalist Enabler

China's Growth Story as Commonly Understood

As discussed in the previous chapter, China, in an almost desperate bid for national salvation, embraced the global economy in the 1990s. What has emerged in the fifteen years hence, however, looks anything but like a nation in despair. We are all familiar with the broad outlines of the story. During the opening years of reform in the 1980s, China grew steadily but primarily on the basis of domestic changes that permitted the system to regain ground lost during the era of command planning. Areas that had long been suppressed—household farming in the countryside, small-scale rural industry, service-related business in the cities—were all to varying degrees opened up. Citizens, especially in the countryside, responded enthusiastically and with great entrepreneurial spirit. In the most forward-thinking locales—the southern province of Guangdong, for example—the goal was to make up for lost time and catch up with the higher status industrialized heartlands of China's North and Northeast.[1] For the country as a whole, the period was about growth in response to newly unleashed domestic demand, which had previously been suppressed under command planning. At least in the countryside, it was also about basic institutional change: the elimination of collective farms and the opening up of household agriculture. Such changes allowed China's most important assets, its people, to be deployed in economically far more productive ways. Equally significant, rural citizens were deployed in a manner of their own choosing rather than the state's, a change that upped the incentives for productive economic behavior.

Yet, for all these exciting developments in rural areas, change in urban areas was tentative and inconsistent at best. For most city dwellers, change was hardly evident at all in their daily lives. The impact of Chinese reform was also minimal for everybody else in the world. China was a good public interest story—a hermit kingdom creeping out of its shell—but hardly something that affected our own day-to-day existence.

How different things would look by the 1990s and 2000s. What had been steady growth in the 1980s became torrid growth in the 2000s. And now, rather than just meeting newly unleashed domestic demand, the Chinese economy was being fueled by global demand. Trade and foreign direct investment absolutely soared. Way back at the height of the Maoist era in 1960, total trade (imports plus exports) amounted to only 8 percent of China's gross domestic output. By 2008, that figure had soared to 59 percent.[2] Real exports grew by roughly 500 percent between 1993 and 2008 alone, thus making China the world's third largest exporter, ahead of Japan and behind only the United States and Germany.[3] In early 2010, China in fact surged forward to the top slot, becoming the world's single largest exporter. On a global scale, China effectively became a market maker.

By the early 2000s, China's growth story became one not just of total trade but of substantial net exports. Trade surpluses began showing up consistently in the Chinese economy in the mid-1990s but really ballooned in the mid-2000s. By Beijing's official accounts, the nation's total trade surplus in 2008 amounted to 7 percent of annual gross domestic output. One-third of America's total trade deficit that year was attributable to goods coming from China.[4] China in all appearances had become a nation supercharged by the consumerist desires of people abroad, especially Americans.

In the midst of all this trading, China was receiving massive infusions of investment from abroad. It wasn't investments in stocks and bonds that were pouring in, the sort of hot money that can enter and exit a market at a moment's notice. Rather, what was pouring in was foreign *direct* investment (FDI), purchases by outsiders of substantial ownership stakes in China-based factories.[5] People from overseas were investing in existing Chinese factories or building entirely new ones of their own. Presumably by doing so, they were bringing with them technology and expertise, benefits that stick. Foreign direct investment at the start of reform had been negligible. In 1983, by Chinese official accounts, it amounted to only US$1.73 billion spread over 470 projects. By the 2000s, FDI was everywhere in China. In 2006 alone, US$193 billion of overseas money found its way to 27,514 projects. Between 1993 and 2006, approximately US$1.34 trillion worth of accumulated foreign direct investment had flowed into Chinese factories.[6]

Equally striking, the Chinese economy over the course of this period experienced what to the naked eye appeared to be incredible upgrading. Not only was China exporting, but its exports were growing ever more sophisticated. In the 1980s and early 1990s, China's exports had primarily come from soft industries like apparel, textiles, footwear, and toys, sectors presumably driven less by know-how and innovation than the availability of low-cost, low-skill labor. Through the mid-2000s, though, Chinese exports moved rapidly up into electronics, telecommunications equipment, office machines, and appliances, sophisticated items presumably requiring considerable expertise to produce.[7] No longer about just cheap labor, the story now seemed to be one of technology-intensive, skill-intensive, state-of-the-art production, the sort of thing we would expect of nations far richer than China.[8] Somehow, this nation seems to have emerged from nowhere to become a global industrial powerhouse.

At least in terms of how it is educating its population, this powerhouse now appears poised to become a global leader in innovation as well. Since the late 1990s, the Chinese educational system has dramatically expanded its training of science and technology (S&T) personnel, the kinds of engineers, scientists, and technicians needed to push the frontiers of innovation. As Denis Simon and Cong Cao document in their definitive work on Chinese S&T training, while the country between 1991 and 2006 experienced a nearly 20 percent increase in its total workforce, it realized a more than 200 percent increase in the number of scientists and engineers involved in S&T activities.[9] Beginning in 1999 and continuing over the course of the next decade, Chinese universities expanded the size of their incoming classes by well over 20 percent per annum.[10]

It is easy to become swept up in the enormity of such numbers, and one should remain cautiously skeptical about both the quality of the S&T training provided and the skill level of the graduates produced. However, even the soberest assessments of China's expansion efforts in education are mind-boggling. The country today is training vast amounts of human talent, an obviously critical ingredient for industrial upgrading and economic growth.

All in all then, the outlines of the story appear clear. A concerted embrace of the global economy permitted China to shift to an externally focused, trade-based mode of growth. Inflows of foreign investment and knowledge then interacted with a massive training of domestic talent to move the country swiftly up the ladder of industrial sophistication. As a result, its portfolio of global exports shifted from low-value, labor-intensive products in areas like apparel and footwear to high-value, knowledge-intensive products in sectors like computers and electronics. The move into higher value, higher productivity industries thus led to an even greater acceleration of growth and an even more rapid accumulation of resources. In the resulting virtuous circle, resources could then be devoted to more training and upgrading, more influence on the global stage, and so on down the road.

Appearances and the Assumptions We Make about Them

Is the story just described really that clear? How exactly does it all connect up? The narrative, after all, hangs on a series of vague phenomena: some sort of "opening" on the policy front; goods moving around as "trade"; money flowing in as "investment"; people going to school and getting "trained"; and somehow, a national economy, represented by a "basket" of exports, skipping forward from one industry to the next. Such abstractions are fine in a way, but what actually do they mean, and what really do they look like on the ground?

More often than not, it is left to our imaginations to decide. That is, we hear a story bound together by abstractions, and then we make assumptions—often intuitively—about what is behind those abstractions in reality. Making assumptions is fine, but we have to be sure to check on them from time to time. After all, they frequently determine the overall conclusions we draw. Surging levels of trade in a given country, for example, can mean many things. They can mean the country is rising as a self-contained economic giant, a veritable high-tech powerhouse. They could also mean, though, that the country is simply hanging on as a low-end way station in global production, a glorified sweatshop where imported components get slapped together and sent abroad as finished products. The devil is in the details.

Chinese growth is not about abstract movements of money and goods. Those are just data points existing out in the ether. Actual growth is about how those dots are connected. It is about real people doing real things on the ground: bending metal, stamping parts, molding plastics, writing software code, manipulating digital designs, and so on. Our feelings toward China are largely driven by how we believe those dots are connected up. In other words, the conclusions we draw about China (i.e., whether it is a friend or foe, a threat or an opportunity, a rival or a protégé) are driven not by the facts of rising growth numbers or shifting baskets of exports—those, after all, can mean many different things—but rather by what we assume those numbers indicate about the nature of the activities on the ground.

The remainder of this chapter explores what those activities really look like and how they jibe with the assumptions we make about them. What has China's embrace of the global economic order really meant? Does it make sense to associate China with descriptors like "rising economic giant," "shop floor of the world," or "industrial powerhouse"? Terms like these involve a particular way of connecting the dots. Is that the right way? If not, how should the dots be connected? Such questions lie at the heart of not only our understanding of China but also our fundamental beliefs about economics. This chapter examines both.

The chapter's basic message is threefold. First, what we are witnessing in China today is neither a repeat of Japan's rise in the twentieth century nor Germany's in the nineteenth. It is not about an ascendant superpower scaling the heights of technological sophistication and unseating incumbents like us in the process.

Second, it is not the opposite either. China's export economy amounts to far more than trivial, Mickey Mouse assembly operations. That economy is indeed highly dependent on export processing, but export processing in today's globalized world involves far more than just screwing together imported components, stamping a "made in China" label on the resulting product, and then shipping it overseas for sale. This is not about just some kind of massive global-scale sweatshop. Export-oriented manufacturing assembly involves meeting extraordinary managerial challenges at the firm level and equally extraordinary institutional challenges at the systemic level. That China has been able to do all this, and do it better than virtually any other nation in the world, amounts to something worth explaining. Producing cell phones or laptop computers—or even Disney toys—in today's world is anything but a Mickey Mouse endeavor.

Third, the sort of globally focused production that takes place in China, while unquestionably allowing the nation to realize substantial growth and domestic skill upgrading, has induced equally astounding upgrading abroad. China's integration into the global economy has unleashed extraordinary innovative capacity, most conspicuously in the United States and in American companies.

The Mystique of Manufacturing

Let's consider for a moment what worries us about China's meteoric rise into high-tech production and what lies behind our concerns when we see the "made in China" label on cutting-edge products. Let's also examine why so many of us feel jobs in manufacturing are important and why we worry when they seem to disappear from our own country. What is it about manufacturing? Why should jobs in this area be considered more important, more vital, and more strategic than jobs in services (i.e., health care, education, business consulting, finance, etc.)?

Answers to these questions are often as strongly felt as they are conflicted. In many ways, the confusion mirrors decades-old or even centuries-old divisions among economists over what fundamentally drives growth. Within the economics discipline, all manner of creative thinking and sophisticated research methods have been thrown at the problem. Yet, despite the generation of so much new knowledge and insight, economic growth in many ways remains a mystery.[11] We still cannot say for sure what catalyzes it, what sustains it, and what causes it to cease. There are so many variables involved—technology, social institutions, governmental policies, cultural factors—almost all of which change over time and vary from place to place. What appears to work in one place often fails in another, and what seems applicable under certain historical or technological circumstances often appears irrelevant under others.

To some extent in the broader public discourse, though, especially in the United States, one explanatory perspective—that of market liberalism—has dominated in recent decades. Americans, not entirely without reason, generally accept the idea that what drives growth more than anything else is markets. And we have certainly been inclined as a nation to urge other countries, especially poorer developing ones, to open their markets up to achieve prosperity. The underlying logic is that as long as markets are permitted to function—that is, as long as prices are freed up to reflect supply and demand, and goods are permitted to move in response—then basic laws of comparative advantage can kick into gear. Impoverished nations, flush with cheap labor, can specialize in low-end, labor-intensive manufacturing, exporting the output to the rich countries that need it but could never produce it as inexpensively. Rich nations, in turn, blessed with technology and skilled labor, can specialize in high-end, knowledge-intensive manufacturing, the kind of production that exists at the frontiers of innovation. The rich, then, can export their highly specialized output to one another and to the poor nations that need it but could never hope to produce it. Everybody would presumably benefit and grow in the process.

The added bonus, at least theoretically, is that if everything is done properly, the poor should be expected to grow more rapidly than the rich. The poor, in other words, should benefit disproportionately. This should be true as long as conditions on the ground worldwide actually reflect diminishing returns to scale, a situation in which the gains realized from an additional input of investment decline as more and more investment is made. Diminishing returns to scale is not hard to imagine conceptually. Consider for a moment the case of a very simple factory with just a handful of employees. The addition of another worker might conceivably increase output, and such increases could be expected to go on for a while as a few more workers are added. Relatively soon, though, things would start to get crowded as each new entering worker began butting up against and reducing the productivity of the people already there. Adding more workers, then, would ultimate cease to increase output. That, basically, is diminishing returns to scale. If you keep adding inputs, eventually, you are no longer going to realize any increase in outputs. In fact, you will ultimately start suffering decreases as the system bogs down.

Moving from the level of the firm to the country, one could easily imagine a similar situation applying to nations competing in the global marketplace. Rich countries presumably already have lots of money and human capital (skills and knowledge), so the returns on additional investments in those areas should be relatively small. Poor countries, however, suffer scarcity in these areas, so the returns on investment should be much larger. After all, a small investment in new equipment in a barely mechanized rural factory can lead to major gains in productivity and profitability. Presumably, then, people across the world in possession of resources—whether money or their own human talent—will direct those resources to the places that can yield the highest returns. In the aggregate, we should expect to see capital and talent flowing from rich places to poor ones. And as these resources flow, a positive growth dynamic should ensue. Infusions of money and talent should lead to industrial upgrading; industrial upgrading should permit production of higher value, higher margin exports; such production should lead to greater income; and so on. The flows from rich to poor should tail off only as the endowments of the poor—their money, their talent, their skills—equalize with those of the rich. How long that may take is anybody's guess. Nonetheless, over time, we should expect to witness an overall trend of income convergence between rich countries and poor ones.

Unfortunately, as most economists acknowledge, things have not played out this way in reality. Income convergence between rich and poor has failed to take place. Quite to the contrary, over the last 150 years the rich have tended to get richer, and the poor (at least relative to the rich) poorer. Rich nations on the whole have tended to grow faster than poor ones, and the poor have fallen progressively behind.[12]

This fact of income *divergence*, of course, neither proves nor disproves any particular theory of growth. After all, divergence could be the product of a variety of different phenomena. It could, as some have argued, be caused by markets not being opened quite enough.[13] *We didn't go far enough with marketization.* Or as others have argued, it could be caused by excessive politicization of—and state intervention in—the markets that have been opened.[14] *There is still too much governmental intervention in markets.* Alternatively, it could be caused by inadequate governmental oversight and regulation of liberalized markets, an explanation that today carries a particular air of credibility given our recent financial problems.[15] *There is not enough (of the right kind of) governmental intervention in markets.* Then again, regardless of what the government is or is not doing, maybe markets can work only if supported by the right cultural factors, norms of reciprocity or trust.[16] *Some people and cultures just are not cut out for markets.*

In an entirely different vein, our expectation that markets should generate convergence may be plain wrong. That is, we may have misconstrued the underlying conditions. What if, whether for technological or other reasons, the prevailing fact in the world is not *diminishing* returns to scale but instead *increasing* returns?[17] That is, maybe the returns on an additional increment of investment are higher in those areas already flush with the resource in question. Particularly in industries with huge start-up costs—silicon wafer fabrication, for example—the immediate returns on upgrading an existing facility might be much greater than the returns on building a new plant entirely.

Depending on the technologies involved, a large steel plant might produce more efficiently than a small one. We routinely see these sorts of things with human capital, though we often do not think about it. A trained physician is likely to earn a much higher income (i.e., realize greater returns on investment in education) in Boston than in Harare, even though doctors are far scarcer and more desperately needed in Zimbabwe than in New England. If more aspects of industry than we suspect work like this, then markets really are not the friends of the poor. Should market conditions be allowed to prevail under increasing returns to scale, resources—seeking their highest returns—would flow from regions of scarcity to regions of plenty. Income divergence would be the normal, natural outcome of markets. Indeed, for the poor to develop under such circumstances, they would have to pursue policies that somehow subvert or sidetrack market forces.[18]

Many of these issues have yet to be understood in definitive fashion. And, as often seems to be the case, just as soon as we get our finger on any one of them, the underlying conditions change. New technologies appear. New modes of organizing production arise. New ways of thinking proliferate. And new kinds of best practice developmental strategies get pushed.

Perhaps understandably, then, in our public discourse, we frequently mix and match difficult-to-reconcile views about markets. On the one hand, as noted before, most Americans are comfortable with the idea that poor nations should be advised to pursue market liberalization. We are equally comfortable with the idea that such efforts will lead to growth, presumably through the export of low-end goods. That is, we implicitly accept the story about diminishing returns to scale. In the political arena, we may complain from time to time about the proliferation of goods "made over there," and we may level accusations of dumping on overseas manufacturers, but at an intellectual level, we accept the idea that a developing country, as long as it liberalizes correctly and plays fairly, will move naturally into low-end export industries, the usual suspects of textiles, toys, shoes, and apparel. We buy those goods and do not feel existentially threatened in doing so. When nations like Sri Lanka, the Philippines, Indonesia, or Bangladesh move into textile production, we do not suddenly see them as rising powers or even serious global competitors. But why not?

Here, many of us switch over to a belief in increasing returns to scale. That is, we see low-end, low-tech production (what poor countries do) as something categorically different from high-end, high-tech production (what rich countries do). We are prepared to believe that movement into low-end production is all about diminishing returns to scale and normal global resource flows from the rich to the poor. We are ready to accept that if you are a poor nation, markets will take you where you need to go. At the same time, many of us feel implicitly that high-end production is all about increasing returns to scale. Few of us really believe that low-tech countries, simply by allowing markets to function, just upgrade naturally and seamlessly into advanced industrial production. Indeed, in the few cases in which we have seen poorer nations move up into high-tech production (i.e., South Korea and Taiwan in previous decades or China today), we have often accused them of unfairly distorting markets through trade barriers, government subsidies, or other preferential measures.

Regardless of the merits of (and politics behind) these sorts of accusations, we actually have good reason for believing that ability to engage in high-end industry stems from something more than just markets. Whether railroads and steel in the nineteenth century or automobiles and semiconductors in the twentieth, a select handful of industries at any given historical moment seemed to have separated the wealthiest, most advanced societies from everybody else. Difficult to enter and requiring huge amounts of skill to sustain, these industries stood out as a class unto themselves. The few nations in history that have successfully mastered them—Germany in the nineteenth century, Japan in the mid-twentieth century, South Korea and Taiwan in the late twentieth—also happen to be among the few that have successfully played the game of global catch up. That is, they were among the few that actually did experience income convergence with the wealthy.[19] They effectively entered the elite club of advanced industrial nations and left the rest of the developing world in the dust.

Anybody can make textiles, the thinking goes. Very few, however, can—fill in the blank for the historical period in question—make locomotives, roll steel, assemble automobiles, or fabricate semiconductors. Markets can get you naturally into apparel. They cannot, it seems, get you naturally into automobiles, aerospace, or biotech. Indeed, that is precisely why China's meteoric rise into advanced electronics, computers, and telecommunications equipment appears so unsettling. It is one thing to see "made in China" stamped on a shirt but another entirely to see it on the latest laptop or wireless device. The latter really does smack of "rising Japan" or "rising Germany."

But what exactly do we think differentiates advanced industries from their low-tech brethren? What do we imagine taking place in high-end electronics production that is different from, say, sock manufacturing?

Why should increasing returns to scale apply to the former but not the latter? How do we expect things on the ground in a rising global powerhouse (whether a Germany, Japan, or China) to look different from what goes on in an ordinary industrializer (a Bangladesh, Sri Lanka, or Philippines) that might be deeply enmeshed in global apparel production?

To arrive at an answer, we need to step back for a moment and think about something people do not normally associate with industrial production—information. Industrial production is at one level about machines and tangible products. At a different and arguably more intrinsic level, it is about information. The making of any product—high- or low-end—involves the transfer of designs (information, really) onto physical materials.[20] Hypothetically speaking, somebody coming up with a new product first sketches a design on paper. The design specifies the material to be used—say, wood, in this case—and the dimensions to which that wood needs to be cut. A craftsperson, then, looks at the designer's sketch (design information), chooses the appropriate saw (which, as a tool with a particular type of blade, has a certain amount of additional design information embedded in it), and then cuts the wood. By doing so, the craftsperson imbeds design information into a physically material, effectively transforming a chunk of wood into a part or component. As more and more components are cut, more and more design information is imparted to material. Finally, as long as the design information was reasonably accurate, the parts can all be fit together into a rough product.

Often, though, the design information is not quite complete—things get left out, pieces end up cut imprecisely, and so on—so the parts initially do not fit together perfectly. To compensate, the craftsperson then sands a bit here, recuts a bit there, and everything works out fine. In essence, the craftsperson, relying on his or her own knowledge and experience, imparts additional design information onto the material, and the final product turns out fine.

For low-end industry—sneaker or apparel manufacturing, for example—the information necessary for transforming raw materials into finished products is generally thought to be fairly straightforward. It can effectively be codified in widely available rules that describe standardized processes. The design for something like socks is simple, and the skill required to transfer that design information onto knitted material is fairly minimal, at least in theory.

These qualities amount to both a blessing and a bane. They make getting into low-end industries easy (or to put it somewhat differently, they ensure that barriers to entry are low), but precisely because so many players can jump in, competition becomes intense. Moreover, standardized production processes lead to standardized, difficult-to-differentiate products—commodities, essentially. Hence, competition can take place only over cost (as opposed to product differentiation), and cutting costs in these industries is all about cutting wages. In the end, firms compete by squeezing their workers and chipping away at their own and their competitors' margins.[21] In other words, they race one another to the bottom. Such conditions explain both why such industries crop up in poorer, marketizing countries and why the countries hosting them rarely prove able to upgrade into higher value endeavors.

Advanced high-tech industry (whether the steel and railroads of yesteryear or the autos and semiconductors of more recent times) has traditionally been understood as a totally different animal. Historically, these industries have been associated with huge upfront capital costs: expensive production facilities and lots of heavy equipment. Such equipment and tools—presses for the stamping of metals, lasers for the precision cutting of plastics, and so forth—are phenomenally costly because contained within them are extensive quantities of knowledge and design information. Just to acquire them, one has to mobilize considerable capital, a major barrier to entry in itself.

Having overcome that hurdle and jumped in, one still needs extensive knowledge and skill to carry out production. The processes involved, at least traditionally speaking, are anything but standardized. They involve huge amounts of information, more than could possibly be set down in designs or embedded in machines. Sophisticated as the designs and machines may be, even after they are brought to bear, huge amounts of know-how—information "stored" in the minds of skilled technicians—are still needed to get to a usable finished product. Put somewhat differently, participation in these industries requires titanic quantities of tacit knowledge, the kind of know-how that comes from experience and that can never quite be recorded as a recipe in a book. In these industries, you get ahead by learning, and you learn by doing. If low-tech soft industry is like a paint-by-numbers kit—you buy the kit, you fill in the colors as indicated, and you get a recognizable if uncreative painting as a result—high-tech industry is one-of-a-kind art. Rather than paint-by-numbers, it is, in a way, a Michelangelo original, something only a select few artisans can approach.

Such industries—again, at least according to the traditional understanding—are all about proprietary processes and highly differentiated products. Only a small number of firms hailing from a small number of advanced economies are ever capable of engaging in this form of production. As a result, competition tends to be oligopolistic. Only a few firms are in the game, and their profit margins tend to be large. They can then pump those profits back into innovation and new product development, thus ensuring their standing at the top. The story becomes one very much of increasing returns to scale.

And we often associate this story with a particular type of production organization: the massive, vertically integrated corporation.[22] Whether it was German steel firms in the nineteenth century or American auto giants in the twentieth, such firms for many people even today define modernity. To some degree, this makes sense given the sorts of challenges such firms were historically able to overcome. Advanced industry for well over a century was one and the same with advanced manufacturing, the coordination of multiple assembly-line steps and the fitting together of multiple highly complex components. The whole chain had to work exactly right for the final product to come out decently. Massive amounts of tacit, uncodifiable information had to be brought to bear to make this happen. Regardless of the efficacy of initial designs, final products involved so many different parts interacting in so many different ways that designers could not possibly predict performance characteristics in advance.[23] They may have known how they would like the product to perform, but realizing that goal in the initial design was almost impossible. Instead, engineers, technicians, and skilled assembly-line workers, with all their combined creativity, had to hit the shop floor, tweak parts, shift designs, reposition machines, or fine-tune processes so as to come up with a product that reflected in practice what designers had envisioned in theory.

From this perspective, then, what really makes advanced industries work—whether in the past or present—are large manufacturing-focused organizations armed with tacit knowledge. The knowledge accumulates through the act of manufacturing itself—the bending of metal, the stamping of parts, and the constant movement of engineers back and forth in the trial-and-error process of making components fit better and final products perform more effectively. Precisely because the knowledge is tacit, it must be transmitted through face-to-face interaction—conversations, meetings, and on-the-fly consultations on the shop floor. Hence, it follows logically that the various pieces of production—product definition, detailed design, design for manufacturability, component design and manufacture, subsystem assembly, and final product assembly—all need to be located in the same place and under one corporate roof. When this process works right, all the knowledge that accumulates over years of manufacturing experience—all the trial-and-error experimentation, all the problem solving, all the refined techniques—becomes embedded in the organization. The firm, in effect, becomes a vessel for innovation, a sort of national industrial treasure.

This national treasure, from its basis in technology- and capital-intensive manufacturing, then develops a series of complementary, knowledge-based skills.[24] It develops managerial expertise in handling large-scale operations. It develops marketing expertise as it pushes a steady stream of products into new locales and learns to respond to new customer demands. It develops financing expertise to fund its own operations and its customers' credit needs. It develops research capabilities as it seeks to place itself even further out on the frontiers of technology. All of these capabilities are understood to derive from manufacturing, and each for the company becomes an additional source of differentiation and competitive advantage.

All this knowledge, in turn, repeatedly feeds back into better and better manufacturing. Such learning can manifest itself in a variety of ways. Information might be managed more efficiently in the existing production process, thus allowing for higher product quality, fewer discards, and leaner inventories, all important issues for cost reduction. Or accumulated knowledge might permit upgrading into entirely new, innovative products. Either way, the firm effectively innovates and upgrades into activities that few if any competitors can duplicate.

To many Americans, this story should sound familiar. It is basically that of the U.S. auto industry in the first half of the twentieth century. So too is it the story of the Japanese, who supplanted the Americans by the end of the century. Large conglomerates like Toyota, often with a certain amount of governmental support, aggressively focused on learning and skill development.[25] At first, they concentrated on low-end products but almost always with an export focus. Global markets served as benchmarks for cost and quality. If the product proved uncompetitive globally, then the firm would be deemed a failure, and its practices would have to be changed. If the product proved successful, the firm would then focus on further cost cutting, further quality enhancement, and movement upward into higher value, higher margin products.[26] Time and again, this happened with Japanese firms. Later, the process would repeat itself with South Korean conglomerates. Whether for Nissan, Toyota, Komatsu, POSCO (Pohang Iron and Steel), Hyundai, or Samsung, export-oriented, globally focused manufacturing became the linchpin for catching up with leading firms from the United States and Europe. No wonder Americans worry about the apparent decline of U.S.-based manufacturing, and no wonder they are looking over their shoulder at China.

Indeed, the rarity with which nations have successfully pulled off "catch up" just adds to its mystique. Numerous countries have tried and failed. Several undoubtedly had the money and basic expertise to jump in—the Soviet Union, East Germany, and Czechoslovakia, for example, in autos, or the Chinese early in the 1970s in commercial airliner production. They bought all the right machines, and they duplicated existing, proven designs. In effect, they accessed all the codified information that was available. In some cases, they were able to turn out products—Lada sedans, the (in)famous Trabant subcompacts, Skoda hatchbacks, and in the Chinese case, a single flyable Boeing 707-like Y-10. Producing a poorly performing product, however, is different from producing a usable one. And a usable product is still different from one actually produced on a commercially competitive basis. In a way, these industrial aspirants mistakenly thought they could achieve Sistine Chapel-like products by purchasing paint-by-number kits. That they ended up with the equivalent of cheap motel room art—cars whose doors did not shut or airplanes whose excessive weight made carrying passengers or freight impossible—confirms how truly important tacit knowledge really is in these special industries and how difficult it is to capture commercially in a firm.

That, of course, makes the cases of success even more conspicuous in our minds. Virtually every great nation in modern history has been associated with storied industrial conglomerates. Some of these commercial titans remain today. Others have departed the scene. Their names, though, are recognized worldwide: Krupp, Thyssen, U.S. Steel, General Motors, Toyota, IBM, Philips, Standard Oil, Bell Labs, among others. And now from China, we seem to be witnessing the emergence of a new set of titans: Lenovo (which acquired IBM's PC business in 2005) in computers; Huawei and ZTE in telecommunications; PetroChina, SinoPec, and CNOOC in oil and gas; Haier and Galanz in appliances; Gome (Guomei) in retail; and so on. Somehow, China appears to have achieved that which has eluded so many other countries: the quantum leap from commodified, low-end production to state-of-the-art, advanced industry. Just consider what China and its leading companies were able to accomplish in the opening ceremonies of the 2008 Beijing Olympics. The event's unparalleled technological wizardry, its sheer scale, and the incredible amount of coordination involved were breathtaking, to say the least. And now China holds the largest reserves of foreign currency in the world. It appears unstoppable. Why shouldn't it be understood as Germany and Japan redux? Why shouldn't it be seen as the latest instance of an emerging great power rising on the basis of its manufacturing-based, industrial might? And why shouldn't we be concerned?

Shadows of Doubt: Four Puzzling Aspects of Chinese Industrial Development

Arguing that China has become a global hub for high-tech manufacturing makes a lot of sense. Arguing that it is thus duplicating the developmental trajectory of earlier risers (i.e., Germany, Japan, South Korea, etc.) makes a lot less sense. China is most definitely involved in high-tech industry but not in the way that such involvement traditionally is supposed to look. That is, the activities going on in China today bear almost no resemblance to what we saw in prior eras in Germany, Japan, or South Korea. Either China is not what we think it is, high-tech manufacturing is not what we think it is, or both.

Four factors, in particular, make China look different from previous risers. First, as mentioned, Chinese industry, particularly in export-oriented sectors, exhibits extremely high levels of foreign investment and ownership. In 2008, foreign invested enterprises accounted for 55 percent of China's total exports and 54 percent of the nation's imports.[27] In China's higher tech, higher value consumer product sectors (i.e., DVD players, TVs, high-end electronics, microwave ovens, etc.), foreign-invested firms by the mid-2000s were accounting for almost 90 percent of exports.[28] Those are incredibly high numbers, historically unprecedented for large, export-focused economies. Japan and South Korea grew with almost no FDI or foreign ownership, and even Taiwan—an island exporter once relatively reliant on multinational firms—never approached the levels of FDI dependence seen in China today.

Second, much of the advanced production going on in China today—much like in lower tech soft industries—involves export processing. Semifinished or finished components are brought in from overseas locales, usually neighboring Asian nations, assembled into finished products, stamped as "made in China," and then shipped out to markets in North America and Europe. From the early 1990s to the present, China's strongest export growth has occurred in electronics, computers, and telecommunications equipment, areas that have increasingly supplanted traditional soft exports like apparel, textiles, footwear, and toys. Yet, these higher end, high-tech areas are also the ones in which the export processing trade has grown the fastest. In 2006, for example, "electrical machinery and mechanical appliances" (i.e., televisions, MP3 players, DVD players, etc.) accounted for about 47 percent of China's total exports.[29] About 70 percent of those electrical appliance exports, though, pertained to processing trade.[30]

The Apple iPod is a typical example of the phenomenon. Accurately stamped "assembled in China," the product is for the most part composed of components brought in from beyond China's borders. As described in an extremely interesting 2007 report by researchers from the University of California, Irvine, a thirty-GB iPod in 2005 retailed in the United States for around US$299.[31] The rough cost of all the inputs—in other words, the price Apple paid for the finished iPod when it came from a Taiwanese-owned, China-based contract manufacturer—was estimated to be US$144.40. Of that US$144.40, 3 percent (US$3.70) went to the Taiwanese assembler operating in China, 51 percent went to the Japanese hard drive producer (who made that component in China, again using imported parts), 14 percent went to the Japanese display module producer (who made the display in Japan), 3 percent went to the American semiconductor designer (who, as a design house, had negligible production or overhead costs), and 2 percent went to the Korean memory chip producer (who produced those chips in Korea).[32]

One interpretation is that the advanced products being produced in China are based not only on imported components but components that embody the most sophisticated aspects of the finished product. In other words, all the things we associate with advanced industry and high-tech products—the knowledge, the innovation, the sophistication—are embedded in the components, which for the most part are made outside China by non-Chinese companies. Even when pieces are made in China—again, often with imported subcomponents—they are generally done so by non-Chinese companies. Indeed, even product assembly, an activity we rarely view as a high-tech or high-value endeavor, is done in China by foreign-owned companies.

Third, many of the ostensibly advanced, high-tech products that come out of China today—regardless of who produces them—behave on the market in ways we associate with commodities rather than in ways we associate with cutting-edge goods. Items like DVD players and microwave ovens, all classified as high-tech exports in the statistical compilations of China's Ministry of Science and Technology, can now routinely be purchased in the United States for under US$50. They have effectively become inexpensive, undifferentiated products—commodities. Personal computers, at an obviously higher price range, have taken on this quality as well, a factor that contributed to IBM's decision to sell its PC division to China's Lenovo.[33] All but the highest end cell phones and digital cameras also now behave increasingly like commodities. They are sophisticated and high tech, but they have come down substantially in cost and are treated by consumers as undifferentiated, routine purchases. Today, buying a "made in China" MP3 player or microwave oven is for many consumers not so different from buying a "made in China" T-shirt. Products like the iPhone, gadgets people are willing to buy at a substantial premium, seem now more the exception than the norm, and even then, the value appears to be captured by the firm doing the design and branding rather than the manufacturing.

And that leads to a fourth point. Whirlwinds of innovation are taking place in advanced industry today but not primarily—or so it seems—in the companies actually doing the manufacturing. The latest innovations in wireless devices, for example, seem to involve battles between Apple, Palm, Research in Motion (the maker of the BlackBerry), and Google, companies that outsource their manufacturing to others. We do not hear much in this context about the China-based assemblers of those products, and we hear even less about indigenous Chinese firms. Furthermore, many new innovations seem to involve components rather than final products: Intel versus AMD processors, Palm-powered versus Microsoft-powered PDAs, Apple versus Windows operating systems, and so on. Nowhere really do we hear about Chinese players in the mix, though almost all the innovations we see are in one way or another embedded in products made in China.

None of these observations is definitive. Taken together, though, they describe an overall pattern. China is growing economically by deepening its involvement in export-oriented manufacturing. Yet, that manufacturing is managed in large part by foreign-owned and foreign-invested companies. In addition, that manufacturing appears in many cases to be detached from knowledge-intensive activities and products. Much of the innovation that we witness appears to be carried out by companies quite removed from the ones actually bending the metal, so to speak. And a number of the advanced products coming out of China are sold not as highly differentiated specialty items but instead as commodities.

We need to step back and figure out what this all means both with respect to China and global production more generally. Why are so many of the production activities that once had to be colocated in a single industrial conglomerate now dispersible across different firms and geographies? How and where is innovation happening now that the activities are so broken up and spread apart? Why do so many of the innovators appear not to be engaged in the physical act of manufacturing? And why is so much of the manufacturing going on in China managed by overseas firms? What does this all mean for China, and what does it mean for us?

The Shifting Architecture of Global Production

For many people, globalization amounts to a set of new circumstances fundamentally shaping our lives—a speeding up of activities all around us, an extension of activities that were once local to the farthest reaches of the globe, and a drawing in of activities from those farthest reaches right to our own doorsteps. Everything now—from new technologies and newly rising nations to new global climatic patterns and new security threats—seems so sped up and interconnected. In many ways, this is what globalization is all about. Yet, in a deeper sense, these aspects are derivative of something else, a completely new way of organizing production. That new mode of organization, in turn, is derivative of the most fundamental new capability of all: digitization.

Digitization, the ability to represent almost anything—an object, an image, a sound, a signal—in a structured sequence of binary digits, has enabled virtually everything we associate with globalization. It has revolutionized our lives in the process. More precisely, digitization, coupled with technologies like the integrated circuit that permit the storage and handling of almost limitless quantities of binary data, has revolutionized the nature of information. Information of the type once too complex to be represented as a set of discrete steps and rules can now easily be set down as code. The codified data, in turn, can now be easily stored and recalled, as we ourselves know in our everyday use of laptops, cameras, USB drives, and other digital devices. So too can that information be easily transmitted anywhere in the world, instantaneously, and at extremely low cost, again something we take for granted in our daily downloads, uploads, and e-mails.

All of this has changed the way we as individuals live. More profoundly, it has changed the way we as a civilization produce. Human civilization, from the Bronze Age to the Computer Age, has in large part been about making stuff. And making stuff, as we noted previously, has always been largely about managing design information. Throughout history, revolutions in production—revolutions in the way we make stuff—have marched hand in hand with revolutions in information management. Digitization has ushered in the latest of these revolutionary moments.

How exactly, though, does digitization—the ability to specify, codify, and transfer huge amounts of data—change production? As we discussed earlier, for much of history, the defining characteristic of advanced industry—that which separated it from ordinary industry and restricted it to a select few elite players—has been informational complexity. These were the kind of industries that produced complex products through complicated multistep production processes. Vast amounts of design information had to be transferred onto physical materials. Given technologies available at the time, however, only a small portion of this information could be codified in blueprints, schematics, or production rules. The rest had to come through the accumulated experience and knowledge of people, who were then generally organized hierarchically within a single firm.

But now, digitization and computerization have erased much of that. By permitting the codification of almost all information, they have effectively eliminated what made advanced industries "advanced." Today, design information, down to the most detailed specifications, can be set down in code. Codified information, in turn, can be transmitted to a variety of different players or programmed directly into the operating software of machines that can then stamp out precisely formed components. Those components can then be fit together again through codified information—highly specific standards and formal rules of connectivity. Components no longer need to be codesigned and coproduced but instead can be made as stand-alone modules by separate highly specialized companies. Because so much design information can be codified, the production process itself can be modularized—broken apart into separate stand-alone steps that can each be done by a specialized firm.

The manufacturing know-how of a single massive conglomerate has ceased to be the "secret sauce" needed to make production work. No longer is so much tacit knowledge—so much of the shop-floor-based engineer's or machine operator's Mr. Fix-it know-how—needed in the production process to make up for the informational gaps that used to exist in formal designs. No longer do people, bound by a single firm's way of doing things and imbued with their own experience-based problem-solving skills (developed, generally, through an entire career spent in that same firm), have to continually move back and forth across the whole production process, tweaking here and refining there. In the past, especially in advanced industry, production was about complex processes glued together through the tacit knowledge of a single organization. Today, with digitization and modularity, production in all industries—from the most sophisticated to the least—is about complex processes linked by codified standards but spread across a bewildering array of individual producers.[34]

At times, it feels as if almost anything can be done anywhere by anybody. Take computer production as an example. In the 1960s, during the early days of the mainframe computer, leading innovators like IBM—all massive conglomerates—designed and produced not only the machine itself but all its key components (transistors, processors, memory chips, switches, terminals, etc.), its operating system, and its related software. For years, much of that was done in a single facility in Endicott, New York.[35]

Now, as we all know, things couldn't be more different. A typical laptop computer most likely is branded by one company, one based perhaps in California or Texas, but is assembled by another, one likely headquartered in Taiwan but doing the hands-on assembly operation in China. Design work may be shared across the engineering teams of both firms. Meanwhile, the computer's high-value "guts" are made in a variety of places by a variety of different firms. The microprocessor, a branded component in its own right ("Intel inside"), may be produced by an American company in a U.S.-based semiconductor fabrication plant ("fab") but is then assembled and tested by the same company's operation in Malaysia. The screen may be produced by a Japanese or Taiwanese company, the disc drive by an American company operating in Singapore, the operating system by another American firm operating worldwide, and so on. Thus, for the production of a single high-tech product, manufacturing activities end up spread out across North America, Europe, and Asia.

But this new architecture of production involves more than just outsourcing and offshoring, the migration of manufacturing to new people and places. It is not only—or even primarily—a story of new competitors moving up rungs of a ladder and displacing old competitors in the process. Instead, it is about organizing the ladder in an entirely new way. The ladder has become totally transformed—bent in different directions, flipped end on end, and multiplied in a variety of different incarnations. Along all these new ladders, players from emerging and advanced economies alike are on the move and interacting. Competitors from China are scurrying upward but so too, and even more impressively, are ones from the advanced industrial world. Often, they are doing so in complementary, interrelated ways. Indeed, what is now being done in emerging markets has enabled transformative upgrading in places like the United States.

China undoubtedly now plays a central role in the new architecture of global production. Yet, this story is as much about us as them. It is as much about our own transformative upgrading as theirs. In fact, our respective experiences in rapid industrial upgrading are deeply intertwined. In the sections to follow, we examine how this is so as we march through a variety of manifestations of twenty-first-century modularized production.

The Effect of Modular Production, Take 1: The Barriers (to Entry) Come Tumbling Down

By permitting the codification of information—and thus reducing the importance of prior experience and tacit knowledge—digitization has opened up high-tech industry to new commercial entrants. As we all know, Chinese firms have rushed in en masse. Yet, though they are now present in industries like information technology and high-end electronics, their presence is for the most part confined to the simplest, most codified activities within those industries. That is, they are in, but not in deeply. They may be producing only a small, relatively simple part of a much more complex final product. Or they may be doing final assembly of a series of components produced by others outside China. Or they may be supplying a low-end IT network that leading global providers have long since moved beyond.

The point here is that to understand what many Chinese firms are doing—indeed, what anybody today is doing—one cannot think as we once did about industries. Instead, we should think about activities. It no longer makes sense to suggest that certain industries on the whole—whether IT, computers, aerospace, or any other—are inherently complex or inordinately lucrative. Now, production processes in virtually all industries—whether advanced or ordinary—can be split up into separable, discrete steps. Some of these steps—again, both in advanced and ordinary industry—have become standardized and commodified. Relatively simple to enter, some of these steps—activities, really—behave much like our prior understanding of low-tech industry as a whole. Meanwhile, other activities today still defy codification and standardization. They remain deeply knowledge intensive, exclusive, and highly profitable. In effect, they behave like our prior understanding of advanced industry. Modularity, by breaking up production processes across the board, has lowered barriers to entry in virtually every industry, high-tech and low. But where those barriers have really fallen is not in any single industry as a whole but rather only in particular kinds of activities across many industries. Now, therefore, whether we are thinking about apparel or aerospace, we need to think about low-value versus high-value activities within each and every one of those industries. A company today can jump into aerospace but end up doing nothing more exclusive than what it had been doing previously in basic electronics assembly. Conversely, a company can be in apparel today but doing highly specialized, difficult-to-replicate, high-value activities.

In the Chinese case, we have seen producers rush into newly opened industries but largely in the low-value end of the activity spectrum. What appears as upgrading from soft industries to high-tech ones, then, often involves very little upgrading at all, at least in the way many of us understand the term.

A survey of Chinese firms that I conducted in 2001 in cooperation with the World Bank illustrates the point.[36] The survey focused on high-tech industries—sectors like electronics, IT, and automotives where one would expect to find more sophisticated commercial activities. Several things became immediately apparent. First, the Chinese companies that participated in the survey—1,500 enterprises spread across five major cities—were unquestionably engaged in global production. Almost all were either producing components whose designs and specifications were set by foreign firms or doing export processing and final assembly for foreign-branded products. Second, the survey respondents were generally operating at much smaller scale and with much narrower profit margins than global counterparts in the same overall industry. Third, the Chinese firms, though engaged in high-tech industries and integrated into global production chains, clustered around the most standardized and nondifferentiated activities in those chains. Only a small portion of the firms surveyed, roughly 15 percent, reported doing any design work for foreign customers.

An even smaller portion, 7 percent, reported doing any R&D work or any provision of specialized, proprietary services to customers. In fact, deeper relationships with other players up and down the supply chain—let alone with consumers of the final completed product—seemed to elude these firms entirely. Most just moved their output through trading companies, effectively "throwing their products over the wall" instead dealing directly with actual end users.

All in all, these firms were rule takers rather than rule makers in the game of globalized production. They had rapidly moved into activities thrown open by modular production and digitization. Once in, though, they were having a difficult time moving up. As survey respondents themselves reported, they were struggling just to survive in an intensely cost-competitive environment. Pump money into R&D and upgrading? Where were such funds supposed to come from? Where was the time to devote to research going to come from? Rather than squirreling away profits for investment in upgrading, these firms were doing the opposite—cutting their margins in a bid for survival.

Chinese firms, though, do have to make substantial investments just to stay in the basic manufacturing game. In this sense, it is not quite accurate to say that jumping into standardized manufacturing is a trivial matter. It is also not completely accurate to suggest no upgrading takes place in these new participants in global production. Just to participate in supply-chain-oriented work, firms have to substantially upgrade their capital equipment and their managerial capabilities. Complex supply chains, though they involve many different firms, are frequently driven by the demands of a few dominant players such as Boeing, Coca-Cola, Siemans, Johnson Controls, Nike, or Wal-Mart. Such firms set the standards, define the products, issue the designs, and push the delivery schedules. Although neither omnipotent nor immune from hold-up problems by partners in the supply chain, these firms are extraordinarily powerful, particularly relative to those performing truly commodified activities like basic product assembly or basic component fabrication. Those firms at the bottom of the food chain have to meet exacting specifications, quality standards, and schedules, all passed down from above. Moreover, they need to respond to frequent changes along all these dimensions. If they cannot respond, particularly if they are performing a basic assembly function, supply-chain leaders will take the business elsewhere.

So what is the product assembler to do? How can it firm up its position in the chain? One thing it tries to do is invest in the latest capital equipment—state-of-the-art knitting machines, advanced metal stamping machines, precision machine tools, or whatever else is required for the activity in question. By purchasing machines that are embedded with complex design information—the kind of information that previously could be conveyed only through the tacit knowledge of a skilled technician—the assembler can more easily meet the quality and flexibility standards demanded by supply-chain leaders. Most of these tools are imported from abroad.

This story unquestionably has positive aspects. After all, on an aggregate level, purchases of such infusions of technology have driven economic growth in China. Much of the country's growth story has been about productivity gains achieved through movement from low-technology conditions—minimally mechanized agriculture and basic industry—to higher technology ones. That is, by purchasing foreign technologies—know-how embedded in machines—China's industrial economy has been able to realize higher output per worker, greater returns, and all the attendant effects of wealth generation.

This story also has positive aspects for those outside China. China may be a massive exporter today, but it is also a massive importer both of knowledge-intensive components used in export processing and of capital equipment necessary for modern manufacturing. In 2008, U.S. exports to China amounted to US$71.5 billion, about 5.5 percent of all American exports that year and an increase of nearly 10 percent from the previous year's exports to China.[37] China today is the third largest purchaser of U.S. goods globally, trailing only Canada and Mexico. What kinds of things have American companies been selling to Chinese customers? Electrical machinery and equipment (i.e., computers, computer-aided design systems, etc.), medical equipment (CT scanners, MRI machines, etc.), power generation equipment, heavy transport equipment (construction vehicles, excavators, cranes, etc.), and of course, aircraft.[38] The story is similar but even more pronounced in Germany's trade with China. China is Germany's second largest export market outside the European Union, trailing the United States but ahead of Japan.[39] And what are Chinese companies buying from the Germans? Again, plant machinery, electrical equipment, optics, transportation equipment, and so on. When a semiconductor fab (fabrication plant) goes up in China, more likely than not it is using hundreds of millions of dollars of nanomanufacturing equipment from the likes of Lam Research, Applied Materials, and KLA-Tencor in the United States or ASML in the Netherlands.

When Chinese companies purchase such equipment, they are, in a sense, upgrading from low-technology conditions to higher level ones.

What they are not really doing, however, is upgrading to higher value activities. In other words, they are purchasing know-how that has been codified and embedded in machines. Those expensive machines, then, permit a Chinese factory with a low- or semiskilled workforce to manufacture a high-quality component consistently, flexibly, and rapidly—performance characteristics absolutely essential for playing in the global supply-chain game. Worth remembering is that all this has to be done just to participate in the basic manufacturing—the straightforward assembly—of fairly simple commodity products. Consider, then, how much more is needed to move into higher value activities like R&D, product design, branding, or customer service.

Moreover, all of this technology adoption and operational flexibility must be managed, which is a tall task in its own right. Some kinds of know-how can be purchased as embedded information in machines. Other kinds—managerial know-how—while not available in machines, can still be purchased in a sense. It is purchased as foreign direct investment (FDI). When a Chinese corporate entity sells a piece of itself—an ownership share—to an outsider, a two-way transaction is taking place. The foreigner is acquiring an ownership stake in the Chinese firm (often a majority one), which carries with it a substantial amount of managerial control and a claim to future revenue streams. What does the Chinese entity get in return? Some scholars, including my friend and brilliant colleague at MIT, Yasheng Huang, have suggested that they don't get much, save for decent treatment in a poorly designed, politically misguided Chinese regulatory environment that affords foreign-owned entities better treatment than domestic private firms.[40] According to this perspective, the Chinese entrepreneur, simply to get a fair shake in his or her own country, must sell out to the foreigner. Huang is undoubtedly correct that private entrepreneurs have suffered considerable discrimination at the hands of the state in China. Nonetheless, I would argue that such discrimination is not the only, or even primary, reason for the prevalence of foreign ownership. Instead, what drives demand for FDI—the willingness of Chinese industrial entities to sell shares to outsiders—are the managerial challenges associated with operating in global supply chains. By selling off stakes in themselves, Chinese firms are effectively purchasing managerial know-how not unlike how they purchase know-how in imported manufacturing tools. And just as know-how embedded in a machine often remains in the machine (the machine is not easily reverse engineered), so too does managerial know-how often remain embedded in the foreign manager. That is, the knowledge is slow to transfer over to

Chinese managers. Hence, we see persistent patterns in China of high levels of sophisticated technology purchases and high levels of foreign ownership of domestic industry.

This need not be viewed either positively or negatively. It should by no means be taken as a slight to the Chinese system. That China has been able to purchase the machines, welcome in the foreign owners, and build the supporting market institutions, and do it better than virtually every other developing world locale, is a credit to the nation and its population. At the same time, what the Chinese experience indicates is that for low- and middle-income nations, the era of modular production has brought anything but a flat world. Many have fallen behind. China, the greatest success story among them, can claim the signal achievement of having kept pace, playing its part in a global production system effectively controlled by—and often convulsed by—foreign commercial entities.

Because the focus for Chinese industry is now so much on basic manufacturing assembly, outcomes in high-tech sectors look much as they do in ostensibly lower end areas like apparel. The relationship between Wal-Mart and Chinese suppliers in the knitwear industry is fairly typical.[41] Wal-Mart since the early 2000s has operated a major sourcing network in China. By the mid-2000s, the company was annually sourcing from China roughly US$18 billion in goods—mostly clothing, home decor items, and toys.[42] The exact figure is hard to determine because Wal-Mart reports only direct purchases by its China-based sourcing operation, leaving unstated the purchases done through China-based agents with whom it works closely. By splitting the figures in this way, a practice dating from 2005, Wal-Mart can distance itself from some of the political headaches that come from racking up high levels of Chinese imports, not to mention the public relations headaches that come from reports of substandard conditions in China-based suppliers.

Regardless, for many Chinese suppliers, particularly in areas like knitwear, Wal-Mart is far and away the largest customer. The Boshan Linar Garments Company in China's Shandong Province is typical. In 2006, roughly 80 percent of the company's output went to Wal-Mart.[43] Similar numbers obtained for the "king of the sock industry" (*waye dawang*), China's Langsha Knitting Company. Suppliers like Langsha, Boshan, or the Jiaxing Yishangmai Fashion Company, a major sweater exporter in eastern China, generally operate in one-industry towns surrounded by hundreds or even thousands of similar firms producing similar kinds of goods. Yiwu City, an apparel manufacturing hub in China's Zhejiang Province and home to Langsha, has more than 14,000 enterprises spread across everything from hosiery to zippers and accessories.[44] To distinguish themselves from the crowd and attract the business of major buyers like Wal-Mart, suppliers, as discussed earlier, often must import expensive capital equipment—knitting machines, embroidering equipment, cutting machines, and so forth. Such equipment is necessary for achieving the tighter weaves, higher quality standards, and more varied production runs expected by overseas customers. The financial and managerial demands of these teched-up operations then push producers to demand FDI—that is, enter joint ventures or other co-ownership arrangements with foreign manufacturers, whether from Europe, North America, or Australia, thus adding claimants to already narrow profit margins.

Having done all this just to enter the supply chain, producers still get squeezed by rising production costs and increasing competition. By 2007, Chinese garment producers, as in so many other manufacturing sectors, were facing rapidly escalating wage bills, energy prices, and raw material costs. At the same time, new competitors from places like Indonesia and Vietnam were nipping at their heels, luring away North American retailers and their purchasing agents.[45] In 2007, Langsha, insisting it could not survive on the profit margins offered by Wal-Mart, severed the relationship for a period of time. That same year, Jiaxing and Boshan also lost all or some of their Wal-Mart orders. Meanwhile, these suppliers were stuck with the capital equipment and attendant financial obligations they amassed simply to participate in global production in the first place.[46] It is an awfully tough, unforgiving game to play.

The Smile Curve

One way to conceptualize the phenomenon is through what Stan Shih, the founder of the Taiwanese computer company Acer, terms his "smile curve" for value creation.[47] The curve, derived from Shih's observations of the IT industry, attempts to compare the relative profit margins of all the different activities needed to produce a finished product—a computer, say—in a high-tech knowledge industry. In many respects, though, it can be applied to any industry today. As indicated by figure 4.1, the high-value portions of the curve appear at the extreme edges—upstream in knowledge-intensive and highly proprietary R&D, product definition, and design and downstream in equally knowledge-intensive branding, marketing, distribution, and customer service. The activities surrounding the invention of new technology,

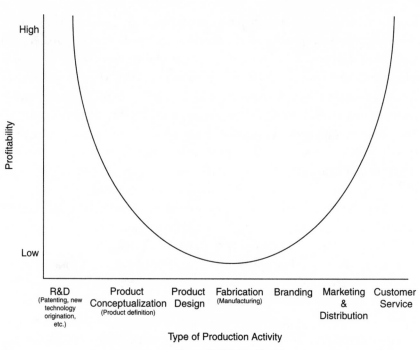

FIGURE 4.1 Stan Shih's Smile Curve

like those involving actual engagement with end users, involve firm- and person-specific know-how rather than standardized, codified routines. Hence, such activities remain proprietary and high value.

Manufacturing, however—or more precisely, product assembly—ends up as a standardized, low-value affair. As long as you buy the right machines and, for slightly more sophisticated manufacturing activities, relatively easy-to-obtain foreign managerial expertise, you are in. But so too is everybody else who does the same. The lesson is clear. If you want to survive over the long run, and especially if you want to make money, you have to get out of the smile's trough and up into its dimples.

If the curve were applied to China, one could argue—somewhat accurately—that producers there are stuck almost exclusively in the trough. They are suffering the plight of developing country manufacturers worldwide. The very thing that granted them entry into manufacturing—codification of information—now haunts their existence as they struggle for dwindling profits in completely standardized operations. The only difference in China is that producers there have struggled better than counterparts elsewhere. Thus, while their entry into commodified production may have displaced workers in comparable activities in the United States—whether in footwear, apparel, furniture, or similar industries—most of those activities departed American shores decades ago. Instead, the workers who have really been unseated by the Chinese are those in other developing world locales: Southeast Asia, South Asia, Mexico, and much of the rest of Latin America. As indicated by the Langsha example, though, some of these locales—Vietnam, the Philippines, Indonesia—are fighting back, thus inducing further cost cutting by the Chinese and a more rapid "race to the bottom" for producers everywhere.

The Effect of Modular Production, Take 2: Upgrading by Foreign Contract Manufacturers in China

Despite all the challenges just discussed, there is nothing about modular production that absolutely precludes movement up the smile curve. Indeed, within China, there are several noteworthy examples of manufacturing-centered upgrading. Where they have occurred, though, are primarily in overseas-owned, especially Taiwanese-owned, firms. Such companies, while maintaining a substantial presence in China, are actually multinational manufacturing specialists that have been able to integrate China-based operations into a broader set of activities. In so doing, they have become potent global players. Some of the best examples are companies like Quanta, Foxconn, Delta, and ASUS, Taiwanese-owned multinationals that now perform vital roles in global electronics and IT production.[48]

These firms share a set of basic characteristics. First, they all started as contract manufacturers, specialists in the fabrication of all manner of electronics products and componentry. No matter what the component—motherboards, graphics cards, cables, power supplies, and so on—they could produce it inexpensively as long as its design was fairly well established. Their expertise lay neither in product definition (the initial conceptualization of a product), product design, branding, nor marketing. They simply knew how to build stuff cheaply and almost always for somebody else—whether IBM, Dell, Hewlett-Packard, or any other brand leader—whose name ended up on the product and who garnered the bulk of the profits.

Second, over time, in large part through huge manufacturing campuses that they located across the Taiwan Straits in mainland China, these firms have grown to tremendous scale. Foxconn today, in its main manufacturing site in Shenzhen, China, employs upwards of 300,000 people and manufactures virtually every laptop computer and printer sold by Dell and HP.[49] Taipei-headquartered ASUS, with manufacturing sites in Suzhou and Shanghai, by 2008 was producing more than 24 million motherboards (40 percent of the global market) and hundreds of thousands of notebook computers annually.[50] Quanta, arguably the largest laptop manufacturer in the world, makes in its China-based facilities, among other things, virtually all of Apple's solid body laptop computers, high-end machines like the MacBook Pro and MacBook Air, not to mention Apple iPhones. Delta, in addition to the many other things it does, produces the power supply "bricks" for most of the branded laptops sold worldwide.

The pattern fits Timothy Sturgeon's characterization of electronics-related contract manufacturing more generally.[51] The outsourcing of manufacturing by brand leaders has not led to an explosion of small-scale contract manufacturers operating in every corner of the globe. This isn't the flat world of limitless opportunity for the little guy. Instead, even in ostensibly commodified manufacturing assembly, the piece of the supply chain with the lowest barriers to entry, we witness a world composed of a small number of scaled-up, highly specialized conglomerates operating in a select few global locales, China paramount among them.[52] These large contract manufacturers compensate for razor-thin margins by achieving tremendous manufacturing volume. Equally important, they develop managerial expertise that enables further cost cutting, more rapid turnaround times, and deeper, longer term relationships with brand leaders. By attaching tacit knowledge, managerial know-how, to an otherwise standardized activity—that is, by coupling basic assembly with the ability to achieve especially high yields, especially rapid turnaround times, or especially flexible small-batch production—they elevate the activity to something special and something difficult to replicate by potential competitors. Assemblers that have upgraded in this way still face narrow margins, a reality, perhaps, of their power relative to other players up and down the supply chain. However, within their own sphere of activity—assembly—these firms drive out less skilled competitors, amass tremendous production volume, and achieve a certain position of dominance.

That leads to a third point. Taiwanese-owned contract manufacturers have over time moved from doing only manufacturing assembly to coupling assembly with the provision of design services. That is, they are not just assembling products for brand leaders but are now doing much of the design work for those products as well. The whole evolution has a sort of push–pull feel to it. Brand leaders, on the one hand, have pushed design work, especially the detailed design work needed to ensure a product's manufacturability, down onto contract manufacturers. The brand leaders, naturally, want this work done for free. The more successful contract manufacturers, on the other hand, have sought such work, for by developing proprietary design capabilities, they can lock in relationships with brand leaders and even move toward establishing their own brands. Once a company like Delta not only assembles but also designs the power supply brick for a MacBook—and when Delta proves faster than anybody else in minia-turizing successive generations of those power bricks with ever-smaller versions of the MacBook—it becomes difficult for Apple to turn on a dime and have its products produced by somebody else. In a sense, by taking on design work, the contract manufacturer, though still squeezed by tight margins, insulates itself from the race to the bottom, dog eat dog conditions of purely commodified manufacturing assembly. After all, taking on design work entails the development of capabili-ties (i.e., building and running R&D centers, recruiting and retaining trained engineers, etc.) that elude many firms worldwide, including most in mainland China.

And that raises a fourth point. The Taiwanese that prove capable of doing this are multinationals who can bring together operations across a variety of geographical locales and functional areas. These firms, in terms of where their greatest number of employees reside, are China-based product assemblers. But they are actually much more than that. They are Taiwanese-headquartered managerial operations, pan-Asian (Taiwan, Hong Kong, China, South Korea, etc.) R&D centers and in some cases global marketing operations. Moreover, at the mana-gerial and engineering level, they are populated by individuals with extensive international experience, often in global technology centers like California's Silicon Valley. Such individuals—"Argonauts," as the scholar AnnaLee Saxenian terms them—move smoothly to and fro between Taipei, Shanghai, and Silicon Valley. As they weave together complex activities and relationships among leading firms, research centers, and universities, they become key bearers of cutting-edge knowledge.[53] Their employers, then—the more elite, Taiwanese-owned contract manufacturers—end up operating at the frontiers of innovation.

Fifth and related, these firms are now upgrading into new product development and branding. This, of course, involves a delicate dance because it suggests possible competition in the future with the con-tact manufacturer's current customers. One of the solutions involves inventing entirely new product categories rather than competing in areas already occupied by brand leaders.

The recent case of netbooks is a great example. In 2007, ASUS, in part motivated by work being done by rival Quanta, began marketing an ultrasimple, ultralow-cost machine based on a novel combination of established technologies—a seven-inch LCD screen, flash memory, and a Linux operating system.[54] The stripped-down netbook, easily transportable and useful primarily for Web surfing and checking e-mail, became an instant sensation at its roughly US$400 price point. Marketing the product as the Eee, ASUS sold out its complete 350,000-unit inventory well before the close of the year.[55] By the end of 2008, ASUS had sold roughly 5 million netbooks. Other companies, witnessing the appeal of the category, rushed in with their own versions and sold another 10 million units. Within a year of their introduction, netbook sales came to represent almost 10 percent of the entire global market for laptops.[56]

The development is interesting because it says something about the nature of innovation and upgrading in modular production. Taiwanese contract manufacturers moved up the smile curve by building a combination of manufacturing and design capabilities, thus deepening their relationship with brand leaders. On the down side, they could not continue moving up the smile curve—to the extent that curve is understood as applying to a single product like a standard laptop computer—for doing so would put them in direct competition with their main customers. On the plus side, because they were modular producers, their ultimate fate was not tied to any single product, any single smile curve, in other words. They could use the knowledge garnered from manufacturing an existing product—say, a high-end Dell laptop—to jump to an entirely different product like a netbook. In effect, they could employ the knowledge accumulated on one smile curve—knowledge about componentry, knowledge about designs, knowledge about user preferences—to jump over to and simultaneously operate on a different smile curve. The basic point is that in a world of modular production, upgrading may very well involve not so much moving up the smile curve but instead operating simultaneously on a variety of curves, all of which intersect at the given firm's activity of specialization.

The other interesting point about the netbook innovation is that although it amounts in some respects to just the cobbling together of off-the-shelf parts, it also reflects a very different way of thinking about how computing devices are structured and used. For well over a decade, debate has existed in the industry between "thin" and "thick" client architectures. In thick client setups, computers are built with maximal processing power to allow them to run virtually any kind of software and conduct virtually any kind of operation internally, relying on servers only to store information and communicate with the outside world. In thin client setups, computers are built with minimal capabilities—often inexpensively—and then most of the processing activities are carried out on the servers they connect with. High-end laptops, with the fastest processors and most robust software, reflect the thick client approach. The netbook, in contrast, very much fits a thin client model.[57]

In pushing something like the netbook, a modular producer like ASUS is not just introducing a new low-end product. Rather, that producer is catalyzing the development of a whole series of technologies, products, and commercial activities associated with thin client computing—more powerful servers, software designed to be run from them and accessed remotely, services for remote data storage, better wireless networks, and so forth. Concomitantly, other kinds of technologies associated with thick computing—smaller and smaller disc drives, longer lasting batteries, and better heat management systems, just to name a few—could potentially be de-emphasized. The point here is that the modular innovator, by popularizing something like the netbook, ends up shifting barriers to entry across a variety of different industries and technologies. New kinds of businesses become enabled, and others are forced into obsolescence.

So, what does this story of Taiwanese contract manufacturers tell us about upgrading in China? It tells us that upgrading is going on there and that innovation can still percolate up from manufacturing. At the same time, at least at present, much of that upgrading and innovation is happening not in indigenous Chinese firms, but instead in the Taiwanese and other multinational firms with China-based operations. Moreover, they are achieving this upgrading not by focusing exclusively on activities within China but instead by linking their China-based operations with people and capabilities located elsewhere. Thus, this is not a story of *China* upgrading per se. Instead, it is a story of China and Chinese-based operations at once enabling and being pulled into broader patterns of global upgrading. Global is used in two senses here: global in that the companies doing it tend to be multinationals, and global in that it is happening through networks of operations across multiple countries. China is playing a key, but not autonomous, role. And its participation does not, at least up to this point, suggest rise at somebody else's expense. It is still too early to say exactly what this model is. What it clearly is not, however, is traditional mercantilism or even traditional state-led development à la Japan or South Korea.

The Effect of Modular Production, Take 3: "Upward Commodification" by Chinese Producers

What about all those emergent indigenous Chinese producers we keep hearing about, automakers like Chery and Geely, appliance makers like Haier and Galanz, telecommunications systems providers like Huawei, or a computer maker like Lenovo? They have obviously moved into some very sophisticated business activities, branded their own products, and in many cases, introduced those products into overseas markets. How should we understand this? Does it signify upgrading? Why or why not? How does it differ from the upgrading efforts of the foreign-owned contract manufacturers described previously?

What so distinguished the best of the Taiwanese subcontractors was their ability to scale up, dominate globally their respective segments of the value chain, and build a set of unique managerial capabilities in the process. In so doing, they fit themselves into a global division of labor with a number of other scaled-up, leading firms. At the same time, while remaining primarily within their specialized activity of manufacturing assembly and design, they situated themselves across a variety of products and industries: computers, cell phones, automotive electronics, among many others. In other words, they positioned themselves on several smile curves at once.

A small subset of Chinese indigenous firms—the few that the Chinese government has tried to build into traditional conglomerates—has attempted something different and much more timeworn. They have sought not to deverticalize and specialize but instead to integrate across the supply chain. That is, they have sought to stay on a single smile curve but add activities on the upward curving ends to those they already perform down in the trough. In doing so, they have sought to build themselves—often with considerable governmental support—into "national champions," the sort of conglomerates that were dominant worldwide prior to the era of modular production, and that were hallmarks particularly of the East Asian model of state-led development.

Their very existence is interesting because it suggests that even as the Chinese system as a whole plunges headlong into deverticalized, globally integrated production, elements of traditional industrial policy still linger in Chinese governmental and commercial circles.

Firms like Haier, Huawei, and others—all with expertise in low-cost manufacturing—have in many cases successfully marched up the learning curve. Huawei is now selling telecommunications networking systems and equipment in Europe and North America. Lenovo, as many people know, purchased IBM's PC division and now owns the Thinkpad brand worldwide. Haier today is the world's fourth largest white goods (home appliances) manufacturer. Chery has ambitions of soon selling vehicles in the United States.

Nonetheless, the march up the curve has not always delivered on its promise of enhanced profitability and control. Lenovo, for example, even after the IBM acquisition, has struggled to build global market share. In terms of worldwide personal computer sales in 2008, Lenovo, with 7.5 percent of the market, substantially lagged global leaders HP, Dell, and surprisingly, the Taiwanese multinational Acer. Indeed, whereas Lenovo experienced a 5 percent decline in market share between 2007 and 2008, Acer was up a whopping 25 percent.[58] The industry inevitably exhibits volatility from year to year, but if anybody was rising in 2008, it was Acer and Apple, not Lenovo. Meanwhile, nipping on Lenovo's heels were contract manufacturers like ASUS who were at once producing the PCs for leaders like HP and Dell and introducing the next generation of products that could supplant PCs.

In telecom network provision, Huawei has clearly situated itself as a low-cost provider, but it substantially lags global leaders like Cisco, Ericsson, Alcatel-Lucent, and Nokia-Siemens Networks in terms of technology, value-added service provision, and overall revenues. That is not to say Huawei lacks either dynamism or innovative zeal. By early 2008, it had emerged as the global corporate world's fourth largest patent applicant (with 1,365 patent applications in 2007), trailing only Matsushita, Philips, and Siemens. Where a firm like this will be in several years is difficult to say. Yet, its overall development arguably fits a pattern that obtains across many of China's most advanced indigenous firms. Each time the Chinese champion moves up into a more sophisticated activity, the activity seems to commodify, while leading global competitors race forward into something yet more sophisticated and more difficult to replicate. In other words, as the indigenous firms race up the smile curve, as indicated in figure 4.2, the curve seems to drop downward right under their feet.

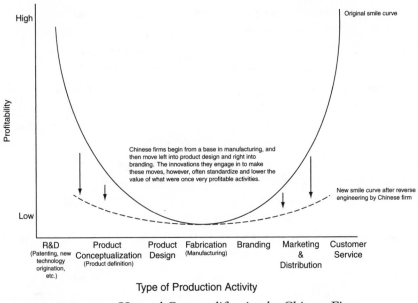

FIGURE 4.2 Upward Commodification by Chinese Firms

This drop is not coincidental. Rather, it has to do with the particular kind of innovation and upgrading the Chinese firms are engaged in. In essence, what they have specialized in is a kind of innovative reverse engineering. They find completely novel ways to standardize the previously uncodified, proprietary activities of industry leaders. Products and production processes that had once been uncodified and extremely difficult to replicate end up fully opened and standardized. This is not to say that Chinese firms are necessarily stealing existing designs or violating competitors' intellectual property. Those are issues for legal experts to decide.[59] In purely production terms, these firms are devising new ways of dealing with design information that dramatically lower the cost of producing a product.

A good example comes from the Chinese motorcycle industry.[60] During the 1980s and 1990s, globally dominant Japanese motorcycle assemblers like Honda, Yamaha, Kawasaki, and Suzuki had ambitions to enter the China market. Their entry strategy, in part dictated by Chinese governmental regulations, usually involved the establishment of joint-venture manufacturing operations with a Chinese partner. There were many to choose from, for like much of Chinese industry—both then and now—the motorcycle sector was characterized by extreme fragmentation. Many players existed, but few if any operated at commercially viable economies of scale. Even today in a typical motorcycle manufacturing hub like Chongqing, one can still find a bewildering array of both state-owned and private assemblers, companies like Jianshe, Jialing, Lifan, Zongshen, Shineray, Hi-Bird, and many others.[61]

When some of the older state-owned players like Jianshe and Jialing entered these initial joint ventures, they were exposed to a particular variety of Japanese-style production. That style, as the scholars Dongsheng Ge and Takahiro Fujimoto have observed, involved an assembler-led, design-focused system that placed great emphasis on new product development.[62] Lead Japanese assemblers would come up with detailed designs for the product as a whole and for every component. Maintaining full control over those designs, they would then divvy up production tasks among a series of essentially captive suppliers. The assembler set all the parameters beforehand and then managed a closed production network that supplied parts precisely tailored to specific motorcycle models. In contrast to so many of the modularized, deverticalized supply chains that we see today, this was an almost organically interconnected, stand-alone entity under the proprietary design control of the lead assembler. This resulted in high-quality, high-performance motorbikes. What it did not result in, though, was very inexpensive bikes. And it did not provide opportunities for Chinese participants in the network to break out and market their own bikes.

Those firms, though, ultimately found ways to break out, and they did so by innovating, in a sense. They learned how to take a nonmodular, highly integrated system of new product development and convert it into a highly modularized, highly deverticalized mode of production. As Ge and Fujimoto point out, Chinese assemblers and parts manufacturers alike—whether they had worked directly with the Japanese or not—selected certain Japanese motorcycles as focal models and then disassembled them. Once the focal models were broken down, the indigenous assemblers and parts makers worked in parallel to reengineer individual parts and entire models. Parts effectively had to be redesigned for manufacture. In some cases, the parts were simply copied. The problem, though, was that the parts had been originally designed to work only with specific models. In some cases, Chinese parts makers (rather than final assemblers) were now doing the reverse engineering, so they wanted to ensure that the parts could be used in the widest variety of motorcycles possible. That is, they wanted their reverse-engineered parts to be salable to a wide variety of customers. Hence, they redesigned parts in ways that made them much more standardized—modular, in effect.[63] At the same time, assemblers, who were also trying to reverse engineer entire motorcycles, did not have the design capabilities to do the whole task. Hence, they outsourced detailed design for key parts and subsystems to the components makers, thus almost by definition forcing previously integral, top-down designs to become much more modular. The Chinese assemblers, in effect, gave up the kind of design control that had been at the heart of the Japanese system.

The upshot by the late 1990s and early 2000s was an extremely dynamic and competitive manufacturing environment in places like Chongqing. Local assemblers and component manufacturers were introducing one reverse-engineered motorcycle after another. Call them what you will—"knockoffs," "pirated goods," "low-cost alternatives"—but these Chinese-produced "Yamehas," "Suzakis," and "Honeas," all essentially reverse engineered, modularized variants of Japanese models, became all the rage not just in Chinese markets but throughout much of Southeast Asia.[64] These bikes may not have been as reliable as the Japanese focal models on which they were based. They may not have performed as well or been as fun to ride. Yet, they were much less expensive to produce and, thus, much less expensive to purchase and maintain for the consumer. Plus, as the Chinese assemblers improved their techniques, the bikes became much more reliable. Even today, they still cannot compete in high-end markets with the likes of Honda or Harley-Davidson, but they have established a solid foothold at the low end of the product spectrum.

Legal issues aside, the story is unquestionably one of skill upgrading and innovation by Chinese manufacturers. After all, working from somebody else's production architecture, they created a new one of their own and, in so doing, substantially lowered production costs for a complex product. In many ways, this is similar to what Chinese producers have done in a number of other areas: home appliances, electronics, toys, telecommunications switching equipment, and so on.

The problem, however, is that by opening up and modularizing production processes that had once been closed, Chinese manufacturers end up lowering entry barriers for everybody. That is, they induce tremendous competition and undercut potential avenues for differentiation and profitability. In a way, one can think of it as the Chinese producer moving up the smile curve in a fashion that ends up wiping the smile off the curve entirely (see figure 4.2). When Taiwanese contract manufacturers have upgraded, they have tended either to move up the smile curve by deepening relationships with brand leaders—usually by providing propriety design work in addition to manufacturing assembly—or to effectively jump onto new smile curves by introducing new products. Chinese indigenous manufacturers generally have done neither. They have instead worked to standardize previously proprietary, closed products and processes.

Having done so, the Chinese manufacturers often still lag in the ability to effectively integrate activities across the supply chain. The Chongqing motorcycle manufacturers, for example, can effectively reverse engineer existing designs, but they are still unable to come up with designs of their own. As an expert from a major European design consultancy that works with these firms noted, "In China, they [the motorcycle manufacturers] make nice parts, but they still do not do designs... They have weak project management skills, and they neither see the need for, nor have the ability to control their suppliers in order to implement a project."[65] Such management skills—often involving coordination across multiple firms—are, unlike actual motorcycle designs, difficult to reverse engineer. They are the still uncodified, tacit element of production, which separates a low-end, commodified product from a high-end, high-performance one. Such skills are likely to be acquired over time, but it is going to take a lot of learning across a lot of trial-and-error experimentation. Meanwhile, Chinese manufacturers are generally relegated to the lower cost, more commodified end of the consumer products spectrum.

Although not ideal for these manufacturers, the situation is great for consumers worldwide. It makes for very inexpensive, reasonably high-quality TVs, DVD players, microwave ovens, low-end servers, computers, and other products that now behave as commodities. The Chinese producers then scramble to put their brands on these products, but as commodities, the products are no longer easy to differentiate. Do consumers care now what kind of basic microwave oven they buy? Do they care what name is on the US$40 DVD player they purchase on a whim? For many of these products—precisely because Chinese producers have figured out how to standardize them and produce them so inexpensively—brand has ceased to matter. In their admirable efforts to move up, Chinese manufacturers have in many cases undercut the profitability of doing so. Once they move in, brand leaders know it is time to move out.

That, in some sense, explains why IBM was willing in 2005 to sell its PC division—and its marquee Thinkpad brand—to Chinese computer maker Lenovo. At least in the minds of some IBM managers, the laptop had ceased to be a differentiated product. Producing and selling it had become a thankless task, a commercially suicidal endeavor in which the only way to win was to keep cutting one's profit margins.

Whether this is simply post hoc self-justification is hard to say, but more than a few senior managers at IBM felt they had dumped the computer business on Lenovo, thus freeing IBM to move onward to the next generation of proprietary, high-value activities: provision of tailored business solutions for high-end industrial customers, cutting-edge R&D, new technology development, IT network provision, and a variety of other high-margin endeavors. To the extent the example is generalizable, one can say that indigenous Chinese firms are upgrading into advanced manufacturing at precisely the time global industry leaders are upgrading out.

The Effect of Modular Production, Take 4: Modular Innovation in Advanced Industrial Economies

The advent of modularity has brought more than Chinese-made knock-offs, low-priced gadgets, and supercharged contract manufacturers. It is about more than just rising firms, whether from China or anywhere else. Rather, in this new way of structuring production, everybody is on the move. Indeed, modularity has enabled change in North American and Europe no less impressive than what has occurred in developing locales like China. As Chinese firms move up into—and commodify—high-end manufacturing, they undoubtedly cause problems for people engaged in those same activities elsewhere. Frankly, they in some respects create problems for themselves as they drive down entry barriers for potential competitors. The broader reality, though, is that they are participating in, and even fostering, production changes that catalyze entirely new and extremely profitable commercial activities in places like the United States.

Our earlier version of the smile curve suggested that modularity has lowered profit margins in manufacturing and raised them in areas like design, branding, and tailored customer services. In some respects, that is an oversimplification. By pulling apart the production process into separable, stand-alone stages, modularity has enabled the creation of entirely new manufacturing industries. For example, when companies like IBM managed the production of all facets of a computing product, it would have been hard to imagine the rise of firms like Intel or AMD wholly devoted to the design and manufacture of a component, the semiconductor, or the rise of Microsoft on the basis of an operating system.

In its own way, modularity lowers barriers to entry not only for low-end manufacturers but also for highly skilled, highly specialized firms that previously would never have had outlets for their products. "Vertical specialization" is how a recent study from the U.S. National Academies aptly termed this.[66] In some ways, an even better term might be "deverticalized specialization." When the computer industry, for example, deverticalized (moved away from a single firm doing everything to multiple firms doing just one or two activities in the production process), it was not only Microsoft and Intel that blossomed. So too did semiconductor foundries, firms specialized in making chips but not designing them. Those operations, then, fostered the development of fabless design houses, firms, often based in places like Silicon Valley, that specialize in the creation of new semiconductor designs. New designs allowed new kinds of capabilities to be built into new kinds of products. As indicated by figure 4.3, the smile curve for a product like a personal computer has become full of high-profit peaks even as the product itself commodifies. These peaks are often dominated by companies which, though their names may not be recognizable to ordinary consumers, enable whole waves of innovation.

Indeed, a number of these companies, through innovations directed at personal computers, have made possible follow-on products like the smart phone. Because of various innovations in chip design, screen design, miniaturization, and heat management, the handheld smart phone can do today what only the desktop computer could do yesterday. Indeed, the smart phone can do more. It can also do what the film camera used to do. But that function, of course, first migrated to a semiconductor-enabled digital camera, and then to a credit-card-sized camera, and then to the phone.

And now with the smart phone, another set of activities—or industries—has been enabled as the phone has become a platform for new applications (apps) created by independent software developers. Some of those software apps—GPS-based turn-by-turn navigational programs, for example—might replace what previously had been stand-alone hardware devices. The phone also evolves hand in hand with new screen technologies—again produced by specialized firms—that permit users new ways to view (digitally delivered) media. That creates many new opportunities for media providers. In fact, savvy computer companies like Apple reinvent themselves as media companies, pushing new ways to deliver digitized entertainment to the users of their devices. Apple's iTunes software is a good example. At the same time, the traditional media providers—namely, network television and

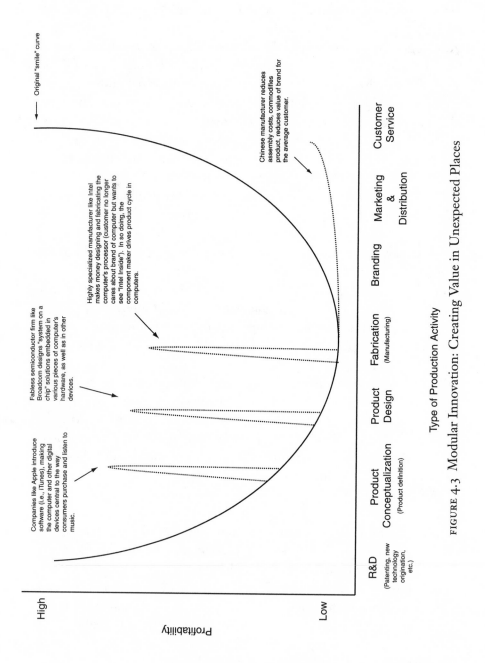

FIGURE 4.3 Modular Innovation: Creating Value in Unexpected Places

radio—face big problems as their advertising-based revenue model gets the rug pulled out from under it.

The point is that citizens in the world's wealthiest countries are not just being challenged from below by overseas competition. And they are not only being showered as consumers with a bewildering array of novel and often quite affordable products. Rather, they—we—are now as producers participating in completely new ways of value creation. Production is now no longer just about finding the right spot on a single smile curve. Nor do the points on even any one curve so simply come together as a smile. All sorts of new value opportunities are opening up along those curves. What are in some cases extremely lucrative industries today—semiconductor design, data storage and security, Internet search engine development, and so on—were not even industries at all yesterday. At the same time, once lucrative activities have in some cases become either far less profitable or utterly obsolete.

More specifically, modular production, the very kind of production both facilitated and accelerated by China's economic rise, can be understood as impacting advanced countries like the United States in the following ways. First, modularity has made it easier for small entrepreneurial start-ups to enter the market. Now, new enterprises can join the electronics, telecommunications, automotive, or virtually any other industry without having to own a single piece of capital equipment. They need nothing on the scale of a multibillion-dollar semiconductor fab or a massive auto assembly plant. They may, for example, just need a small number of computers to produce highly proprietary, industry-enabling semiconductor designs. Or perhaps they develop algorithms for the creation of new kinds of data storage devices. Possibly they design and manage networks upon which digitized medical scans can be sent for reading anywhere in the world.

Second, many of the highest value portions of production have been detached from the physical act of manufacturing. Some Americans rue the demise of U.S.-based manufacturing, partly—and understandably—because they worry about the disappearance of jobs. Partly, though, they worry more existentially that in its shift to a postindustrial economy, the United States is losing know-how, innovative capacity, autonomy, and power. This latter set of concerns for the most part misses the point. Modularity has blurred once-firm distinctions between manufacturing and services. Research and development and design-related activities in the past were inseparable from physical manufacturing. Hence, they were all previously treated as manufacturing. Today, many of these activities are carried out by highly specialized firms that do no physical manufacturing at all. The jobs appear as services, but they in fact claim the bulk of the profitability and power in the broader production chains they feed into. They often end up as the biggest repositories of know-how in the entire manufacturing process.

Thus, whether Intel, Google, Cisco, Qualcomm, EMC, Lam Research, Nvidia, Marvell, and so many other U.S.-based entities, these are firms that hold the keys to the manufacturing kingdom, for they are the ones that drive the most innovative and knowledge-intensive aspects of production. Some actually bend metal; others focus only on design. Some have branded products; others operate far upstream in the shadows, pushing R&D and innovation in componentry or network infrastructure. However, all are creating jobs, in some cases directly through their own operations, and in other cases indirectly through the wealth they generate. All, by defining the frontiers of innovation and new technology development—the most difficult-to-replicate, innovative aspects of global production—set the tempo at which everyone else in the supply chain must march.

That they do leads to a third point. Because many of the high-end producers in the United States are modular and rarely invested in the capital-intensive aspects of production, they are no longer tied to any single downstream consumer product. These firms frequently end up straddling multiple industries simultaneously. A fabless design house may one day design a chip that permits new functionality on a laptop computer, only to follow up the next day with a design enabling products that wipe out the laptop entirely. Or it may create a design that ends up having applications in automobiles, a downstream product whose value increasingly resides in its electronics and software.

Similarly, Microsoft grew originally on the basis of a computer operating system, but now it is seeking to become the dominant operating system provider in the cell phone industry. Just as it determined a key standard in the computer industry, now it is trying to do so in cell phones. Of course, in trying, it has to compete against other American companies like Google, which, like Microsoft, may not be associated with telecommunications but have managed to move into that domain from a variety of different starting points. Meanwhile, Google, with its recent announcement of the Chrome Operating System, is itself moving into Microsoft's computer operating system business. Microsoft, in turn, with the announcement of its Bing Internet search engine, is moving onto Google's home turf. Both of them, however, as they now try to dominate software standards in the smart phone business, compete with Palm, Apple, and Research in Motion (BlackBerry), all major players in this area. None looks like what we would traditionally understand as a manufacturing firm. None, in fact, really amounts to a telecommunications company. Yet, each is trying to control the standards, the rules of connectivity, that serve as key enablers of products and key drivers of the production chain.

Why engage in physical manufacturing—product fabrication—if you can control the high-value rules and design parameters that those doing manufacturing must scramble to meet? Even if those manufacturers reverse engineer your designs—which they may be wary of doing if you are their primary customer—you will have already moved into new products or jumped across into new industries. After all, as a modular player, you have the option of operating on multiple smile curves simultaneously. You are free to do this precisely because you no longer have to invest in all the capital equipment, facilities, and infrastructure associated with product fabrication in any one industry. Somebody else—namely, China-based contract manufacturers—has done that for you.

Fourth, because their specialized activities can straddle so many different industries, American firms are freed up to pursue a particular kind of unbridled, modular innovation. When producers were vertically integrated—that is, when they had invested in all the facilities and equipment necessary to make a single complete product—their fates effectively became tied to that product. They may have been inclined to innovate, at least in the sense of improving the product to meet evolving consumer preferences, but they would have resisted new technologies or ideas that might unseat the product entirely. To use management scholar Clay Christensen's terminology, they would have engaged in "sustaining" but not "disruptive" innovation.[67] In the era of modularity, however, everything is about disruption, especially for innovation leaders in places like the United States. As noted previously, a modular producer—a design house, for example—may innovate today in ways that knock out its previous innovation from yesterday. As long as it keeps moving and stays at the cusp of value creation, it remains not just a viable business but a business effectively in the driver's seat.

Hence, we see firms like IBM and Apple continually reinventing themselves. What really is Apple today? A computer design company? A smart-phone company? A media company that is just using all those electronics devices as platforms for iTunes? And what about IBM? It very clearly and publicly has moved out of computer manufacturing and into the provision of proprietary business software and IT networks. In the process, it is trying to shape IT industry standards by pushing open-source, Linux-based computer operating systems, a move that could unseat potential competitors like Microsoft while catalyzing entirely new avenues of software development. Meanwhile, in its upstream research labs, IBM, through concepts like "racetrack memory," is pioneering new ways to store and manage digitized data that could revolutionize the computer hardware industry and the myriad devices that flow from it.[68]

Time and again, just as the competition starts busting down the door, these innovation leaders jump to new products in which they can embed their own proprietary, uncodifiable know-how. For Apple, this know-how may come in the form of software for selling and listening to digital media. For Google or Microsoft, it may be software delivered online or through a handheld device. For Cisco, it may be in software and designs embedded in routers and servers that it may have branded but subcontracted to somebody else to manufacture.[69] In moving forward into knowledge-focused activities, these companies continually leave behind other activities that have been opened up and commodified. Indeed, leading companies actively encourage the commodification of activities they seek to exit or activities that are the heart of their rivals' competitive advantage. Hence, IBM dilutes the value of brand generally in laptop manufacturing by selling the Thinkpad name to Lenovo, but presses ahead on proprietary innovation in the high-value guts of computing devices or the design of tailored IT systems for large corporate customers. Similarly, it actively encourages open-source computer operating systems, potentially undercutting products like Microsoft's Windows, and at the same moves into the provision of Linux-based IT networks or software solutions for large corporate customers. Not entirely unlike what the Chongqing motorcycle manufacturers did to the Japanese, these firms find ways to open up and commodify the activities of their competitors. Yet, they do so only because they can simultaneously take the next step by offering a proprietary, high-value product that then rides on the back of that which has just been commodified.

One way this is manifested for consumers is in the rapid product cycles that exist today across so many industries. In the past, it was only items like apparel that changed across four, five, or six seasons per year. Now, it is computers, cell phones, data storage systems, home networking systems, digital cameras, and so many other kinds of products. The gadgets come and go with incredible rapidity, with each new one bringing with it enhanced capabilities, new functionality, and in many cases, lower prices.

Conclusion: China and
The Modular Revolution

China in recent years has achieved extraordinary growth by plunging into the center of a global production revolution. Having carved out a particular place in a new global division of labor, Chinese firms now perform critical manufacturing functions in virtually every consumer product category. In some cases, their innovations have substantially lowered production costs and changed the nature of the products themselves, transforming high-end, brand-specific goods into commodities. In almost all cases, often by buying new technologies and developing better managerial techniques for employing them, these firms have realized major productivity gains. Productivity gains translate into long-term wealth creation and national growth.

At the same time, China as an industrial nation has been thrust into an extremely challenging situation. The rapid product cycles typical of modular production impose unprecedented pressures for flexibility and cost cutting on the part of those doing the physical manufacturing. Product fabricators must become adept at absorbing new designs, managing small-batch production, and responding quickly to shifting orders, all while keeping costs down and volumes up in inherently narrow-margin businesses. In essence, they must learn to operate in environments of intensely high "clockspeed."[70] Rapid turnaround times, new innovations cascading down from above, compressed product cycles, and lots of competition have all become the new normal.

A select few firms in China have proved particularly adept at meeting these challenges while remaining focused on manufacturing. They happen to be Taiwanese-owned multinationals that couple substantial operations in China with their other business units located abroad.

Indigenous Chinese producers could conceivably compete with them in the future. One problem at present, however, is that the most advanced of these indigenous companies, though impressive, appear held back by the particular manner they have pursued upgrading. Whether by choice or in response to governmental pressure, they have tended to move toward vertical integration rather than specialization. In other words, they have sought to couple the basic manufacturing they are already doing with new efforts in downstream product branding and upstream R&D, often within narrowly defined, single industry boundaries. Thus, they end up doing many things, but none particularly well, and all within the confines of a single industry. The products they brand often end up commodified. The manufacturing they engage in, while often quite good, is not managerially flexible or adept enough to compete with the Taiwanese. The fact that they are single-industry defined and single-industry branded makes them less inclined to move, as Taiwanese contract manufacturers do, across multiple product areas. Moreover, because they are often manufacturing for their own branded product lines, they get cut off from some of the interfirm partnering efforts—the sort of joint design work that goes on between Apple and Quanta, for example—that lead to skill upgrading and knowledge transfer. This is not to say that they are failing. Rather, it is to say that they are struggling to keep up, struggling to keep pace with those who seem to have responded more adroitly to the challenges of value creation and value capture in a world of modularized production.

Of course, in a world of rapid innovation, those at the top at any given time may not remain there tomorrow. Interesting to note, however, is that much of the churning that takes place today is not between incumbents from wealthy nations and new entrants from developing ones but rather among the rich country firms themselves. In computers, Dell and HP get squeezed by Apple and Acer, not China's Lenovo. In computer operating systems, Microsoft fends off challenges from Google, not indigenous Chinese software companies. Even in areas suddenly opened by disruptive technologies, wealthy-nation firms are consistently first to jump into the void and reap the gains. GPS-based navigation systems are a good example. Sales of handheld and in-car devices surged in the early and mid-2000s, only to come crashing down in 2008 with the growing availability of navigation apps for smart phones. In the process, the fortunes of companies like Garmin (founded in Taiwan but now headquartered in the Cayman Islands) rise and fall, but not at the hands of upstart Chinese device makers producing low-cost substitutes. Instead, the new competitors are U.S.-based software developers, the people coming up with the new apps for smart phones. To compete, device maker Garmin, in turn, must scramble to reinvent itself as a software company.

Examples like these and many others typify an overall trend. As illustrated in figure 4.3, modular production—a key part of which involves China-based manufacturing—is facilitating extremely rapid, almost unbounded innovation in places like the United States. American and other innovators, then, are competing fiercely among themselves, introducing new products, blowing away old ones, creating opportunities in new activities, shutting them down in others, establishing new standards, forcing the obsolescence of old ones, and so on. As a result, various new corporate entrants have been able to find their way onto the ever-expanding competitive landscape, one far more complex and interesting than a simple smile. Few if any of the new profit peaks, however, are being claimed by Chinese domestic industry.

Who exactly owns the current architecture of production is impossible to say. It is perhaps the wrong question to ask. Yet, far more certain is that as much as the modern era is about China emerging as a global manufacturer, so too is it about the United States advancing faster than ever before as an innovation leader. Had it not been for the advent of modern modular production—globalization, in effect—neither outcome would have been possible.

FIVE

Capitalist Enabler, Capitalist Converger

C HINESE FIRMS MAY not be leading the charge, but in the new global division of labor, China has had to change substantially just to stay in the game. To carve out and sustain its position as a global manufacturing hub, China has had to undergo transformative institutional change defined as much by outsiders as by the Chinese themselves. Here is where the story of institutional outsourcing becomes so critical.

To participate in global production, a country need not slavishly imitate a particular institutional model. As economist Dani Rodrik suggests, there are many institutional "recipes" for dealing with a single global economic reality.[1] Over the years, China certainly has pursued a variety of idiosyncratic reform efforts, some of which have flown in the face of internationally recognized best practice. Its government has continued to hand pick particular industries for special support, even as interventionist industrial policy has fallen out of favor in much of the world. It continues to throw up regulatory barriers against entrepreneurship and new enterprise starts, particularly ones hailing from the private sector.[2] Whether for reasons of domestic surveillance or just broader governmental control, it has repeatedly sought to impose intrusive regulatory standards in sectors like information technology. The Green Dam (*Lu Ba*) affair of 2009, an abortive effort to require personal computers sold in China to have Internet censoring software preinstalled, is a recent example. Others include efforts to require search engine providers like Google to restrict politically sensitive terms—Tibet, Falun Gong, June 4, and so on—from Chinese versions of the software. There is no doubt that China has an intrusive government willing to engage in regulatory practices that make global counterparts, not to mention some of its own citizens, blanch.

That said, although some idiosyncrasies can persist, participation in global production—particularly to the degree experienced by China—requires harmonization of certain core domestic practices with prevailing global norms. Put simply, capitalism with Chinese characteristics is fine on the margins but not at the core. In its most elemental social constructs and rules, China today is defined not by its own version of capitalism but rather by that of the world's leading commercial pacesetters, Western companies and consumers.

Outsourcing Restructuring
to Foreign Owners

Much of this is reflected in the changing nature of ownership within Chinese industry. In 1989, before the real acceleration of Chinese reform began, the size of the total industrial sector was relatively small, and more than half of all output was produced by traditional state-owned firms. Another 35 percent of output came from "collectives," enterprises owned by local government. Five percent came from "individual" (*geti*) firms, nascent private enterprises emerging during an era when "private" was a term still too sensitive politically to be used openly. A final 4 percent of output came from the only other officially recognized ownership designation of the period, a catch-all category termed "other types of industry" (*qita jingji leixing gongye*).[3] This category included foreign-invested firms.

By 2007, the industrial sector alone had expanded almost twentyfold. So too, in a sense, had the number of officially recognized enterprise categories. In addition to state-owned and collective firms, there were now private firms, joint-stock firms, limited-liability corporations (LLCs), publicly listed LLCs, and foreign-invested firms, among others.[4] State-owned firms by this point accounted for just under 9 percent of total output and collectives roughly 3 percent. Private firms, once forbidden, now accounted for almost a quarter of all output. Meanwhile, foreign-invested firms (including those with investment from Taiwan, Hong Kong, and Macao) accounted for almost a third. As noted previously, foreign-invested firms by this point were producing more than half of China's total exports and nearly the entire amount of Chinese exports in high-tech areas like office equipment and electronics.

As my colleague Yasheng Huang has elegantly shown, foreign ownership across all exporting sectors in China—from the most technologically sophisticated to the least—is much higher than what is seen in other countries. Moreover, it is higher than what existed historically in neighboring locales like Taiwan during their most rapid period of development.[5]

Professor Huang attributes such high levels to a kind of distortion in the system stemming from the Chinese government's ambivalence or even outright hostility toward private entrepreneurs. Facing discrimination, entrepreneurs—the argument goes—need to move themselves into the more politically favorable foreign-invested ownership category either by moving their own funds overseas and then bringing them back as foreign investment or, more likely, by selling off a piece of their firm to a foreign investor. That is, they sell to a foreigner, presumably at a discounted price, just to receive fair treatment by their own government. That high levels of foreign investment obtain even in low-tech sectors—such as silk, for which the Chinese presumably have centuries of accumulated know-how—is taken by Huang to mean that the actual contribution of managerial or technological know-how by the foreigner is minimal.

Perhaps because of my focus on the overall architecture of global production, I interpret the findings differently. As suggested earlier, participation in globalized modular production—regardless of whether we are talking about semiconductors or silk shirts—entails substantial managerial challenges. These include phenomenal cost pressures, high demands for flexibility on the part of purchasers, rapid product cycles across almost all industries, high-quality standards (which often necessitate the use of technology- and capital-intensive equipment), and in many cases, cooperative design efforts with other modular producers in the supply chain. On top of all that, the modular producer—which, in China, often amounts to a contract manufacturer—is often producing for multiple customers who are themselves competing with one another. For example, a footwear subcontractor is likely producing simultaneously for Nike, Adidas, and Mizuno. Similarly, a computer assembler may be producing simultaneously for HP and Dell. A key managerial skill, therefore—one necessary for basic survival in the business—involves protection of the customer's most valuable intellectual property: its designs. It is not only that designs must be protected from outsiders beyond the firm. They must also be protected from other competing customers *within* the firm.

Pulling all of this off requires substantial managerial expertise, a kind of know-how that is not easily codified. Moreover, it is a kind of expertise which was not required in previous periods of export processing-led development when supply chains were not nearly as complex, product cycles not nearly as short, quality standards not nearly as high, and the overall nature of innovation neither as rapid nor disruptive. It is a kind of expertise now required across all exporting sectors, whether ostensibly high tech or not. That the Chinese invented something like woven silk in 3000 B.C. arguably has no bearing on the ability of a Chinese producer to serve global demand for silk apparel today. What counts now more than handicraft traditions are abilities to coordinate with European designers, North American major retailers, global innovators in weaving equipment, among many others. The challenge today comes not from the technological sophistication of any particular sector but rather from the managerial complications of supply-chain participation in any globalized sector, from silk to semiconductors.

Thus, high levels of foreign ownership in China say more about the nature of global production today than they do about the (distorted) nature of Chinese reform. China may be an outlier in terms of how many of its exporters are foreign owned, but so too is it an outlier in terms of how much worldwide manufacturing assembly takes place within its borders. It is completely conceivable that over the long run, the managerial know-how required for deep participation in global supply chains will migrate to indigenous Chinese producers. Indeed, it clearly already has in certain sectors. Yet, for the time being, the ability to directly own the export operation, among other factors, is what is drawing manufacturing giants like Foxconn, Quanta, and ASUS to locate their facilities in China. Other nations are free today to organize their participation in global production on the basis of arm's-length contracting rather than direct foreign ownership. Those that do so, however, appear to be losing business to China. The market, or more precisely, those market players with power in global supply chains—the major North American retailers, the major brand leaders and product designers, the major global manufacturers, the worldwide sourcing specialists—are voting with their feet, and their feet are taking them primarily to China.

China has become a manufacturing hub by outsourcing to foreigners the power to structure Chinese domestic industry—or at least substantial portions of domestic industry—in ways those foreigners see fit. For other developing nations, the lesson of the Chinese experience may very well be that extensive foreign ownership is now the price of admission for extensive participation in global production.

Saving the Revolution
by Ending Socialism

But what really has all this global engagement meant for China in terms of institutional change? China, after all, is still an authoritarian country, one in which rule of law seems nascent at best, corruption almost omnipresent, checks on governmental power decidedly weak, and individual rights honored more in the breach than in the observance. This is hardly a model society. Nonetheless, the presence of so many problems—including the accumulation of new ones in recent years—cannot be taken, prima facie, as evidence of absence of change or even resistance to change.

As indicated in chapter 1, extensive foreign ownership—particularly at the level reached by the early 2000s—was possible only with the complete obliteration of socialist-style workplace organization. For those foreign-invested firms to become such major creators of value, both within China and globally, the whole system of socialist workplace organization had to go: the work units, allocation of jobs through state assignment, permanent attachment of workers to employers, widespread conditions of "unemployment on the job,"[6] housing owned and assigned by employers, health care delivered entirely through employers, and political surveillance and control channeled through employers. At one level, by permitting and even encouraging foreign ownership over industry, the state—whether through farsightedness or just reflexive hostility toward domestic entrepreneurs—outsourced management restructuring across Chinese industry to foreign commercial players. Foreign-led restructuring efforts could proceed, however, only because the state tolerated (for reasons discussed in chapter 3) the rapid dismantling of institutions that for decades prior had been the cornerstones of state power. Thus, on a deeper level, to save itself and some semblance of the revolution it created, the state permitted changes that would at once end Chinese socialism and position China as a major enabler of global capitalism. For the revolution to be saved, socialism had to go.

Something, though, had to fill the institutional void that was opened up. In other words, the state, beyond dismantling old structures, had to provide new ones both to maintain social order generally and complement specific restructuring efforts already under way within firms. Here is where the importance of harmonization with global norms becomes apparent. China could, and did, chart its own independent course in a number of areas. It maintained high levels of state ownership in industry, high levels of state intervention in the economy, blurry boundaries between public and commercial actors, and a robust party apparatus extending across much of society. In some particularly critical areas, however, the state had little choice but to push convergence toward global norms.

To put it somewhat differently, the state had many choices, but if it was really going to rely on national enrichment as a primary basis for legitimacy, if enrichment was going to come through integration with global production, and if integration was going to be achieved through foreign-led, supply-chain-focused restructuring efforts, then certain kinds of institutions would be needed. Many of these—commercial legal codes, labor laws, and currency conversion mechanisms, among others—would evolve in fits and starts, and would function erratically all along. Nonetheless, for all the justifiable criticism of their performance, their very existence represented a stark departure from China's prior mode of revolutionary governance, and an equally stark convergence toward practices found throughout the advanced industrial world. Just as the state, whether by default or design, had become dependent on foreign-invested and foreign-focused firms to drive growth, so too would it take its cues from abroad in building the domestic rules needed to support those firms' efforts.

Convergence toward Overseas Applications of Law

One example of this outward reliance involves the development of enterprise law. China's first company law, promulgated in 1986, was specifically written to apply only to foreign-invested firms. In a sense, enterprises in years prior had not been relevant social entities in pre-reform China. They, of course, existed and were important for production, but they were subsumed within broader concepts—the state and its bureaucratic planning apparatus (of which enterprises were a part), the means of production (within which enterprises, as instruments of labor, fell), and class struggle (which could occur in the enterprise). In some cases, enterprises were "independent accounting units" (*duli yusuan danwei*), but administratively, they were but the production arms of a broader state bureaucracy. They certainly had no legal status of their own. Indeed, the entire notion of legal status was not only irrelevant but in many respects politically suspect. Politically legitimate change proceeded through class struggle, mediated, of course, through the guidance of the party-state. Neither enterprises, as extensions of the state production bureaucracy, nor individuals, as both grassroots producers in that bureaucracy and members of contending classes, had independent legal status. Law itself was viewed contemptuously as an instrument of capitalist exploitation, an atavistic, prerevolutionary impediment to progressive change.

With the rise of foreign-funded companies, those attitudes would need to change. These new producers—divorced from the self-contained revolutionary logic of struggle, bureaucracy, and class—had to be given some kind of definition, some kind of status within the system. From the government's perspective, such status was necessary as a basis for regulation.[7] Defining the firm was a precondition for regulating it. At the same time, from the firm's perspective, basic legal status was necessary for engaging in even the simplest cross-border transactions. Without such status, how could China-based operations ever enter sales agreements with overseas customers, purchasing agreements with international suppliers of capital equipment, long-term contracts with logistics providers, and any number of other basic commercial transactions? Even for the less high-profile players investing early on, let alone the massive, foreign-owned contract manufacturing operations that would develop later, export-oriented business could proceed only if mechanisms existed to define the firm's boundaries and the extent of ownership claims (particularly when joint ventures and multiple investors were involved). Thus, all the parties involved —state and nonstate alike—needed a basic vocabulary, a basic set of rules, by which they could manage or even just sensibly discuss their evolving commercial relationship. The revolutionary tradition offered nothing on this front. Western-style capitalism, however, did—law.

Through the course of the 1990s, the this new law-based framing flourished.[8] By 1993, with China's first broadly defined enterprise law, that which previously had been held out only to foreign-invested firms—"legal person" (*fa ren*) status—was now extended to all companies. Terms like *shareholder, limited liability*, and interestingly, *rights* began to enter the normal discourse for everybody. As it evolved and expanded over the next decade, Chinese enterprise law functioned creakily, and its protections often remained out of reach for key domestic players. Critics justifiably claimed that rule of law often failed to obtain in practice. Yet, the new legal framing proved sufficient for shepherding the growth of a foreign-invested sector that was at once firmly embedded in China and deeply linked transactionally to global supply chains. In the process, rule of law—and all its attendant vocabulary of legal person rights, protections, and status—evolved from being something needed only instrumentally to facilitate international commerce to something far more profound: an aspirational goal for the nation and a fundamental basis for state legitimacy.

Convergence toward Overseas (American) Approaches to Labor Relations

Export-oriented business needed more than specific legal definition on the one hand and dreamy governmental pledges to build a rule of law society on the other. It needed to be able to control its workforce. To respond to the pressures of modular production—the price competition, the short product cycles, and the continual onslaught of new technologies—the China-based firm, often a manufacturing assembly operation, had to do some basic things: hire workers during market upswings, fire workers during downswings, maintain control over wages, and enforce discipline on the shop floor. None of this looks even remotely extraordinary from the perspective of normal market-based economics. It was more than extraordinary, however—indeed, even anathema—from the perspective of revolutionary China. Workers were a social class, not a set of stakeholders in the firm or parties to transactions with management. The firm itself was an extension of the state, not a competitive market actor that dealt independently with labor.

All that had to change with the advent of foreign ownership and export processing.[9] Once again, law—in this case, labor law—rose to the fore as the new definer and mediator of societal relationships. China's first national labor law, passed by the National People's Congress in 1994, set the tone for what would only deepen over the next fifteen years.[10] Laborers were defined not as a class—revolutionary or otherwise—but rather as individuals with legal rights. Those individuals, then, were conceived of as being in a commercial relationship with independent entities—enterprises—that also had a series of rights and obligations under the law. The relationship itself would be defined by contract, a formal legal agreement of specified duration, with specified terms of remuneration and specified conditions of termination.

In practice, as political scientist Mary Gallagher points out, the move toward law shifted the balance of power away from workers and toward management. The labor law's stipulation that workers were entitled to union representation (even if only by the sole union allowed in China, that of the Communist Party) generally went unenforced. Enterprise-level party officials frequently ended up serving as human resources administrators working shoulder to shoulder with managers to meet commercial goals.[11] This in no small part explains why foreign-invested firms, including wholly foreign-owned enterprises, through much of the 1990s and 2000s often welcomed the establishment of in-house party organizations.[12] From management's perspective, in-house party officials—often beholden to local governments more interested in commercial growth than labor representation—were crucial for disciplining the workforce, settling disputes, and providing cover in the event of layoffs. Workers, in turn, through a combination of the law's emphasis on contracting and the de facto reality of no collective representation, were put in the position of having to negotiate individually with management.[13] In the event of a dispute, they could "use the law as their weapon," as government slogans urged, but they would have to do so as lone individuals and often with precious few resources at their disposal.[14]

Matters of justice and fairness aside, the reality is that by the first decade of the twenty-first century, China had moved toward a pattern of labor relations wholly removed from its revolutionary past and increasingly consonant with practices in the capitalist West, especially the United States. The order of the day would be flexible employment, individual contracting rather than collective representation, and substantially curtailed nonwage benefits. Public goods like health care, housing, and retirement pensions would be handled primarily outside the firm and on an individual self-help basis. If you as a citizen wanted them, you paid for them. Thus, China, in playing its part in worldwide production, provided the kind of stripped down, decidedly nonsocialist employment structures deemed necessary by producers to compete.

Foreign Exchange: Convergence toward Developed World Macroeconomic Management Techniques

For Chinese reform architects, accommodations for modular production went beyond the law. In fact, they extended into the fundamental mechanisms by which the government managed the macroeconomy. The most salient example involves the handling of foreign exchange, which itself affected the management of the money supply more generally. For China in 1978, just as the first hints of reform were appearing, total trade (imports plus exports) amounted to less than 10 percent of gross domestic output. Two decades later, by the end of 2007, trade—in an overall economy that had grown nearly seventy-fold in nominal terms—now amounted to 67 percent of gross domestic output.[15] In the 1970s and 1980s, when the economy was small and trade was minimal, foreign currency exchange could be managed through rigid mechanisms of socialist control. The state administratively fixed the renminbi's (RMB) price relative to other currencies (namely, the U.S. dollar) and did so at a level significantly above that which would have resulted if market forces of supply and demand had been allowed to operate. Of course, when an official price diverges from underlying demand conditions in this manner, alternatives to the official price frequently emerge in the underground economy. Basically, black markets for foreign currency develop. This is precisely what happened in China. As anybody who visited the country in the 1980s would likely remember, foreign currency could be converted to RMB on the street at rates far better (more RMB to the dollar) than the official rate offered by state banks.

That black markets for currency existed is not surprising. It is also not surprising that firms involved in overseas transactions could access these markets to some extent. More interesting, though, are the other mechanisms the state employed to marginalize black markets and keep them in check. If price alone could not control the supply of foreign exchange, then direct administrative measures would be employed in the effort as well.

This is exactly the approach the Chinese government took from the 1950s all the way through much of the 1980s. Under most circumstances, individuals and firms were forbidden from accessing foreign currency at all. On top of that, as per the socialist system's "double airlock" system of capital controls, they were also forbidden from moving goods across borders. Enterprises needing to import something—whether capital equipment or production inputs—could do so only after receiving governmental permission and, even then, only by working through a select few centrally controlled trade corporations. Furthermore, to obtain the foreign currency actually needed to make the purchase, the importer again had to apply for permission and—provided it was granted—had to purchase the currency (with RMB) at the state-determined price. Conversely, enterprises seeking to export had to work through state-controlled trading firms. Any foreign exchange received from overseas sales had to be sold back to the state at the state-determined price that—given the RMB's administratively set, overvalued status at the time—was highly unfavorable to the exporter.[16] Indeed, exporters never even touched foreign currency because it was received, and subsequently converted back to RMB, by the state trading corporation that had brokered the overseas sale. For a small foreign currency transaction—payment in dollars for a small overseas purchase or reimbursement for a foreign visitor, for example—a firm could certainly use the black market. In fact, by the late 1980s, these markets were gradually being legitimized and legalized. For serious business, however—the purchase of a piece of capital equipment from overseas or the sale of goods abroad—the firm had little choice but to navigate the official system, effectively applying for a quota to the State Administration for Foreign Exchange to access foreign exchange at state-determined prices.[17]

On the whole, the system proved effective for insulating China's domestic economy from world market prices. Unfortunately, it also proved effective for largely shutting China out of worldwide commercial flows. This was a system far too cumbersome for traditional Asian-style export-led growth. It was still more unsuited to the even higher transactional tempo of present-day worldwide modular production. Had this system persisted, China could never have become the global manufacturing hub it is today.

For export processors and contract manufacturers, the problem is straightforward. Based in China, they on a day-to-day basis need renminbi to pay wages, energy bills, taxes, and other local operating expenses. At the same time, they need foreign currency—U.S. dollars—to pay for all the production inputs they source from abroad. They, of course, also receive foreign currency from the overseas firms whose orders they are filling. Just as accommodation must be made for orders that suddenly ramp up or down, so too must funds be available in various currencies to finance those shifts. On top of that, particularly if the firm is a joint venture, profits have to be paid out to China-based stakeholders in renminbi and to overseas stakeholders in dollars. The basic point is that for all this to work, not only physical goods but also money must move fluidly across borders. Clearly, this is something a socialist-style double airlock system could never accommodate.

But what arose in its stead? The answer is Western-style capitalism or, more specifically, a system of market-based exchange rate valuation roughly similar to what exists in advanced capitalist systems like the United States or Hong Kong. That is not to deny that the Chinese government manipulates, influences, and otherwise manages its exchange rate. It clearly does. But it does so through the open-market operations of its central bank, thus influencing price while at the same time permitting relatively seamless convertibility for commercial actors. In this sense, its policy between 1997 and 2005 of pegging the RMB's value directly to the U.S. dollar and its establishment since then of a managed float based on a basket of global currencies (still largely based on the U.S. dollar) are quite similar to what Hong Kong, a bastion of market capitalism, has practiced since the early 1980s.

More broadly, the Chinese government's effort to shape a key price in its macroeconomy—in this case, the price of its own currency relative to others—is not entirely different from what the U.S Federal Reserve System does when it sets interest rates. Comparable open-market operations—the purchase and sale of government securities— are involved, and in both the U.S. and Chinese cases, central bank operations influence currency value. The difference is in the particular price the respective central banks are targeting. In the U.S. case, the targeted price is the domestic interest rate—the price of borrowing money—and the primary goal is to manage inflation by controlling the money supply. That price, though, because it shapes the attractiveness of the U.S. economy to foreign investors, clearly influences demand for the dollar, and thus the price of the dollar (relative to other currencies). Without thinking twice about it, we can speak sensibly of a strong or weak dollar policy on the part of the U.S. government.

In the Chinese case, the targeted price is the value of the RMB relative to other currencies, namely, the dollar. The Chinese government maintains that price by having its central bank, the People's Bank of China (PBOC), purchase dollars from domestic holders in exchange for RMB. In so doing, the Chinese government creates a series of knock-on effects for China's domestic money supply, not to mention interest rates in the United States. Like the Fed, then, it must make additional choices about how to deal with any inflationary effects.

The difference between the two countries, arguably, involves the focus of their respective macroeconomic interventions. The U.S. Fed in recent years has concentrated on inflation control through the interest rate. The PBOC has focused on export promotion through the exchange rate. Both, by their own estimates, are striving to manage stable, long-term economic growth through macroeconomic management. Interestingly, the PBOC, unlike the Fed, describes its particular kind of intervention as a transitional stage toward a more advanced form of macroeconomic management. And what is that more advanced form? The interest rate measures employed by the Fed.

What is of importance here is not the fairness of the respective nation's macroeconomic management techniques. That can be debated until the cows come home. Both nations are now major global financial players, and both engage in macroeconomic control techniques that not only influence exchange rates but also induce a variety of other knock-on effects both domestically and abroad. The more important point is to illustrate how in China's case, movement toward open-market modes of currency management is consistent with—indeed, absolutely necessary for—participation in globalized production. In the "old" days of the 1960s, 1970s, or 1980s, rapid developers like Japan or South Korea could pursue export-led growth while maintaining administratively cumbersome exchange controls.[18] In the new era of modular production, such policies are not an option. Nations like China may be able to manage exchange rates today, but they must do so through open-market operations, modes of management that for developing nations create as many headaches as advantages.

One can get a sense for this by tracing in rough terms the way money has been flowing in recent years. This flow is presented schematically, in somewhat simplified fashion, in figure 5.1. In the figure, U.S. consumption habits are marked step 1, but because the flow is circular, one could make arguments for placing step 1 at other points. Some people argue that the cycle is driven by America's appetite for consumption, and others argue it is driven by Chinese currency interventions (steps 3 and 8 in the figure). We do not resolve such debates here. In some ways, given the circularity of the flows and the interdependence of the processes involved, questions of who caused what may never be resolvable. For the sake of the present discussion, though, we focus simply on the overall flows.

We start with the overall global flow of goods in the mid-2000s. By that point, China on the whole was importing components from neighboring Asian nations (with whom it was running bilateral trade deficits) and exporting finished products to North America and Europe (with whom it was running bilateral trade surpluses). Because of the huge size of the particular bilateral surplus with the United States, China ended up running a net surplus on its overall trade account. What this meant was that there was a net inflow of U.S. dollars into China; people in China were selling more goods to the United States than they were purchasing from it.

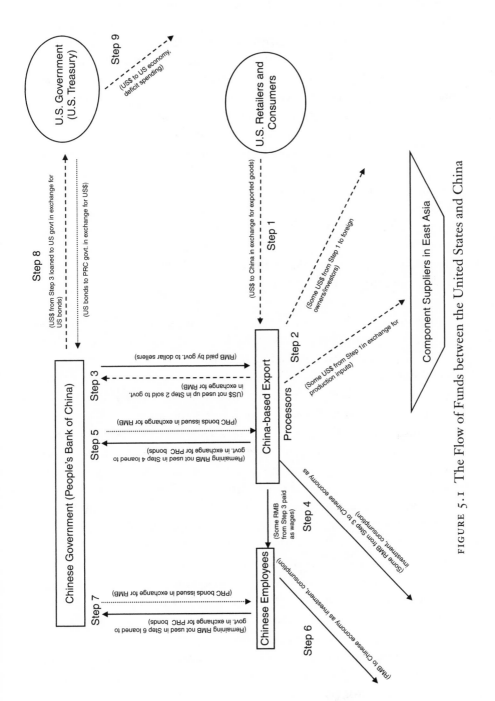

FIGURE 5.1 The Flow of Funds between the United States and China

But as we know, this is not really about Chinese people per se selling to American people. The picture on the ground could more accurately be described as one of Taiwanese-owned contract manufacturers employing China-based workers to turn components sourced from across East Asia into computers. Those computers, then, are purchased by American companies, branded, and sold onward to American consumers. As sales of computers—not to mention virtually every other consumable—skyrocketed in the United States in recent years, dollars flowed to those overseas-owned contract manufacturers in China. They then faced choices about what to do with those dollars. In some cases, they had to use the dollars to purchase production inputs—computer componentry, for example—from across Asia. In other cases, they had to use those dollars to fund their R&D and design teams operating in Taiwan or the United States. In still other cases, they repatriated those dollars as profits to Taiwanese or U.S.-based owners and investors. And in all cases, they had to convert some of those dollars to RMB to pay workers and other operating costs incurred within China.

Still, though, there was the issue of what to do with the surplus dollars, the growing profits that came from booming sales. Pay higher wages? Expand the production facilities in China? Hold onto the funds as retained earnings within China? To some extent, all three avenues were pursued, and each involved converting dollars to RMB. There was, in fact, a strong incentive to convert funds to local currency. The Chinese government was offering a very favorable exchange rate. By publicly committing itself to a dollar peg (at 8.28 RMB to the dollar), the Chinese government was effectively promising all comers that it would purchase their dollars for RMB at the pegged price. Had the government not been willing to commit to these purchases, holders of dollars would have had to sell them for RMB to those people or entities in China who needed dollars—for instance, enterprises seeking to purchase U.S.-made capital equipment. Hypothetically, the more dollars they tried to convert, the more the value of the dollar would sink relative to the RMB (i.e., sellers of dollars, to unload them in a saturated market, would have to accept fewer and fewer RMB from buyers). With rising RMB values, the cost of China-based manufacturing operations, at least in dollar terms, would go up. Those rising manufacturing costs would then get reflected in higher computer prices for purchasers in the United States.[19] American consumer demand would presumably drop as a result, and concomitantly, so too would the net flow of U.S. dollars to China. Indeed, at least in theory, the flow would reverse as Chinese consumers, armed with cheap dollars, would be more inclined to purchase U.S.-made goods.

That whole process, however, was not permitted to unfold. Just as the U.S. government is unwilling to let domestic interest rates fluctuate willy-nilly in the face of unbridled market forces, the Chinese government is unwilling to allow the same to happen to RMB values. In both cases, the governments step in as market makers, huge players that can shape market prices through massive purchases and sales of the asset in question. In the Chinese case, the Chinese government offered China-based holders of dollars better prices for those dollars (in RMB terms) than other potential purchasers in the market would have offered. If left unimpeded, the market, flooded with dollars being sold for RMB, would have driven the dollar's value down in RMB terms. The market, however, was not left unimpeded. Instead a major dollar purchaser, the Chinese central bank, stepped in to hold up values.

Once the government committed itself to a peg, not only ordinary holders of dollars but also speculators had reason to exchange their dollars for RMB. After all, they could have reasonably bet that if they sold their dollars to the government today at the current price of 8.28 RMB per dollar, the government, facing such a huge inflow of dollars, would eventually have to lower the price (in RMB terms) at some point in the future. It could not keep flooding so many RMB into the Chinese economy. Thus, the speculator or any other holder of dollars (e.g., a Taiwanese-owned contract manufacturer) could sell those dollars at a high price today and then hope to buy those dollars back at a lower price in the future. This, in fact, is what happened when, starting in 2005, the Chinese central bank began steadily lowering the RMB price at which it was willing to purchase dollars (in other words, it permitted the value of the RMB to rise in dollar terms). Nonetheless, right up to the U.S. financial collapse in the fall of 2008, dollars were flooding into China, and the Chinese government, as evidenced by its globally unparalleled accumulation of foreign exchange reserves, was buying them up.

Where did those funds go, though? What happened, at least through 2008, when so many commercial entities in China sold dollars for RMB? One thing that happened was that large quantities of RMB were pumped into the Chinese economy. These infusions of cash found their outlets in everything from real estate speculation and consumer purchases to infrastructure expansion. The Chinese economy boomed.

At the same time, the Chinese government, like most of its counterparts worldwide, remained deeply concerned about inflation.

Determined to avoid excessive expansion of the money supply, the government had to find ways to pull back from circulation the floods of RMB it was creating through its purchases of dollars. That is, it had to find ways to "sterilize" the expansion of the money supply induced by its purchases of foreign exchange, purchases that were themselves driven by the government's goal of holding the exchange rate at a specific level.[20] This pullback was achieved through the Chinese central bank's sale of RMB-denominated government bonds to domestic investors—whether households, firms, or financial organizations. In other words, the Chinese government borrowed money domestically, pulling in cash today in exchange for a promise to pay out more tomorrow when the bond came due. According to Yi Gang, the vice governor of China's central bank, China's foreign exchange reserves expanded by roughly US$1 trillion between 2003 and 2007. During that same period, the central bank pulled back approximately RMB 7 trillion (roughly US$900 billion) from the Chinese money supply by issuing bonds and raising reserve requirements for domestic banks.

This contraction of the money supply was helped along by the propensity of Chinese households to save rather than consume. The government could effectively sell large quantities of bonds without having to substantially raise interest rates, the returns guaranteed to bond purchasers. The purchasers—savers, really—were inclined to sock away their funds rather than spend them, in large part for precautionary reasons. As discussed earlier, with its deepening integration into global production, China had hurtled rapidly toward American-style workplace relations and social welfare provision. For the average Chinese citizen, employment had become flexible, benefits had become scarce, and things like health care, housing, and education—all previously available for free—had become exceedingly expensive. Understandably scared, people were inclined to save. Less understandably oblivious to similar circumstances in their own lives, Americans were more than willing to help out by spending with abandon. In the broadest sense, as long as Americans were willing to spend more than they had and borrow the rest, the Chinese could spend less than they had and save.

This connection becomes clearer if we consider what the Chinese government did with the dollars it was accumulating. In most cases, rather than holding them as noninterest-bearing cash, the Chinese government invested its dollars in the United States by purchasing U.S. Treasury securities (i.e., T-bills).[21] In so doing, it accomplished several things. By purchasing dollars in the first place, it forestalled any appreciation of the RMB relative to the dollar. By using those dollars, then, to purchase U.S. Treasury securities, it amassed interest-bearing, ostensibly safe, dollar-denominated assets (loans to the U.S. Treasury). For Beijing, those investments served to back its RMB-denominated liabilities, the bonds it had sold to Chinese households. And by purchasing U.S. Treasury bonds, the Chinese government effectively pumped credit into the U.S. economy, thus permitting the U.S. government to run massive budget deficits without driving up U.S. interest rates. Consumer credit, therefore, remained readily available in the United States, and American household spending could continue unabated.

Several things are worth noting about this whole pattern. First, for all our complaints—justified or not—about RMB valuation, China's current system of managing foreign exchange represents an absolute sea change from that which previously existed under socialism. In the past, the Chinese government employed direct administrative controls to make price essentially irrelevant for shaping supply and demand. It dealt with foreign exchange basically by ordering people to keep their hands off it. Today, in an economy highly dependent on cross-border trade and financial flows, the government has to employ a completely different approach, the use of indirect market instruments to move demand for—and therefore, the price of—Chinese currency. Like the U.S. Fed in its management of interest rates, the Chinese central bank proclaims a target price—in this case, a price of the RMB in dollar terms—and achieves that price in the market by buying or selling cash. In broad governance terms, then, the Chinese state has moved from a standard socialist approach to an equally standard capitalist one.

Second, had this shift not happened, China would never have been able to take on the role in global production that it plays today. Chinese financial management, in effect, has evolved hand in hand with the nation's integration into global production. By replacing a system of crude exchange controls with one focused on price stabilization through open-market operations, the government made large-scale export processing—participation in global supply chains, basically— possible. Through its reforms, it created a situation in which businesses, whether foreign owned or domestic, could count on relatively seamless currency conversion both into and out of the renminbi. Furthermore, businesses could count on a stable currency price, which is an important issue for modular producers who both buy inputs and sell outputs on a dollar basis in overseas markets.

Third, although this system of foreign currency management has enabled China's positioning in global supply chains, that positioning itself distributes costs and benefits in complicated ways. In the American political arena, China's currency practices are often presented in stark "us versus them" terms—the Chinese government manipulates its currency, and Americans pay the price. The reality, however, is decidedly more complex. During the heady years prior to the 2008 global downturn, China-based export processors certainly benefited, but of course, a substantial number of them are foreign owned. Thus, some of the profits went to overseas investors, including those in the United States. Component manufacturers throughout Asia also benefited because they were selling primarily to China-based assemblers. American companies doing the branding and marketing of the finished goods benefited as consumer credit in the United States remained plentiful, and U.S. sales went through the roof. And of course, U.S. consumers benefited, in a manner of speaking, by being able to access unprecedentedly low-priced consumer products with equally low-priced credit. Those were fat years for many constituencies on both the American and Chinese sides.

Whether the boom was somehow *caused* by Beijing's currency policies, Chinese citizens' abnormally high savings rates, or anything else having to do with China is impossible to say. There were simply too many other things happening at the same time—including an easy money policy by the Fed, rapid housing sector expansion in the United States, and subprime lending and other "innovative" practices spreading like wildfire across the American financial landscape with little regulatory oversight.

Nonetheless, that Beijing's currency policies complemented the Fed's interest rate policies and that Chinese savings financed American spending are indisputable. In these typical chicken and egg problems, what caused what is impossible to determine. Absolutely clear, though, is that like the chicken and egg, the United States and China in financial terms are inextricably linked. As America's biggest global lender by far, China has effectively financed America's trade deficits and the American penchant for oversized consumption more generally. As the world's largest purchasers of Chinese exports (manufactured goods that are at least assembled in China), again by far, Americans in recent years have driven growth in the Chinese economy. Since the mid-2000s, both nations have been engaged in a mutual handshake of sorts.

Now that the boom has gone bust, the underlying risks in that handshake have become clearer. In the United States, consumers have lost purchasing power, the economy has ground to a halt, and joblessness has reached levels unseen for twenty-five years. With falling U.S.

consumption, China-based manufacturers have experienced precipitous declines in orders, thus necessitating layoffs in China's coastal East and South, areas specialized in export-oriented manufacturing. Because these firms employ migrant workers from all over China, the effects are felt throughout the country and arguably most acutely in the rural hinterland. The effects are also felt in neighboring countries that export into these supply chains.

The U.S. government has been put in the position of having to bail out domestic banks and insurance companies to avert collapse of the nation's entire financial system. Meanwhile, the Chinese government is left in a difficult quandary. Through its purchase of U.S. Treasury securities, it has amassed a considerable amount of dollar-denominated assets that will tank in value if the U.S. economy crashes. China's officially reported foreign exchange reserves stood at US$1.95 trillion as of March 2009. Economists estimate that 65 percent of that portfolio, roughly US$1.5 trillion, is held in dollar-denominated assets, primarily Treasury securities (US$760 billion), but also agency bonds (Fannie Mae, Freddie Mac, etc.), U.S. corporate bonds, U.S. corporate securities, and bank deposits.[22] These assets back a comparably large amount of RMB-denominated liabilities (domestic bonds) owed to the Chinese people. Just as Americans are still potentially threatened by the financial risk lurking in their troubled system, so too are the Chinese. If the U.S. economy were to suffer additional shocks and the value of the U.S. dollar were to plummet, Beijing would be left in the position of watching its dollar-denominated assets evaporate while its RMB-denominated liabilities remained nauseatingly robust.

Over the long run, Beijing may seek to diversify its foreign exchange holdings across a broader range of currencies, but it must proceed cautiously to avoid having the bottom drop out of the dollar. Similar caution applies—or at least should apply—to those Americans demanding RMB appreciation vis-à-vis the dollar. Appreciation over the long run is appropriate. Sudden appreciation—that is, a collapse of the dollar—serves nobody's interest.

And that leads to a fourth and final point. Chinese exchange rate management should be understood as playing by our rules in two different respects. In a sort of static fashion from roughly 2003 to 2007, China's currency policies complemented, for better *and* for worse, American consumption patterns. Thus, these policies meshed with our own by permitting us to engage in the economic behavior of our choice, however ill-advised that choice may have been. In a deeper sense, though, Chinese currency management can be understood as playing by our rules in terms of the evolutionary direction in which it is heading. Over the course of less than two decades, China departed from a fairly traditional, socialist-style system of capital controls, and headed forward through a series of stages—a unified exchange rate regime, a fixed dollar peg, and a managed float—each more similar to modern capitalist practice than the last. The trajectory is fairly clear. In exchange rate management, China is converging toward the currency practices of advanced industrial nations like the United States. Of course, for the movement to be complete, China will have to continue pursuing additional domestic reforms: more robust social welfare provision (to avoid the need for precautionary savings), continued urbanization (thus leading to greater domestic demand), and better environmental and labor standards (thus raising domestic costs and potentially lowering the trade surplus).[23] Most of these efforts are currently under way. Some, namely, the encouragement of domestic demand, primarily through bank lending, have been catalyzed by the Chinese government's domestic stimulus package in the wake of the 2008 downturn.

As numerous officials in China recognize, these institutional changes, coupled with further currency appreciation, will place China in a more balanced financial relationship with the United States and in a better position to achieve long-term growth. Thus, the broader point is that while the 2008 crash created pressures for China to ease off complementing American policies as a lender and financial enabler, it created opportunities for China to move closer to the forms of modern market governance and macroeconomic management practiced in advanced industrial nations. "Capitalist enabler" increasingly morphed into "institutional outsourcer" or, perhaps more accurately in the case of currency management, "institutional converger." The lesson of 2008 is that while neither the United States nor China can continue playing the former game, both must work assiduously to improve their performance in the latter. Just as the collective fates of those two nations are now inextricably linked in global production, so too are they linked in global finance. For China, then, institutional convergence—at least along the lines outlined in this chapter—has evolved from national aspiration to national imperative.

SIX

Playing to Win?

China's Advance into High-Tech Research and Development

As SUGGESTED IN the preceding two chapters, China has played what might be termed a "best supporting actor" role in global production. Serving as a low-cost provider of the most commodified pieces of production, China has created opportunities for wealthier nations—the lead actors—to deepen their command over commercial innovation and global commerce more generally. To maintain a supporting role, and to do it more effectively than virtually any other developing nation, China has had to undergo radical domestic transformation carried out largely in the image of the advanced industrial West. That China has benefited immeasurably in the process is beyond doubt. Like any great supporting actor, though, China has had to make accommodations throughout, many of which cut against natural inclinations for autonomy and control. It has had to hew closely to scripts written by people other than its own, and it has often had to take direction from those outsiders. And all the while, despite the occasional thrown elbow or vitriolic tirade, it has had to studiously avoid upsetting the lead.

Who is to say, though, that this won't come to an end at some point, even some point soon? After all, even if China were subordinating itself today, why wouldn't it seek to call the shots tomorrow?

Once a best supporting actor scales the heights of his profession, does all that others have expected of him, and lands a coveted Oscar, presumably he will seek—indeed, demand—lead roles and, better yet, lead roles of his own choosing. China may be playing by our rules today, but why wouldn't it seek to change those rules and even one day change the entire game to better suit its interests?

It is in this sense that China's much-publicized ambition to become a global leader in science, technology, and commercial innovation becomes so interesting. The Chinese government in 2006 proclaimed a nationwide campaign for "indigenous innovation" (*zizhu chuangxin*). In cities across the nation, billboards went up imploring citizens to "construct a harmonious society" (*goujian hexie shehui*) and "strengthen our nation's capacity for indigenous innovation" (*tigao woguo zizhu chuangxin nengli*). The official position from Beijing was clear. China would be catapulted to the very frontiers of scientific and technological innovation.

There was more to this drive than just slogans, and it had in fact been going on since well before 2006. From 1995 to 2005, China's investment in research and development (R&D) increased nearly 20 percent per annum, a rate that researchers at the OECD (Organisation for Economic Co-Operation and Development) justifiably term "stunning."[1] China's ratio of R&D to total national economic output (GDP) more than doubled from 1995 to 2006, climbing from 0.6 percent to 1.42 percent.[2] Conservative estimates now place the country sixth on the list of worldwide funders of R&D.[3] Some observers, using broader definitions of R&D, put China even higher, in third place behind only the United States and Japan.[4] As noted previously, China during this period and right on through the present has made massive investments in higher education. In 1994, Chinese universities graduated just fewer than 640,000 students, 14 percent of whom were in the sciences and 36 percent in engineering. By 2006, the annual number of graduates had swelled to 3.77 million—a nearly sixfold increase over twelve years. Just over 5 percent of the graduates in 2006 were in the sciences, 36 percent in engineering, and more than 17 percent in a major that did not even exist in 1994, management.[5] In terms of headcount, China's pool of science and technology workers is surpassed only by that of the United States.[6] The numbers are jaw-dropping.

Several of China's indigenous companies appear to be making good use of this talent. Huawei, China's leading supplier of telecommunications networking equipment, now devotes roughly 10 percent of its annual revenues (which in 2008 stood at US$23.3 billion) to R&D.

It currently operates fourteen R&D centers in locales ranging from Silicon Valley and Stockholm to Moscow and Bangalore.[7] Computer maker Lenovo is also recognized as a major R&D player, with seven research centers in China, one in Japan, and one in Raleigh, North Carolina.[8]

More striking than Chinese efforts to "go out" have been foreign efforts to "come in." The world's leading technology companies have scrambled in recent years to initiate R&D operations in China. Microsoft, Motorola, Intel, Google, Nokia, Ericsson, and many others now run major China-based research centers.[9] In 1997, there were only 24 foreign-owned R&D centers across all of China, but by 2007, there were 1,140.[10] As anyone could plainly see, the drive for indigenous innovation was on. The Chinese government was taking the lead, and foreign corporations seemed to be gamely helping out.

"Believers" Versus "Doubters"

Nobody disputes that massive investments have been made. Whether those investments have paid off, however, is a matter of major debate. Two diametrically opposed views have emerged, neither one far-fetched or irrational, but each with a markedly different conclusion about how far China has advanced and whether people in the United States, Japan, and Western Europe should be concerned.

The first school of thought, what we will term the "believers," argues that China truly has surged forward and done so in ways that imperil American interests. The view is well represented in the 2008 report of the U.S.–China Economic and Security Review Commission (USCC), a public body set up by the U.S. Congress to draw annual assessments of the national security implications of America's economic relationship with China.[11]

The argument begins with a particular characterization of Chinese intentions, asserting that Beijing "has been pursuing a government policy designed to make China a technology superpower and to enhance its exports."[12] "China's government," it continues, "intends to create a more knowledge-based and technologically proficient economy."[13] The point is that the pace and direction of China's science and technology push are governmentally determined and pursued with strategic intent.

The argument continues on to tactics. "China's leaders," the report states, "seek to enhance its [China's] advanced technology production through subsidies and other incentives to attract foreign-invested research and technology companies to China. Acquisition of foreign technology is intended to speed China's development of advanced products."[14] The idea here is that foreign corporations—viewed in the report as conduits for Chinese knowledge acquisition—are locating R&D centers in China because that is precisely what the Chinese government wants them to do and, indeed, has encouraged them to do through both legitimate and illegitimate means. The report continues, "Some of its [China's] tactics violate free market principles—specifically its use of subsidies and an artificially low RMB value to attract foreign investment."[15]

The argument's next step involves conclusions about how far China has actually come in the upgrading process. On the one hand, the report strikes a note of caution when it says, "Exactly how many steps up the technology ladder foreign-invested enterprises have boosted China is still disputed among experts."[16] On the other hand, it goes on to say in the next sentence, "But China is making considerable progress in moving up that ladder." In the end, the report is quite clear about its view of the overall trend: China is winning, it is doing so by extracting know-how from American companies, and its victories are coming at our own national expense. As the report states in its conclusion, "Foreign technology companies, such as U.S. and European computer, aerospace, and automotive firms, have invested heavily in research and development and production facilities in China, sharing or losing technology and other know-how. Chinese manufacturers have benefited from this investment."[17] For the believers, R&D is basically a competitive, zero-sum game. If new guys are moving up from below, old guys are getting tossed off the top.

Interestingly enough, one can take an identical set of facts—that is, China's official promotion of indigenous innovation, the rapid increase in R&D expenditures, the build out of the science and technology (S&T) workforce, and the proliferation of foreign R&D centers in China—and come up with a completely different interpretation of what is going on. This brings us to the second school of thought, one that we will call the "doubters." These observers, in stark contrast to the believers, take on a dismissive, even condescending, view of China's S&T endeavors. Well represented in Chinese, American, and European academic circles, this perspective argues that despite the country's economic achievements and despite the nationwide emphasis on innovation, China is lagging, and lagging rather badly, on the R&D front. China is presented not as a rising science and technology powerhouse but instead as an underperforming student, an engineering school wannabee who, though reasonably talented, can't quite come up with the grades necessary for success.

A representative example here is the OECD's 2008 report on Chinese innovation policy. Describing all the funds China has mobilized for R&D, the report states, "This impressive investment in resources has contributed significantly to the rapid socio-economic progress registered in China in the last decade, but it has not yet translated into a proportionate increase in innovation performance."[18] In short, a glaring gap exists between what is going in and what is coming out.

And how do we know that this gap exists? The first piece of evidence, at least as the doubters see it, is that China is not spending as much as it appears to be and, by extension, as much as it should be spending. China's R&D outlays, the doubters argue, have to be put in comparative perspective. The country may be committing a lot of resources but not nearly as much as the world's technology leaders. China spends the equivalent of 1.42 percent of its gross domestic product (GDP) on R&D. The United States, in turn, spends 2.62 percent of its GDP on R&D. South Korea and Japan spend even more, 3.23 percent and 3.39 percent, respectively.[19]

The second piece of evidence has to do with the modest returns being realized. As noted by the OECD, Chinese patent applications filed in 2005 under the worldwide Patent Cooperation Treaty (PCT) amounted to only 3 percent of the global total, a level on par with filings from Sweden or Canada.[20] If nothing else, this indicates that investments have been rather thin for the kinds of basic and applied research that lead to patentable inventions. In other words, when it comes to R&D, China has been doing a lot of D but not much R. In fact, some of the doubters argue that for much of Chinese industry, little R&D whatsoever is taking place. Liu Xuelin, a well-known professor of management in the Chinese Academy of Sciences, argues that Chinese firms, locked into intensely competitive, commodity-focused production, simply lack resources to do R&D. Liu and others have estimated that no more than 10 percent of Chinese indigenous firms do any R&D at all, and no more than 1 percent rely on any of their own intellectual property.[21] And as for all those science and technology workers being churned out by Chinese educational institutions, Simon and Cao in their comprehensive 2009 volume caution us to be wary about the quality of the training and the skill levels actually attained.[22]

For many of these more skeptical scholars, the substantial foreign presence in Chinese R&D efforts is taken as a sign of weakness rather than strength. The idea is that the foreigners are doing R&D because the Chinese cannot, and the kind of R&D foreigners are doing in China is fairly low end, weighted more toward product development (often for products specifically tailored to the Chinese market) than basic research. Thus, in terms of cutting-edge knowledge, the foreigners are hardly handing over the keys to the kingdom. Rather, they are doing what it takes—namely, tailoring products to the Chinese market—to outcompete Chinese firms in their own backyard.

But that still leaves open the question of why this (purported) gap exists between China's nationwide R&D investment and its overall national R&D output. For the doubters, the answer hinges on structural features of the Chinese system. The idea in a nutshell is that the system is far too state centric. Proponents of this view argue that while in China today R&D spending *seems* to be shifting away from government agencies and toward commercial firms, the reality is that many of the so-called commercial firms doing the spending now are just former state bureaus that have hung out a commercial shingle.[23] Given what these organizations are and with whom they are connected, they remain comfortably insulated from what really drives innovation: markets. At the same time, the argument goes, the real commercial firms that truly are operating in markets face an entirely different set of obstacles. Banks refuse to finance them, especially if they are small and private. China's intellectual property laws afford them little protection. Foreign investors, wary about creating new competitors, refuse to transfer anything of value to them. And the Chinese government, the only decent source of R&D funds left in the game, maintains a completely nontransparent process of project evaluation and grant disbursement.[24] It basically funds only insiders.

Hence, from this perspective, China is left in a rather disappointing position. For all its talent and resources—all its tremendous potential to become a leading light in global innovation—it ends up hobbled by a cumbersome, difficult-to-reform state system. Politically connected firms face inadequate market pressures. Conversely, market-oriented private firms face excessive political impediments. As a result of these institutional problems, China ends up achieving less on the innovation front than it should.[25] Progress has been made, the argument goes, but precious little relative to the amount of funding thrown in. Instead of shooting up the ladder the way it should, China is left struggling to mount the first few steps, hardly the believers' image of a rising high-tech superpower.

How can we make sense of these two diametrically-opposed schools of thought? They agree on the overall set of facts but completely disagree on what those facts mean. One view gives us a global S&T powerhouse, and the other a flatfooted S&T underperformer. There is likely no amount of additional aggregate data—whether regarding patent output, numbers of new inventions, types of products introduced, or really anything else—that will persuade one side of the other's claims. In this chapter, we do not pursue that route of dueling aggregate claims. Instead, we focus on something different, the nature of the R&D activities themselves. Similar to what we did in chapter 4 with manufacturing, we consider here what commercial R&D today really looks like on the ground and what it involves. Who really is doing it, and what exactly are they doing? How does what they are doing in China relate to what is being done in other parts of the world? Questions about quantity—whether China is doing a lot of R&D or a little, as much as it *should*, or perhaps even too much—seem pointless if we cannot specify what this thing called R&D is all about. By answering that last question, we may find that issues of quantity are beside the point. At the very least, we may find that in China certain kinds of R&D are being done with great frequency, but others seldom at all. Moreover, we may find that those differences matter greatly for the issues we care about.

In the following sections, we consider broadly what commercial R&D entails in today's world, and then we delve into the specifics of what is transpiring on the ground in China. The perspective presented here comes from extensive company-level interviews I have conducted over the years both on my own and with teams of colleagues from the Massachusetts Institute of Technology.[26] The field interviews, ranging across China, Taiwan, Japan, the United States, and Western Europe, were conducted primarily from from 2006 through 2009.

Research and development is a complicated endeavor involving many different kinds of activities that often vary from industry to industry. Research and development in cosmetics is not the same as R&D in aerospace, and neither of those is exactly the same as R&D in electronics, an obvious point, perhaps, but one often lost in big-picture debates about a given nation's level of R&D activity. At the same time, by focusing on activities within specific industries, one runs certain risks in drawing general conclusions about *all* industries. The four years of field interviews upon which this chapter draws revolved primarily around four industries: energy, telecommunications (i.e., networking equipment, mobile phones, and networking services), IT-related electronics (i.e., personnel computers, handheld devices), and pharmaceuticals. In some cases, they extended into other areas, including consumer care products, aerospace, building materials, and automotives. Whenever possible, my conclusions distinguish between those that are industry specific and those that are more broadly applicable across industries.

The Globalization of Research and Development

Returning to the two schools of thought outlined earlier, we can see that for all their differences, they both identify the phenomenon of China-based R&D by multinational corporations as something new and important, a critical piece of the China story. They do so with good reason. Of all the production activities described in the smile curve (chapter 4), one in particular, at least until recently, has long been considered immune from internationalization: R&D. For years, even as manufacturing activities moved offshore with increasing frequency, research and development appeared to remain firmly rooted in the home locales of major multinationals. Manufacturing, perhaps, was an activity for everywhere, but R&D was something to be done in North America, Western Europe, and Japan. The closer to the headquarters of the multinational company carrying it out, the better.

In the last few years, however, that one remaining bit of geographical fixity seems to have come unstuck. The R&D process appears to have fragmented, though not quite in the same way as production more broadly. With production as a whole, activities got dispersed not only geographically but also across multiple firms. With R&D, the activities certainly now appear disbursed geographically, with many of them going on in places like China, where they had never been going on before. Yet, ownership still seems concentrated in the hands of a relatively small number of multinationals. The supply chain, so to speak, for R&D seems not yet to have fragmented across multiple firms. Instead, leading technology-focused corporations, who had once operated concentrated, highly centralized R&D operations now appear to be managing highly diversified, highly internationalized research networks which they themselves own.[27] Spread across multiple locales, these networks presumably allow corporations to mobilize talent on a global basis and harness it to the task of commercial innovation. Enabled, of course, by the digitization revolution, corporations can now conduct R&D through a sort of global workflow, moving tasks from one international locale to another, often through combinations of e-mail, IP telephony, videoconferencing, and work-flow synchronization software. This is no longer your Thomas Edison working in isolation in a lab in New Jersey. Indeed, it is no longer even Bell Labs, a stand-alone corporate research division concentrated in a single metropolitan locale.

But if it is not Thomas Edison or Bell Labs, what exactly is it? The aggregate quantitative data certainly suggest something new is taking place globally. During the late 1990s and early 2000s, while R&D expenditures still remained concentrated in the United States (R&D expenditures in the United States during those years grew at twice the global average), R&D spending in South Asia, Southeast Asia, and most notably, China began to shoot upward (albeit from a relatively small base).[28] So too did expenditures in Central Europe and Russia. As Dieter Ernst points out, International Monetary Fund balance of payments data from these years suggest rapid growth of cross-border payments for technology licensing and other forms of intellectual property.[29] And as these funds were being disbursed all over the world, it appears that multinational firms from advanced industrial economies were doing most of the spending. According to the United Nations Conference on Trade and Development (UNCTAD), among the 700 largest R&D-spending firms in the world in 2005, 80 percent came from one of five countries: the United States, Japan, Germany, the United Kingdom, and France.[30] Only 1 percent of the top spenders came from developing nations, Central Europe, or Russia. Those 700 primarily advanced industrial corporations, however, accounted for almost half of the entire world's total R&D expenditures in 2005 and well over two-thirds of the world's commercial R&D.[31] Clearly, there is a lot of spending going on, much of it done by multinational corporations and at least some of it done in nontraditional places. Particularly with regard to that last issue, China, having recently helicoptered into position as the world's third largest locale for R&D spending, appears to be at the heart of the action. Again, though, the question remains, what really is this action all about?

Research and Development
Broadly Defined

No matter where it is happening, R&D—specifically, commercial R&D—can be understood as falling within several fairly distinct categories of activities. Scholars and other technology specialists have come up with a variety of taxonomies, but for our purposes, we break R&D into three categories: research on fundamental, new-to-the-world technologies; research and development for new product platforms; and research and development for existing products that need to be adapted to specific customer or country-level requirements.[32]

The first type, research on new-to-the-world technologies, is what most people imagine when they think of R&D. It is also the type more often than not implied when people debate whether China is making inroads on the R&D front. Examples of this kind of research would include our earlier discussion of IBM's efforts on racetrack memory in the IT industry or drug discovery and new molecule synthesis in the pharmaceutical sector. An indigenous Chinese example can be found in the energy sector with Tsinghua University's pioneering efforts on high-temperature gas-cooled (pebble bed) nuclear reactors. This new-to-the-world nuclear power technology—appealing both for its resistance to runaway chain reactions (meltdowns) and its potential deployment in low-cost, small-scale units—has recently moved out of the laboratory and into the field with the construction of a commercial-scale demonstration project in China's Shandong Province.[33] Regardless of where it is happening, this type of innovation, focused much more on the R than the D in R&D, is probably closest to what most people understand as "invention."

A different, second category of R&D pertains not so much to the invention of new-to-the-world basic technologies, but rather the creation of new kinds of products that make use of recently invented technologies. Thus, this second category is not about inventing totally new technologies, but instead taking technologies that are already available, albeit in many cases ones that are still in their infant stages, and combining them to form new products. In many ways, this second type of R&D can be just as innovative and challenging as the first. Examples here would include the netbook products we discussed in chapter 4 or Apple's iPhone. The guts of netbooks are all well-known components, but in the new product, they have been put together in a creative and exciting way that has proved immediately appealing to consumers. The Apple iPhone is roughly similar. Its componentry is undoubtedly advanced, but what really distinguishes it from other smart phones is its user interface, its feel as it seamlessly pulls together voice, data, multimedia, and other communications functions in a single handheld unit. Thus, the platform is clearly distinguishable from those of other competitors like Palm or BlackBerry. The best of these examples do more than just satisfy existing consumer demand.

Rather, they enable the consumer to do things he or she never imagined doing (or imagined needing to do) but then could never imagine living without once the product is actually tried out.[34]

Quite different from this kind of new platform development, a third type of R&D, one usually involving much more D than R, pertains to the adapting of existing products to local market or specific customer needs. In telecommunications, where different countries often have different network standards, such product adaptation is required almost any time networking equipment or a network solution (e.g., Wi-Fi, WiMax, broadband wireless, 3G, IPTV) is sold abroad. At a somewhat different level, consumer products like smart phones or standard mobile phones need to have user interfaces that accord with local languages and culturally bound user preferences. Phones in China, for example, need to have Chinese character input systems, which themselves may involve software changes, keyboard changes, or in some cases, touch-screen or touch-pad changes to the products' original design. Products with voice-recognition capabilities designed originally for one language may need to be adapted to the new challenges that come from another language. In an entirely different industry, pharmaceuticals, drugs approved for use in one country are often subject to different approval standards in another. At the very least, the drug will likely need to undergo local clinical trials before being approved. In still another industry, transportation systems, major customers—usually metropolitan transit authorities—often impose specific design demands, thus requiring adaptation of the supplier's product platform. Thus, things like station entry gates and fare collection systems designed for one metropolitan subway system often need to be adapted and reengineered before they are accepted by another.[35] In many cases, this involves not only physical changes but also extensive reengineering of the operating software. The point is that across many different kinds of industries, localization demands are often both challenging and extensive, even for the most mature products and product platforms.

Research and Development
for Local Customization

Keeping the three types of R&D in mind, let's now consider how they mesh with broader trends in internationalization, including the movement of so much activity to China. We start with the third type, customization to meet local needs. Clearly, one of the reasons R&D, broadly defined, has internationalized in recent years is that with so many new consumer markets coming online during the era of globalization, demands for product adaptation have skyrocketed. Whether it is cell phone networks going up in sub-Saharan Africa, new air traffic control systems being installed in Southeast Asia, new mass transit systems being built across China, or new drugs being introduced into developing countries just now experiencing for the first time the diseases of prosperity (e.g., heart disease, hypertension, diabetes), all of these require R&D for local adaptation and approval. It is by no means surprising, then, that with the spread of sales worldwide, multinational firms have had to spread R&D operations globally as well. It is not that product adaptation requires a development center in every locale, but it often does require regional presence and extensive interaction with local users. It is certainly the case that multinationals face incentives to locate product adaptation centers in the biggest—or potentially biggest—overseas markets. China across so many different consumer sectors jumps out as an obvious choice.

Exactly how much product adaptation is going on in China-based foreign R&D centers is difficult to say. Our years of interviewing, however, suggest that the amount is considerable across a wide range of industries. In numerous product areas, China already represents an extremely large market, but one with idiosyncratic preferences, practices, and standards. As one telecommunications executive related to me in 1999, "If you are in the global mobile handset business, you absolutely have to be selling in China. If you can't produce a product suited to their [the Chinese consumers'] tastes and capture these volumes, you'll never be able to sustain your position in other markets."[36] A major European auto parts maker noted to my MIT colleagues and me in 2007 that because the metals used by private Chinese auto assemblers like Chery and Geely are less advanced than those used in Europe, and because the production process in China often involves hand welding rather than machine welding, the parts it produces must be redesigned for Chinese consumption. Hence, when this European supplier follows major customers (global auto assemblers) into China or produces directly for Chinese assemblers, it moves a piece of its R&D operation over to China as well.[37] In some ways, the European firm is not reengineering its parts up—pushing them to the edge of the industry frontier—but reengineering them down to suit outdated processes. On a somewhat different score, a major global cosmetics company reported that in its view, China represents 100 million potential customers who in many cases demand a somewhat tailored product. According to this company, in-country R&D expansion absolutely has to accompany sales growth. Indeed, one-third of the products it already sells in China are specifically adapted to local tastes and user practices.[38] And of course, global pharmaceutical companies, to get their drugs approved in China, have to run local clinical trials. Several major drug companies reported during interviews that the bulk of the work done in their China-based R&D centers involves precisely these kinds of trials.[39]

The pharmaceutical case is particularly interesting because local clinical trials are also critical drivers of sales. In the Chinese health-care system, hospital and individual physician reimbursements are driven largely by drug sales.[40] The Chinese system attempts to hold down patient costs by limiting fees hospitals can charge for preventive medicine and basic care. At the same time, the systems leaves wide open the pricing of drugs, high-end diagnostics, and surgical procedures. Not surprisingly, Chinese health-care providers, in ways that imitate their American counterparts, are far more enthusiastic today about prescribing high-end drugs and investing in state-of-the-art diagnostic tools than they are about doing basic preventive medicine. The former represents the road to riches, whereas the latter is the path to poverty. With the way the Chinese health-care system has evolved in recent years, it is not just that pricing regulations drive certain kinds of health-care provider behavior. It is also that decision-making authority has been pushed down to the provider level. In this system, key decisions—whether about prescribing a drug or ordering an MRI test—take place at the point of care, often with little if any oversight from outside agencies. That carries two ramifications for medical device and pharmaceutical manufacturers. First, it has a multiplier effect on the size of the market, for there are few if any regulatory measures to prevent redundant equipment purchases or overprescription of high-end drugs. Second, it means that to access this market, the multinational supplier needs to develop networks of relationships extending deep down into the system.[41] As one China-based research director for a global pharmaceutical firm related to me, clinical trials for new drugs and devices are an important way of developing influential allies at the hospital level who will then help sell your product later.[42]

The broader point is that for everything from cosmetics and medical devices to network security software and Internet search engines, a degree of adaptation is required as producers range into new markets. In many cases, particularly when the market is especially large, it makes sense to do that adaptation work "in country," so to speak. It is natural, therefore, that as China has grown, so too has the multinational R&D presence there. It also follows naturally that as a handful of indigenous Chinese firms are beginning to go global—that is, sell products or systems in overseas markets—they too are extending their R&D presence abroad. Huawei, for example, is starting to sell telecommunications networking systems—generally, at the low end of the market—in Europe and North America. Given the centrality of national standards and individual customer preferences in this industry (customer, in this case, referring to network operators, carriers like Verizon or AT&T), Huawei almost has no choice but to develop an R&D presence abroad.[43]

Hence, the fact that we see multinational R&D centers proliferating in China, and even a few Chinese R&D centers popping up abroad, says little if anything about knowledge transfer. It certainly cannot be claimed that the very existence of these centers ipso facto confirms knowledge transfer, a giving up of the keys to the kingdom by multinationals to foreign competitors. And it does not mean that these centers are just meaningless public relations façades, "PR" & D centers set up just to please the local government but not actually to do any serious research. To the extent these centers are doing local adaptation—which our interviews suggest is a considerable portion of their activities—they are not really transferring vital knowledge, but they are playing a vital role in enabling sales. In today's world, if companies are going to increase their penetration of overseas markets, they will also likely need to expand their overseas-based, product-adaptation-focused R&D operations. The persistence of unique local conditions, even for what are thought to be standardized global products, simply demands it.

Research and Development for the Creation of New Product Platforms

With R&D for local customization, the effects of globalization are relatively straightforward: Rising levels of overseas sales drive rising demands for product adaptation. Still, the *process* by which this adaptation takes place remains relatively unchanged from the past. The situation is very different, though, with regard to R&D for the creation of new product platforms. Here, the process really has changed, in large part due to the very same forces of digitization and modularity that have transformed worldwide production more generally.

As discussed in chapter 4, these forces did several things. First, by deverticalizing and fragmenting the production process, they permitted the proliferation of highly specialized firms that may focus on just a single activity on the smile curve. Second, given such specialization and the detachment of modular producers from any single consumer product, the forces of change unleashed disruptive innovation and accelerated product cycles. Third, by enabling China-based producers to flatten the smile curve—that is, by permitting them to codify and thus dramatically lower the costs and profitability of manufacturing activities—they created pressures for global technology leaders to move out of manufacturing and up into higher value, knowledge-intensive activities. For leading multinationals, the imperative to create new product platforms, new services, and even new fundamental technologies became greater than ever. Fourth, just as digitization permitted information flow up and down the supply chain, so too did it permit comparable flows within the firm and within single production activities. Thus, something like R&D, even when pursued within the confines of a single firm, could now be conducted through activities distributed across multiple locales, some far removed from corporate headquarters. Just as production as a whole in the globalization era often became a networked activity extending across multiple firms, R&D—even though it generally remained a single-firm, in-house endeavor—also took on a kind of networked quality. In both cases, people had to come up with new ways to manage distributed activities extending across multiple international locales.

What, then, does this mean for the creation of new product platforms?[44] One thing it means, as noted earlier, is that technology-focused multinational companies face intense pressures to roll out new products and services. The telecommunications industry is a case in point. On the equipment provision side (i.e., routers, switches, fiber-optic cables, core backbone equipment for mobile phone networks, etc.), new entrants like Huawei have driven down profit margins. Indeed, Huawei's driving down of costs can itself be considered an example of R&D-based innovation. It is not so much that a new product was created but instead that new processes were developed for producing older products less expensively. In any case, what this does is to further encourage traditional suppliers of these technologies to hurriedly move into something else.

Demand for that something else was conveniently created by another change in the industry, this time on the network operator side. For a variety of reasons—including deregulation, enhanced competition, and the emergence of substitute technologies—the profitability of fixed-line voice communications has tanked for network operators in recent years. Yet, demand for other kinds of services has skyrocketed. Businesses customers are demanding networks capable of moving ever-increasing quantities of data at ever-increasing speeds. Greater data flow then necessitates enhanced network security and data storage capabilities. Household consumers want not only mobile phones but also broadband access for both home and mobile use. They want smart phones that can handle not just voice and data communications but also video and TV, and of course, they want access to all these things no matter where they travel. These are all services that involve not just the phone itself but the engineering of the entire network.

What we are witnessing now is that all manner of different technologies appear to be converging on this one industry—screen technologies for phones, new kinds of software, new ways of delivering broadband, new modes of producing and selling music and video, and on and on. Should the smart phone ultimately replace the personal computer, network operators would be delighted. Yet, for that to happen, the operators (carriers) need to scramble—often in intense competition with one another—to deliver all the new services smartphone users demand. And where are the carriers going to get those services? From new product platforms engineered by the telecom network equipment providers. The network carriers are hustling to provide customers with new services, and the telecom equipment providers are hustling to provide carriers with networks capable of performing those services. In most cases, the problem is not a lack of fundamental technologies. A plethora of new technologies are now available, many of them created by small, highly specialized start-ups that have proliferated in the United States in recent years. The technologies, though, have to be refined for reliable deployment and, equally important, need to be interwoven with other technologies into a single product, a network solution.

But how is a leading equipment supplier supposed to come up with these new product platforms, especially when the pace of technological change is so rapid? The supplier faces three basic choices.[45] First, it can do the job in house, relying on its own know-how. This is appealing in many respects, and it is often good for the company's bottom line. Yet, given the pace of technological change and given how so many different technologies from across so many different industries (at least as traditionally defined) are converging on telecoms, in-house development is not always a viable option. Second, the company can buy the technology from a third party or even acquire the third party itself. To do that, the company needs not only money but also the kind of search capabilities necessary to find these new technologies and their creators in the first place. That search function is challenging in any industry facing rapid worldwide technological change. An executive at a major European aerospace conglomerate related to this author how his company somewhat serendipitously acquired a technology for shaping carbon composites (used in turbofan blades) from a small U.S.-based firm specialized in building materials.[46] The conglomerate stumbled upon the technology supplier through an Internet search.

Once the technology or technology originator is acquired, though, it still needs to be integrated into the company, which is a substantial challenge in its own right. Such acquisitions are difficult to pull off successfully, but they are often necessary when market pressures are such that there is simply no time to develop the technology in house. If done correctly, these acquisitions can build the core competitiveness of the company and give the firm command over new types of key technologies. Given the challenges involved, though, this is not the kind of thing that can be pursued casually on a one-shot basis (a one-off effort to meet a single customer's wish).[47]

In fact, such one-off, customer-driven pressures often lead to a third solution, temporarily partnering with a third party to come up with a product solution. In these cases—which, as telecom executives ruefully explain, require multitudes of lawyers—the partnership often involves some shared intellectual property and cooperative development of a network architecture. The fact it is being done as a partnership frequently influences the kind of network architecture that is chosen. When leading companies develop architectures on their own, they frequently opt for proprietary, closed systems. However, when partnering is involved, the solution often entails an open, modular architecture that can accommodate and link a series of standardized components, the very sort of components that a company like Huawei might produce. Partnerships like this can also involve situations in which the firms involved come from totally different industries, have no interest in getting involved in one another's business, but recognize that they have an opportunity to interact symbiotically. For example, a telecom equipment supplier seeking solutions for delivering TV to mobile phones may recognize that the product platforms involved will likely require special types of integrated circuits (chips). The equipment supplier, however, is not a chip designer. So, what it may do is partner with a fabless semiconductor design house that already owns the intellectual property (IP) for a chip that can perform the necessary function. The fabless design house has neither the desire nor capability to package that chip into a usable telecom product. Similarly, the telecom supplier is not going to become a chip designer. Hence, they partner on a single product.

What exactly do all these new pressures for technology acquisition and new product development have to do with internationalization? One of the interesting things is that multinationals, which in many cases were already operating multiple overseas sites for product adaptation, have begun in recent years to use these sites for new product development. Put somewhat differently, they have started to distribute product development tasks across both these existing international sites and a variety of new ones, thus creating a sort of in-house network for R&D operations. In some cases, these centers are able to contribute technologies that emerge from the conditions of the local market where they are based. That is, some sort of technology solution to an idiosyncratic local condition proves applicable on a global basis. For example, one major telecom equipment provider explained that its India-based R&D center developed WiMax technologies (for wireless data transmission) because that was a low-cost solution demanded by the Indian network operators. The company globally, then, was able to expand upon those technologies and include them in solutions for higher end European customers. Similarly, the company's China-based R&D operation developed a fiber-optic communications product (involving WDM—wavelength-division multiplexing) for expanding the carrying capacity of in-home cable (for television, phone, and data). Developed locally to meet demand in Shanghai, that product is now deployed globally.[48] Another telecom equipment provider, in this case focused on mobile phone production, noted how its China-based R&D team, in localizing user interfaces for Chinese consumers, developed a series of new capabilities for speech and handwriting recognition (i.e., the conversion of voice and handwriting inputs into digitized data).[49] These advances, involving not just electronics but also linguistics, have been applied not only in the company's other Asian markets but also in the Middle East.

In some cases, it is less the specific demands of the local market than its underlying structural conditions that make it an important site for product development activities. A China-related example here comes from pharmaceuticals. As noted previously, global pharmaceutical firms conduct drug trials in China in part to get governmental approval for the drugs and in part to develop sales networks. Yet, an additional factor also comes into play. Besides having a lot of people and hospitals, China also has a tremendous number of what in the pharmaceutical industry are known as "naive" patients.[50] The term has nothing to do with the patients' knowledge or sophistication. Rather, it describes people who suffer a condition—hypertension or diabetes, for example—but have never previously been treated for it. In most cases, the condition had long gone undiagnosed. Such patients are ideal candidates for clinical trials because no previous treatment history clouds the effects of the drug being tested. As a rapidly developing, urbanizing country, China is for the first time in its history facing the diseases of prosperity—obesity, hypertension, diabetes, and arteriosclerosis, just to name a few. At the same time, relatively few Chinese suffering these conditions, at least until recently, were being appropriately diagnosed and treated. Thus, when they show up at a hospital for the first time now, they become prime candidates for participation in trials. From the pharmaceutical company's perspective, this becomes an ideal environment for testing blockbuster drugs that could potentially meet great demand across virtually all global markets.

In some cases, the international R&D center plays an even deeper, more integral role in new product development. Moving well beyond product adaptation or the occasional throwing off of a locally inspired innovation, some international R&D centers become truly integrated into the parent corporation's global R&D network. They do so by developing specialized skills or talents that can be combined in interesting ways with complementary capabilities existing elsewhere in the parent's R&D operations. What results is a truly global workflow. The company elects to develop a new product platform, and, having come up with the concept, allocates a series of development tasks across its global R&D network. Depending on the given R&D center's specialty, one task may end up in Illinois, another in Silicon Valley, another in Shanghai, and still another in Munich. Meanwhile, a central coordinator handles integration tasks. In some cases, an outlying R&D center may serve on a per product basis as the coordinator. In still other cases, tasks may be performed not in parallel but instead in sequence, with hand-offs moving from one international center to another.

These are among the newest trends in the internationalization of R&D. Although difficult to assess in terms of their extent, they are definitely taking place in China. For example, a major multinational electronic systems provider explained how over time, it was able to identify and subsequently develop particular capabilities in its various R&D centers, which for the most part had been set up originally for product localization.[51] Headquartered in Europe, that company, after determining on an annual basis its overall product development strategy, allocates tasks to its globally dispersed R&D centers. Its China-based center has become highly proficient in developing software for mass transit fare collection systems as well as for network security in banking (i.e., automatic teller machine networks). Work from this center has gone into products sold not just in China but also in South Asia, Southeast Asia, and Europe. The company's Australia-based center, on the other hand, has particular capabilities in air traffic control software and has taken the lead on developing these product platforms globally, including when those platforms are sold in China. That is simply not the area the China-based R&D center specializes in. In numerous cases for this company, work on global product platforms goes on in parallel across numerous centers and then is synchronized through tools like IBM's Rational collaboration software.[52]

In another example, a telecom equipment supplier explained how its various global centers have become specialized in particular technologies that are then combined centrally into overall product solutions.[53] The corporate headquarters define the product requirements; the various global R&D centers, through intense communication, agree collectively on an overall product architecture; and then specific development tasks, often related to specific technologies, are allocated to individual centers. The work proceeds in parallel across the company's R&D network. For this particular company, its main China-based development center has particular capabilities in optics, 3G, WiMax, and several other network technologies now demanded by customers (telecom network carriers) across a variety of global markets.

The interesting thing about this China center, though, is that in addition to having particular capabilities, it also happens to have, on average, far younger engineers than do the company's other centers. These young engineers are also very productive. The China R&D center has been recognized in house as the most productive contributor to the corporation's overall global patents. That is, on a per employee basis, this center contributes more to overall corporate patents than any other center in the network.

That example alone suggests several important points. First, it suggests—or more accurately, reflects—a certain reality about the nature of talent in China. The Chinese educational system is unquestionably training a huge number of science and technology workers, engineers in most cases. Whether in general that system is turning out a high-quality engineer is debatable. Less debatable, though, is the quality of the talent turned out at the very pinnacle of the system, China's top three or four technical universities (i.e., Tsinghua, Shanghai Jiaotong, and Zhejiang University). Simply by virtue of the tracking that goes on in China's highly pyramidal, exam-based educational system, these top institutions are pulling in the crème-de-la-crème, the absolute brightest students from across a 1.3-billion-person population. The university education delivered at the top of the system is a good one, but even if it were not, the individuals receiving it are hyper-ambitious and highly driven. These are precisely the kind of people one would expect to lead a nation's technological development.

So interesting, though, is that these individuals, rather than going into indigenous firms, are being cherry-picked by foreign multinationals. As Simon and Cao point out, in 1995, foreign-invested enterprises employed 3.81 percent of China's total high-tech workforce (S&T personnel in high-technology industries) and 5.38 percent of China's scientists and engineers. By 2006, the proportions had ballooned to 37.09 percent and 41.05 percent, respectively.[54] For newly minted engineers from the most elite institutions, the proportions accepting employment in foreign firms are undoubtedly even higher. As one global software developer with a Shanghai-based R&D center explained, "We recruit at only Tsinghua and Shanghai Jiaotong. There's no point going anywhere else. And, there's no point basing our [China software development] center anywhere but Shanghai. It might be cheaper in Chengdu [Sichuan Province], but the best young graduates want to live in Shanghai or Beijing only."[55]

Indeed, these individuals are often far more eager to work in a foreign R&D center than an indigenously owned one.[56] It is not simply that the foreigners pay more. Salaries are in fact equalizing. Rather, it is that the foreign companies often offer additional training, management education, and in many cases, exposure to an entirely new way of doing things. In other words, employment in the foreign technology leader accords not just tangible benefits but also status and international cachet. Participation in a first-rate global R&D network itself becomes a lure for attracting talent. China may be pushing indigenous innovation, and domestic companies like Huawei may be doing very impressive things. For the time being, though, foreigners are the ones most effectively tapping into China's science and technology talent.

That the foreign-owned firms are doing so, however, leads to a second point. The talented individuals being recruited in China have to be somehow integrated into the company's global operation, a challenging managerial task. Take, for example, the case noted earlier in which a multinational telecom firm's most productive R&D center is based in China. That center's employees tended to be much younger, and presumably lower salaried, than employees in the company's other research sites. As a China-based research manager—himself a Chinese returnee from overseas—explained, "Our employees are young and eager, and sometimes it becomes difficult dealing with [company name deleted]'s other research centers, especially the 'gray hairs' in [name deleted, but it is the company's oldest and best-known research center based in the West]. They [the employees at the best-known center] were panicking about losing their jobs…and saw the establishment of the China center as a threat."[57] As this manager related, the main center for a time refused to cooperate and share information with the China center, a major problem when tasks are supposed to be interlinked through a common workflow. Easing this territoriality became a major managerial hurdle for everybody involved.

What all these examples suggest is that the internationalization of new product development is a multiedged sword. Operating a multicountry network of R&D centers offers a company numerous advantages. It gives a firm access to highly specialized talent that can be harnessed for in-house development of new technologies and technology platforms. It also extends and even globalizes the search function for identifying new technologies that other companies—potential partners or acquisition targets—are just introducing onto the market. In other words, it provides the company with early warning for new technologies it might choose to acquire. Similarly, it provides opportunities to develop relationships all around the world with potential technology partners.

If done right, the globalized R&D network—often including a key China-based component—allows the multinational to stay at the frontier of new product development and drive product cycles. Indeed, in something like telecoms, it to some extent explains what differentiates leading multinationals from indigenous Chinese firms like Huawei. In effect, a division of labor has emerged. Huawei has made impressive inroads into the global provision of basic telecommunications networks. The firm, in particular, has mastered the art of manufacturing sophisticated equipment at low cost. Yet, Huawei is just now taking the first steps into R&D internationalization with the establishment of overseas centers to facilitate product adaptation. Still working to master this skill, Huawei has not yet moved on to the next step: establishing and managing a truly global network for product development. That leading multinationals have these networks and the ability to manage them allows the companies to stay several steps ahead of the product cycle for state-of-the-art technologies and high-end service provision. In many cases, for a given telecommunications customer (a network operator) now, Huawei ends up providing the boxes (i.e., the basic equipment) but a multinational equipment supplier provides the high-value (i.e., high-profit) technology add-ons (i.e., the network solutions).[58] Indeed, even within China, this often is the case.[59]

The downside, if it can be called that, is that managing an R&D network is an extremely challenging, specialized endeavor that can easily overwhelm even an experienced multinational enterprise. Those who find ways to do it well can put substantial distance between themselves and their competitors. They can certainly put substantial distance between themselves and indigenous entrants from places like China. Those who do not, however, can get mired in problems of territoriality, miscommunication, project delays, and loss of focus. These are serious problems that explain to some extent why in the area of new product development, indigenous Chinese firms have not yet even begun to internationalize.

Interestingly, for those firms that have gone global in their R&D efforts, there is one problem that gets far less mention these days than one would expect: intellectual property theft. Particularly in recent years, my fellow MIT researchers and I have found that these concerns, though still present, have receded somewhat for global technology leaders operating in China. The reason seems not so much to involve improvements in China's intellectual property rights (IPR) regime, though some have occurred. Rather, it has to do with the nature of the R&D activities themselves. When an R&D center based in China, or anywhere else for that matter, participates in a workflow distributed across a network, it is not as if the individual center has a particular product to steal. Instead, it has a certain degree of know-how that must be combined with knowledge found elsewhere in the network to result in a new product. That know-how, to some extent, can be carried away if the engineers choose to pack up and move to another company. Yet, removed from the broader network, it is not clear how usable that know-how really is. Or to put it somewhat differently, once a competitor figures out how to build a network to use that know-how, the original company will have long moved on to something else. In some ways, the innovation—whether a new product platform, a new network architecture, or a new software solution—is protected not by a patent or a copyright but instead by its own complexity and the highly distributed, cellular conditions under which it originated. By the time an outsider figures out how to duplicate the innovation, the product cycle will have moved on.

Research and Development
for Fundamentally New Technologies

In general, research on fundamental, new-to-the-world technologies—at least on the commercial front—still remains the domain of companies from the world's richest economies. Moreover, this kind of research is often conducted close to the corporate headquarters. This is not the kind of activity that internationalizes easily.

Nonetheless, in some industries—pharmaceuticals, for example—basic research is being extended across global locales. Several major firms, in addition to operating centers for drug discovery across Europe and the United States, are now experimenting with some centers in China. One research director at a multinational drug company, in describing the opening of a small center in Shanghai to study neurodegenerative disorders, emphasized how it was being treated as a kind of test, a chance for a Chinese PhD returnee from Europe to see whether a viable research group could be developed at low cost in China.[60] Only time will tell whether the new group produces any major contributions.

In at least one industry—energy—fundamental R&D is going on in China. The previously noted high-temperature, gas-cooled (pebble bed) nuclear reactor demonstration project is a case in point. But the phenomenon extends well beyond pebble bed reactors. In certain industries, the needs of a handful of key markets are defining the innovation challenge globally. This is certainly true with energy and China. Whether they are multinational or indigenous firms doing the work, it is in the China market that numerous new-to-the-world energy technologies are being developed and deployed for the first time. Thus, in at least the energy domain, global commercial leaders, if they intend to remain at the frontiers of new technology development, have to be operating and selling in China.

Civilian nuclear power is a good example. Globally today, China has become the single most important market for suppliers of nuclear power plant technologies and systems. In 2008, construction was initiated on ten nuclear power plants worldwide. Five were in China. Through July 2009, construction was initiated on six new plants. Five were in China.[61] For several years now, electric power generation has been expanding in China at a torrid pace. Between 2001 and 2008, China's installed power generating capacity more than doubled.[62] The nation's electric power sector, now the second largest in the world (behind only the United States), is fueled primarily by coal (roughly 80 percent of China's power comes from the combustion of coal, as opposed to 50 percent in the world's other major coal consumer, the United States).[63] Nuclear power today accounts for only 1.1 percent of Chinese electricity production (as opposed to 19 percent in the United States), but a major expansion of the sector is now underway. China today has just over nine gigawatts (GW) of installed nuclear generating capacity, but the government has at various points announced goals of reaching forty to sixty GW by 2020.[64]

It is not simply that China is building a lot of plants. And is it not just that all of these plants are built on the basis of technologies and designs purchased from global suppliers (including the French, Russians, Canadians, and Americans). Rather, it is that the Chinese government today is insisting on building *only* state-of-the-art plants, even if that means relying on overseas suppliers rather than indigenous firms. Basically, the government will not settle for older third-generation plants but is instead demanding the newest fourth-generation designs regardless of the immediate impact on domestic suppliers.

There are several reasons for this.[65] First, government officials, in a view backed by the global suppliers themselves, believe that the newest designs are also the safest. Within China, some nuclear engineering experts, in fact, criticize this attitude, insisting that the greatest safety risks pertain not to the physical technology but rather to the human side, the management dimension.[66] They fear that if the country builds out too quickly, it will exceed the pace with which qualified plant managers and government regulators can be trained. Up to this point, however, the safety record for China's admittedly small fleet of civilian nuclear plants remains good. Nonetheless, though they may differ on the build-out rate, government officials and analysts alike agree on the practice of building state-of-the-art foreign-designed plants. They all agree that China should have the best. If it cannot build the best on its own, it must buy the best from elsewhere.

Second, a number of people in Chinese government and industry clearly hope one day to design and produce state-of-the-art plants indigenously. In other words, there is an openly stated ambition to develop ways to produce plants less expensively, perhaps through modular designs, so that ultimately, China—rather than France or the

United States—can become the major global supplier. In many ways, this "producer's mentality"—this ambition to gain market share by finding new ways to produce existing technologies at lower cost—can be found in many segments of Chinese industry.

And third, beyond concerns about safety and commerce, there are always issues of status. As discussed in chapter 3, China's ongoing quest for modernity and self-definition plays out today through comparisons with the advanced industrial West. Many people in China today are unwilling to settle for second-best technologies. They do not want products intended for the developing world and, in fact, do not see themselves as belonging to that world. They want to be seen as modern and advanced, members of the club of the world's leading nations. In their desire to achieve that status, many Chinese are unwilling to settle for second best, particularly when it comes to highly public, showy technologies like metropolitan subway systems, the elevated MagLev train (Shanghai), and civilian nuclear power plants. Buying abroad to get the best trumps developing indigenously to get the second best. As one executive at a major global energy firm told me in 2007, "The Chinese want and need electricity now, but they also want the latest and greatest infrastructure to produce it."[67]

In nuclear power, precisely because the Chinese demand the best and are willing to purchase it from abroad, the implication for major global suppliers is that they have to secure contracts in China if they intend to stay at the cutting edge technologically. It is not just that in any given year, only a small number of plants commence construction worldwide, though that is of course true. Equally important, for many of the designs and the technologies involved, development and a certain degree of innovation continue to take place in the field after the systems are initially deployed. For the supplier, therefore, landing a contract of course brings in revenue, but so too does it allow, through the project's ultimate implementation, the further accumulation of on-the-ground know-how. Thus, impetus is provided for the next round of innovation. The lesson is that you basically have to be in the game today to cultivate the capabilities needed to remain in the game tomorrow. It is, therefore, not surprising that major global energy firms have opened R&D facilities in China, at least some of which are conducting fundamental research.

This is certainly the case in high-voltage electricity transmission. High-voltage transmission happens to be an interesting area only in part because China is the largest global market for these new-to-the-world technologies. China needs these technologies because its primary fuel for generating electricity, coal, is located far from the major energy-consuming cities on the coast. Furthermore, many of these cities are already suffering severe pollution problems from the myriad, difficult-to-regulate power plants they have built. The hope is that by developing capabilities to generate power in large-scale plants located in the country's interior, and then transmitting that power efficiently to the coast, the government will at once be able to control pollution and provide adequate power. A key enabling factor, though, is high-voltage transmission, a complex technological challenge in its own right. Local industrial players are emerging in low- and medium-voltage transmission, but the crucial high-voltage segment is still the domain of just a handful of major global energy giants.[68] Several are establishing China-based development centers because that is where the new technologies will be deployed for the first time.

As noted earlier, though, China-based demand is only part of the story. While the Chinese market is currently leading the way, high-voltage transmission technologies will likely be demanded worldwide if any serious efforts at greenhouse gas remediation move forward. That is, if the world's biggest energy consumers—namely, the United States but also Japan and Europe—get serious about reducing carbon emissions, they will need to tackle the challenge presented by power generation. Solutions almost inevitably will involve a combination of improved energy efficiency (across power production, transmission, and consumption) and some form of carbon capture and sequestration (CCS). High-voltage transmission will clearly be part of the former and most likely part of the latter (given that power under CCS may very well have to be generated in locales far from energy-consuming areas).[69] Thus, to ensure their position in not just current but also future markets, innovators in high-voltage transmission, virtually all of which are major multinationals, have to be present in China. That is simply the place now where new-to-the-world innovations are being developed and rolled out.

In some respects, this overall situation holds true for basic coal-fired power generation as well. As noted previously, new coal-fired power plants are being built in China at an astonishing rate. Contrary to worldwide perception, however, most of these plants—certainly, the ones built since 2006—are employing state-of-the-art power generation and environmental cleanup technologies.[70] As documented by plant-level surveys conducted by the author and two coresearchers at MIT, Chinese power plants emit extremely high levels of pollutants. At the same time, these plants are being built with quite advanced technologies, many of which have been licensed from foreign suppliers.

There are two relevant points. First, pollution for the Chinese power sector is as much about effective monitoring and regulatory enforcement as it is about a particular fuel (coal) or a particular generating technology. Second, in the area of coal-fired power generation, a form of energy production that for better or worse is likely to remain with us for a long time to come, state-of-the-art suppliers have to be operating in China. This is particularly true for the latest technologies, most of which are still in the early demonstration project stages. Experts predict that several of these, including integrated gasification combined cycle (IGCC) and other forms of coal gasification (whether for industrial applications or power generation), will become important enabling technologies for carbon capture and sequestration. China is one of the only places—and in some cases, the only place—worldwide where coalitions of indigenous and multinational energy companies are testing these new technologies in the field.

The Game Today in Global
Research and Development

What lessons emerge from the preceding examination of international and China-based R&D? First, we should be wary of both dominant schools of thought on China's current capacity for innovation. Contrary to what the believers suggest, we need to be careful about ascribing motives and intentions—whether malign or otherwise—to China or the Chinese government. It is by no means clear that China is collectively bent on becoming an S&T superpower and on doing it at the West's expense. Undoubtedly, the country's senior leadership has promoted the strengthening of indigenous innovation. What exactly indigenous innovation means, though—whether zero-sum competition with outsiders, cooperative efforts to solve common global problems, contributions of proprietary domestic knowledge to globally developed products, or something else entirely—is as unknown to us as it probably is to them. As we will see in the next chapter, the Chinese government, not to mention the country's broader commercial establishment, encompasses multiple stakeholders, each with its own set of attitudes, motivations, and ambitions. Depictions of the Chinese government as a unitary actor, a sort of chess grand master doggedly fixing its attention on a single objective are a bit far-fetched.

Nevertheless, it is fair to say that many people all across the Chinese system want to see their country advance. They do want to see things move forward and do want to participate in and be associated with the most modern trends of global life. That does not necessarily mean they hope to see domestic companies knock off leading multinationals. Indeed, as we will see in the next chapter, China's leading domestic firms are often more focused on crushing each other than on overtaking foreigners. What it does mean, though, is that many Chinese participants in business today—especially those in advanced, knowledge-intensive industries—want to become world class. They want to be taken seriously, and they want to do real work. They aspire to be as good as the best. That is as true of the engineers in the China-based R&D centers of multinationals as it is of researchers working on cutting-edge indigenous projects like the pebble bed reactor. Both sets of individuals want to be worthy of respect within their organizations and across global communities of professional peers. For some of these individuals, the effort may be about building the nation. For many more, though, it is about individual status and a sense of being something other than second rate.

Again, though one needs to be cautious about generalizations, it is also fair to say that across many parts of Chinese S&T-related industry, one frequently encounters a sort of producer's mentality. Perhaps because the likelihood of outcompeting the multinationals on new product development seems remote, many Chinese domestic firms focus on finding ways to produce existing high-tech products less expensively. In a manner akin to the Chongqing motorcycle manufacturers described in chapter 4, these companies—albeit in this case concentrated in cutting-edge sectors like renewable energy—are seeking to come up with modular designs that can reduce production costs while maintaining exacting quality standards. Hence, in areas like wind turbine manufacturing—or even in completely new areas like pebble bed reactors—the most advanced indigenous firms are pursuing design innovations that could allow them to enter global markets with a simpler and less expensive but no less reliable product. As we have seen with telecommunications, when the Chinese find ways to produce technical equipment—boxes—less expensively, those boxes (i.e., backbone networking equipment, routers, switches, etc.) become accessible to a broader range of customers—in this case, new telecommunications carriers. As new low-cost carriers enter, pressures rise on incumbents to hang onto subscribers by offering every new service imaginable. What ultimately appears as a service to the subscriber (i.e., a higher speed 3G network; combined multimedia entertainment, cable TV, and broadband access; video on demand, gaming, voice-over

IP through a single box that plugs into a normal phone jack, etc.) is generally the result of a network solution that the carrier has purchased from a leading multinational technology supplier.

The point is that when the Chinese firms innovate their way into box provision, their actions increase demand for what the multinationals are offering: high-value technology solutions that overlay or tie together those boxes. The multinationals can provide those solutions precisely because they are now managing vast R&D operations that are often pulling in and utilizing the best human talent China has to offer.

That leads to a somewhat related issue about knowledge flows. Just as it is unwise to assume that indigenous Chinese companies are, by definition, competing head to head with multinationals, it is equally unwise to assume that the presence of foreign-owned R&D centers in China in and of itself signifies one-way knowledge transfer. A wide variety of activities take place in these centers. Some involve adaptation of mature products to local market conditions and local user preferences. In such cases, to the extent knowledge is being transferred, it is, ironically enough, moving from the Chinese consumer, through his or her product preferences, to the multinational. In other cases, the R&D activities involve contributions to global workflows conducted across the given multinational's distributed research network. Whether the pieces of this process done in China can be extracted as stand-alone know-how by Chinese participants—engineers, say, who might pack up in the near future to start their own companies—is difficult to say. It is the sort of challenge faced virtually everywhere by every technology company. No matter how many nondisclosure and noncompete forms are signed, the risk always exists that a skilled insider will march off to a competitor. Whether that single individual, with his or her particular slice of proprietary knowledge and particular experience within the original employer's organization, can then turn around and derive value from it on the outside is an open question faced by any company operating in competitive markets for high-end talent.

What is much less of an open question—indeed, what is patently obvious today—is that multinational companies are now making tremendous use of Chinese indigenous talent. That is, multinational corporations are mobilizing and pulling in the best engineers China has to offer. China, loosely speaking, may be on a nationwide quest for indigenous innovation. Huge portions of its educated workforce, however, are being employed by multinationals. In fact, the percentages are largest in the elite segments of the talent pool, graduates from the nation's top three or four technological universities. Foreign firms in *some* research activities may be imparting know-how to local employees. What those firms are doing across the board, though, is securing the best talent available in China and committing it to the kind of distributed R&D efforts that reward winners with unparalleled product-innovation capabilities and commercial dominance.

In this respect, just as we should be wary of the believers' claims that China is outinnovating the West, so too should we be wary of the doubters' claims that China is lagging on the innovation front. Lagging in relation to what or to whom? What is the relevant benchmark? Can we say historically that there exists a neat relationship between level of development and amount of innovative activity? China today in per capita terms is three-and-a-half times poorer than Mexico. Is it three-and-a-half times less innovative? It is sixteen times poorer than the United States. Is it sixteen times less innovative? On what basis could one make such a claim?

In a way, there is a degree of circularity in these claims about a Chinese innovation lag. Many of those making the claims seem to assume that innovation proceeds most effectively under competitive market conditions, a not entirely implausible assumption but one that has to be applied cautiously. After all, we know that in the United States, extremely competitive environments like Silicon Valley and extremely competitive financing mechanisms like venture capital have been associated with periods of rapid innovation. So too, however, have arenas relatively protected from commercial competition: defense contracting, the space program, national laboratories, and research universities.[71] Ecosystems for innovation are complicated, poorly understood entities. Scholars are still trying to grasp the underlying forces involved. To assume a linear relationship between degree of market institutionalization (whether with regard to financing, intellectual property laws, ownership, or anything else) and amount of innovation-related commercial activity is risky at best. Taking institutional weakness (again, whether in finance, ownership, or other areas) ipso facto as evidence of underperformance in innovation is nothing less than tautological. Underperformance is at once described definitionally by a given institutional situation and then ascribed causally to that condition. What inevitably results is cloudy analysis and somewhat dubious policy advice.

That said, it is reasonable to believe that over the long run in China, regardless of the precise direction of causation, the deepening of market institutions will continue to move hand in hand with expanding commercial activity, just as it has done over the past twenty years. So interesting right now, though, is that even with seriously flawed market institutions, China has been able to realize substantial innovative activity. Chinese S&T workers are innovating. Of course, much of that innovation is happening in foreign-owned organizations, and it is happening as part of a global workflow. But that is precisely the point. Foreign-owned R&D centers are not simply isolated islands within the Chinese system. The work they do is not somehow cut off from everything else that goes on in China. These centers *are* the Chinese innovation system.

Whether by design or default, the Chinese system in the area of high-end commercial R&D has permitted foreign companies to substitute for fully functioning market mechanisms. The state has been playing its part by pumping in resources to train the country's top talent at its top institutions of higher learning. The multinationals, in turn, have played their part by employing this talent and plugging it into broader global currents of innovation. In particular, given the various weaknesses of China's domestic system, had the foreigners not been drawn into the country, the nation's investment in training could easily have gone to waste.

Yet, because foreign firms have become so central to China's innovation system and because China's talent pool has become increasingly oriented to serving global R&D networks, it is not so clear that China in the future, should it ever hope to do so, could somehow turn on a dime and switch to fully indigenous innovation. In other words, it is not simply the case that the system can use foreigners as a stopgap, build its domestic institutions in the interim, and then once the building is done, switch on the lights for wholly domestic innovation. Instead, what happens under current conditions of institutional outsourcing is that the very evolution of domestic institutions and domestic talent get affected. That is, their evolutionary trajectory is reshaped through their interaction with overseas players and networks. They effectively evolve with an intrinsic orientation toward a globalized model of R&D.[72]

In this respect, it makes little sense to debate whether China today is innovating too much or too little, too aggressively or not aggressively enough. Nor is the right answer the "Goldilocks" solution: "China is innovating neither too much nor too little, and we on the outside should neither be too alarmed nor too complacent." The real issue is not about the amount of activity going on. Rather, it is that an entirely new way of doing things has emerged. China is a big part of that new way of doing things, and in some respects, Chinese participants have facilitated the new way. The new mode of doing things is being pioneered organizationally by a bunch of multinational corporations. The mode, of course, is enabled by technology but not necessarily technologically predetermined. Modern multinationals, by strategic choice, have in recent years pursued R&D in a particular fashion involving complicated combinations of in-house development, technology acquisitions, and interfirm partnerships. All of that now is done on a global scale, thus unleashing incredibly rapid innovation and new product development. Those multinationals managing this process successfully have surged ahead on the innovation front, thus deepening their hold over the provision of cutting-edge products and services. At the same time, openings have been created for new entrants, box producers, many of whom are Chinese. By driving down equipment costs and making them affordable to a broader array of customers, they stimulate demand for the higher end services that overlay the boxes. In this sense, the emerging system of globalized R&D has created a symbiotic relationship between multinational and indigenous Chinese producers.

Of course, managing global R&D operations is a daunting endeavor that constitutes a sort of proprietary advantage for those who figure it out. Chinese domestic firms may one day develop these capabilities. For the time being, however, they still have a long road to travel.

Nonetheless, the real issue is not about who is winning and who is losing, or how far ahead the multinationals are and how quickly (or slowly) Chinese firms are catching up. Rather, the issue is that a very new way of conducting innovation has emerged. In the process, distinctions, particularly on the commercial front, between us and them have become blurry indeed. To cite one example, when box makers like Huawei partner with software producers like Symantec to produce network security equipment (for the Chinese domestic market), both partners have a common interest in discouraging the Chinese government from adopting technical standards that diverge from global norms. The partners, after all, who joined initially for the purpose of introducing products for China's domestic market, want those products to be salable abroad.[73] Global R&D efforts, like globalized production more generally, make for complicated coalitions of interests.

At the same time, such efforts hold out tremendous promise for the solution of common problems. In the energy domain in particular, China today faces serious challenges across virtually every key issue: assurance of adequate supply, depletion of domestic resources, and dire pollution problems. For each of these areas, the Chinese government, broadly speaking, could have thrown up the barriers and waited—perhaps for an eternity—for an indigenous solution to arise. Instead, for the most part, though with some exceptions,[74] it has chosen a different path. It has opted to have foreigners come in with their own technology solutions. Indeed, those foreign firms—whether in nuclear power generation, coal gasification, solar power, electric cars, and a variety of other frontier technologies—are using the Chinese market to drive their innovation programs. Increasingly, we are witnessing new-to-the-world technologies being rolled out for the first time not in advanced industrial markets but instead in China. In virtually all cases, save for a very few exceptions, these rollouts are done by multinational companies well suited to bringing the same products to other global markets. It may very well end up the case that in an area like climate change remediation, technologies that prove indispensable globally will have had their origins in the Chinese market and will have been generated through multinational corporate R&D. That could never have happened in the absence of the globalization of R&D. And it could not have happened without a Chinese system fully committed and oriented to that new way of doing things.

SEVEN

Energy

The Last Bastion for State Control?

IN PRECEDING CHAPTERS, we saw how globalization has permitted firms from the West to pursue revolutionary new modes of specialization and extend their reach across previously insurmountable geographical and sectoral boundaries. We also saw how China has played a critical and complementary role in all this, throwing open its borders and enabling, in its own headlong pursuit of modernity, the commercial ambitions of producers from the West. As evidenced by so many of the production activities already discussed, a growing and often confusing concert of interests now extends across our respective nations and the economic players within them.

Surely, though, limits must exist to this intermingling of interests. Cooperation over computer production or drug testing is one thing, but what about industries that do not lend themselves to harmonious divisions of labor? What about extractive industries—fossil fuel production, for example—that involve the exploitation of globally scarce, highly strategic resources? How possibly could globalization, institutional outsourcing, and harmonization affect them? If anything, such industries seem to be more about bare-knuckled, zero-sum, nation-versus-nation competition. And for that matter, who is to say that these industries, clearly vital to our future, will not be the ones that shape our collective destiny? Indeed, one could reasonably argue that in China's case, particularly for something like the petroleum sector in which all three of the nation's major domestic producers are state-owned corporations, it precisely this kind of zero-sum, state-dominated industry that overwhelmingly shapes China's strategy for global engagement. At the end of the day, who really is to say that China's relations with the West will be defined more by harmonious production of iPhones than bitter competition over declining energy resources?

Generally speaking, one could hypothesize that at some point and in some industries, limits are reached beyond which the state will no longer subordinate itself to the pressures of external markets. There must be at least some critical commercial domains in which the state, even if just for national security reasons alone, refuses to play any game but its own. This chapter explores the hypothesis by examining one such critical domain: the petroleum industry. If any industry can still be considered a bastion of economic statecraft and mercantilism, surely this must be the one. We have every reason to expect that this sector should be relatively immune to the forces of internationalization, institutional outsourcing, and external control that have swept across so much of Chinese industry and society. Oil and gas should be the ultimate tough case for institutional outsourcing, the one sector that should really allow us to plumb the limits of just how far the playing our game concept can be taken.

To explore these issues, we take a slightly different approach from that used in previous chapters. Instead of looking across a variety of companies and industries, we focus on a single company, the China National Offshore Oil Corporation (CNOOC), one of China's three main state-owned oil and gas companies.

The reasons for doing so are twofold. First, CNOOC in the not too distant past found itself at the center of a controversy that not just stoked, but absolutely epitomized American fears of Chinese mercantilism and global ambition. On June 22, 2005, CNOOC, in what amounted technically to a hostile takeover attempt, publicly announced its intention to acquire the American petroleum producer Unocal, a firm that only weeks earlier had accepted a takeover bid by fellow American oil giant Chevron.[1] CNOOC extended a US$18.5 billion cash offer for California-based Unocal, thus knocking off the table Chevron's previously accepted US$16.8 billion bid. The scramble for Unocal was on, and it would unfold before the glare of the media spotlight. In short order, the story escalated far beyond just competing bids from dueling corporate suitors. It became a veritable tempest of geopolitical competition, cable TV hyperbole, dueling lobbying campaigns, and political theater all wrapped up in one. And perhaps most important for our purposes, it became a touchstone for American popular perceptions of China.

In making its bid for Unocal, CNOOC waded into a situation with all the necessary ingredients for setting the American public's collective hair on fire. Throughout 2004 and 2005, gasoline prices in the United States, to the consternation of most citizens, had been steadily rising, tracking increases worldwide in the price of crude oil.[2] Such price hikes were at least partially driven by American consumers' own rapidly expanding appetite for oil. The economy was booming, and ordinary citizens were using energy with abandon. Rather than dwelling on their own growing appetite for energy, however, Americans were becoming increasingly preoccupied with another global reality, China's rising energy demands. Between 1995 and 2005, Chinese consumption of crude oil more than doubled, far outstripping the nation's domestic production capacity.[3] China by the early 2000s had emerged not only as a major oil consumer but also as a major oil importer whose consumption habits could single-handedly move prices on the global market. China's impact on prices was made even more pronounced by the actions of buyers on forward markets, speculators guessing about the future price of oil—and by extension, future Chinese consumption levels—based on trends they were observing today. Regardless of the complications of forward markets or any other details, for that matter, the story for the average American was patently obvious. China was gobbling up global energy resources, and everybody else was paying through the nose as a result. The longer term implications also seemed clear. Global petroleum reserves were insufficient to satisfy both the United States and China. The world was simply not big enough for both countries. One or the other would need to step back and yield.

It was into this mix that CNOOC announced its offer for Unocal. For Americans, this in a flash became about much more than big business. It became an acute manifestation of Sino–U.S. energy competition, the opening shot in an emerging struggle between the two countries for limited global energy resources. And perhaps even more deeply, it demonstrated that the Chinese were playing by utterly different rules, and effectively eating Americans' lunch, so to speak, in the process. In the minds of many U.S. observers, CNOOC was no ordinary commercial company, no ordinary market producer out simply to make a buck. Rather, as a state-owned entity in a strategic industry, it was seen as but the commercial face of a geostrategically ambitious Chinese government. Beijing, by apparently using its national oil companies to snatch up global reserves and sock them away for exclusive Chinese use, was daring to do what Washington neither could nor would. Even worse, this was happening right in our backyard. A commercial arm of the Chinese government, supercharged by almost limitless state financing, was brazenly intruding on our territory and snatching away that which was vital for our own long-term survival.

Although some industry experts downplayed the seriousness of the situation, their nuanced points on the immunity of global energy markets to state manipulation receded into the background noise.[4] Front and center was a different kind of sentiment, one expressed perhaps most cogently by R. James Woolsey when he testified before the House Armed Services Committee in the midst of the CNOOC affair. Woolsey, who a decade earlier had served as CIA director during the Clinton administration, characterized the Unocal takeover attempt as a critical issue of national security. He declared, "China is pursuing a national strategy of domination of the energy markets and strategic dominance of the Western Pacific."[5] He insisted that CNOOC is "an organ, effectively, of the world's largest Communist dictatorship" and thus should be blocked from acquiring American assets.[6]

Similar logic was employed in a June 30, 2005, U.S. House of Representatives resolution urging blockage, or at least serious presidential review, of the CNOOC bid.[7] China, the U.S. public was told, was on a quest for global dominance in a world of dwindling resources. This quest, carried out by front organizations like CNOOC, had to be stopped. It was a straightforward matter of U.S. national security. End of discussion.

As it would happen, this argument—conducted amid the bewildering din of contending corporate lobbying efforts, media hyperbole, and political grandstanding galore—ultimately won the day. In early August 2005, once Congress's determination to block the deal became patently manifest, CNOOC withdrew its offer, thus permitting Chevron's acquisition of Unocal to proceed unimpeded (albeit at a higher price than Chevron had initially offered).

For our purposes, though, the story does not end here. There are important questions to be answered, after all, about what CNOOC as an entity really was and what its bid for Unocal really meant. CNOOC was, and indeed still is, a Chinese state-owned entity, but so too is it a Hong Kong-incorporated public company listed on both the Hong Kong and New York Stock Exchanges.[8] As such, it was, and still is, subject to the Hong Kong Stock Exchange's listing requirements, corporate governance standards, transparency and information disclosure rules, and a variety of other regulatory mandates. Furthermore, CNOOC, given the listing of its American depository shares (ADSs) on the New York Stock Exchange (NYSE), is subject to a variety of U.S. Security and Exchange Commission (SEC) filing and public disclosure requirements.

Should we view these myriad institutional strictures as completely irrelevant, trumped by the fact, as the U.S. Congress in 2005 argued, that CNOOC is majority state owned and situated in a strategic sector? If such strictures are not irrelevant, how should they be understood? What impact do they have on a company like CNOOC, its operations, and its overall strategy? How did they affect the playing out of the 2005 bid for Unocal? These are all critical questions for understanding the extent—and perhaps limits—of the reach of institutional outsourcing into the ultimate bastions of state authority.

There is a second reason for focusing on CNOOC, one related to my own personal experiences. From 2001 through 2009, I served as a member of CNOOC's five-person international advisory board (IAB) during the full nine years of its existence. This advisory board, not to be confused with the company's board of directors, had no formal legal status and performed no formal corporate governance function. It had no authority to vote on corporate decisions, and its members had no formal fiduciary or other legal responsibilities. It was simply a small group of individuals—comprised over the years of a variety of Western academics, businesspeople, and retired diplomats—who met formally once a year to discuss global affairs with CNOOC's senior management and corporate directors.

Participation on CNOOC's advisory board did not provide me, to the best of my knowledge, with access to company secrets. Instead, it offered something far more valuable as far as I was concerned: an opportunity over an extended period of time to get to know and interact with a group of senior Chinese executives in a rapidly evolving industry. Some of the interactions were formal through annual IAB conferences, and others less so, involving periodic one-on-one meetings and get-togethers in China and the United States. Together, these interactions offered an incomparable window onto how a Chinese state firm in a strategic industry operates, whom it interacts with, and how its senior management both perceives and engages the outside world.

Whether through this experience I somehow got the full story is impossible to say. CNOOC senior managers among themselves would probably disagree about what the full story of their firm really is. What I can say without doubt, however, is that the impressions I received and the patterns I witnessed over time differed markedly from what many outsiders assume goes on in a Chinese state firm, especially one in a strategic domain like oil and gas. A number of fascinating phenomena, some quite ambiguous and subject to interpretation, unfolded before my eyes in CNOOC. The one phenomenon notably absent, though, was that which so many outsiders were absolutely sure was driving the company above all else: the strong arm of a mercantilist, strategically focused state. In other words, of all the things going on in this rapidly transforming national oil company, mercantilist-inspired intervention from above—the one thing we should have most expected to see in a state-owned firm in a geopolitically sensitive industry—was noteworthy only for its apparent absence. This chapter explains just how and why that is so, and what it means for our understanding of China more generally.

Before moving into that discussion, I must offer several caveats. First, the aim of this chapter is not to pass judgment on CNOOC or otherwise assess, positively or negatively, the business acumen of its senior management. I possess neither the sectoral knowledge nor business background to make such a judgment. Assessments like that are better left to industry specialists and commercial analysts. My aim is instead to present a picture of how a company like CNOOC is governed and run. Who exactly are the stakeholders? Which ones speak with a privileged voice? Where does the information upon which managers make decisions come from? Through what channels and by what means do business deals originate? Which rules and whose rules shape the way the company operates? These are questions not about whether a company is run well but about how it is run at all. Thus, the account presented should be read neither as laudatory nor critical. It should instead be understood as a picture of how a Chinese state energy giant is governed and operated; it is a picture drawn from the unique observational platform I enjoyed for almost a decade.

In the picture that emerges, direct state involvement in the company's strategy and business operations appears relatively minimal, but the influence exerted by overseas commercial partners and foreign legal institutions appears profound. The point here, though, is not to suggest anything about Chinese governmental intentions. The chapter certainly does not argue that the Chinese government—or any government, for that matter—seriously treats commercial affairs as some kind of inviolable sanctum in which political intervention and pursuit of national interest are considered either inappropriate or illegitimate. The account presented here makes no assumptions about what the

Chinese government does or does not aim to do. Rather, it describes on the basis of years of close observation what a Chinese company in a potentially highly politicized environment does do. By extension, then, the chapter makes an argument about the limits of what the company's state overseers, regardless of whatever intentions they may have, can do.

Because this is an account of only one company, we must be cautious about drawing overly broad generalizations. Nonetheless, it is also an account of an important company, one of only three Chinese national petroleum companies and one that has already been the subject of considerable speculation and overgeneralization. Unlike much of that speculation, however, the account presented here is based on close-in, essentially ethnographic observation of the company over the course of nearly a decade. The account presented here clearly differs from "large N" (survey) analyses of Chinese companies that increasingly appear in the literature. Many of these are excellent and carefully done. Yet, they tend to examine large numbers of companies from afar, often focusing on their financial performance or other statistically quantifiable features. The individual company, particularly with regard to its internal operations, is treated as a black box. Therefore, in their effort to explain performance outcomes, such studies—rarely able to observe first hand the internal operations of any single company—frequently rely on rough assumptions of what goes on within the firm and between the firm and its various stakeholders.

Taking a very different, albeit complementary approach, the account provided here represents an effort to replace such assumptions with actual observations, actual data about what transpires within the box. In essence, this chapter represents an effort to go deep and test our assumptions by examining microscopically how a single company—and a critically important company, at that—truly operates.

Close ethnographic observation always entails the risk of bias. In my particular case with CNOOC, I have over the years come to like and respect many of the people involved in the company. Several had previously been my students at MIT, and it is indeed through one of them that I got involved with the company in the first place.

In addition, I have had a financial relationship with CNOOC, albeit a rather limited one. As a participant on the company's international advisory board, I attended eight annual meetings and received a modest honorarium for delivering a lecture at each of them.[9] Unlike membership on the board of directors (corporate board), participation on the company's international advisory board carried no formal salary.

On other fronts, I have never held CNOOC stock or otherwise invested in the company. Thus, while my financial tie with CNOOC was limited only to an annual lecture honorarium, I leave it up to the reader to judge whether or how my views might have been biased as a result.

Background: The Corporatization and Public Listing of CNOOC

Established in 1982 at the dawn of Deng Xiaoping's reforms, CNOOC is somewhat younger, and arguably less burdened by traditional socialist legacies, than some of China's more storied state-owned industrial behemoths. Nonetheless, CNOOC over the past two and a half decades has traveled a reform path relatively typical for major state-owned firms.[10] During its early years, it was not really a company in the way Westerners would understand the term. Instead, it was one of the production arms of a major governmental bureaucracy, the no longer extant Ministry of Petroleum Industry. Whereas other ministerial arms were tasked with onshore drilling, CNOOC was charged with the exploration and development of China's offshore oil and natural gas resources. Regardless of its particular role, though, CNOOC, like other Chinese oil companies, represented a collection of smaller—four, in CNOOC's case—regional production bureaucracies. Each was focused on offshore drilling along various parts of the Chinese coast. The point is that in its early years, CNOOC, just like China's other national oil companies, was effectively the production element of a larger socialist command system, the on-the-ground manifestation of a vast governmental hierarchy. It could neither independently chart its commercial destiny nor necessarily control the four constituent units on which it was based. Each of those, after all, had a history of responding to their own respective central and regional bureaucratic bosses. Indeed, the challenge from the perspective of more reform-minded thinkers was how to transform this entity and others like it into something resembling a commercial organization that could somehow absorb new technology, discover and exploit new energy resources, manage its own constituent elements, and accomplish all of that without draining the state's coffers. Profitability in these waning days of socialism seemed a distant pipe dream. Establishing basic commercial operations and achieving basic financial viability were weighty enough goals in their own right, plenty to keep policy reformers and company officials busy.

During the 1990s, CNOOC was swept up in the torrents of change that affected all of state industry. As described in chapters 1 and 2, this was the period during which Chinese policy makers, operating under conditions of pervasive national crisis, pulled the plug on traditional socialism. Tens of thousands of state-owned enterprises (SOEs), particularly smaller and medium-size firms, were simply cut loose, either allowed to collapse outright or left to nonstate actors, namely, foreigners, to restructure and reintegrate into a wholly new production system. Desperate times called for desperate, and often haphazard, modes of triage. Many smaller SOEs and the millions of workers employed within them were effectively abandoned, left to their own devices to figure out how to survive. At the same time, a smaller subset of state firms—ones, like CNOOC, in capital intensive, strategically important industries—became the focus of governmental reform efforts. These were efforts, essentially, to save the state sector.[11]

The number of firms to be "revitalized" (gaohuo)—or perhaps more accurately, protected—by the central government was never entirely clear and indeed seemed to change over time. In the 1990s, the publicly stated number usually hovered around 1,200. Today, the official number of key, centrally controlled SOEs stands at 150.[12] Regardless, CNOOC has always been among this privileged group.

By the early 2000s, as some of these firms—or at least, parts of these firms—were becoming highly profitable, observers marveled at their success and began viewing them as "jewels" in the Chinese government's crown.[13] In the 1990s, however, such firms, including CNOOC, appeared as anything but jewels. They represented massive concatenations of problems—incentive problems, personnel problems, technology problems, and many, many others. Neither commercial companies exactly nor governmental bureaucracies, they appeared in desperate need of reform, but reform of what kind? For smaller, less nationally important state firms, the question was answered by default. Cut loose by the state, such firms, in the archetypical example of institutional outsourcing, were left open to foreigners to resuscitate and remold so as to fit into an entirely new global production order. For nationally critical firms like CNOOC, however, this was not an option. A sell-off to foreigners would have been politically and socially unacceptable, as it would likely have been in any country, let alone one still clinging identitywise to the nominal designation "socialist." After all, CNOOC and its counterparts represented the commanding heights of socialist industry.

Instead of being cut loose, CNOOC and its peers would be exposed throughout the 1990s and early 2000s to a series of aggressive restructuring efforts. The first of these, gaining steam nationally in the mid-1990s, was "corporatization" (*gongsihua*), the transformation of the firm into a modern, publicly listed corporation.[14] The idea here was to formally define the boundaries of the firm, specify who exactly the firms owners were, and clarify how their rights of ownership interacted with the authority and responsibilities of the firm's management. In many ways, this was about moving from a socialist definition of the firm as but the extension of a production-oriented state bureaucracy to a market definition that treated the firm as an independent economic actor with a series of external owners distinct from the firm's internal, professionalized management. As a result, the previous socialist emphasis on hierarchy, state, and party was placed in coexistence with an entirely new lexicon of rights, ownership, professional management, and profit incentives—terms associated obviously with markets and implicitly with capitalism.

At least in its early stages, this approach smacked more of institutional borrowing than outsourcing per se. For the central SOEs being restructured in this fashion, the idea was not to hand over control to overseas owners or regulatory institutions. Instead, the aim was to replicate indigenously a corporate governance model employed in the industrialized West. If the West would have clearly specified ownership rights and managerial responsibilities, so too would China (albeit in China's case, under continued state ownership). If the West would have separation of government bureaucracy (politics) and enterprise management, then so too would China (again, albeit in China under conditions of continued state ownership). If the West would have clear financial incentives for managers, then so too would China. In many ways, these changes were intended to resolve a series of practical problems inherited from the socialist past: the excessive politicization of firms; the inability of managers, operating in bewilderingly complex bureaucratic environments, to control the constituent pieces of their companies; the absence of financial accountability throughout the system; and the pervasive, often maddening, disincentives against commercially sound managerial decision making.

In a more profound sense, however, corporatization represented an effort to grasp at something deeper and more abstract. By continually associating corporatization with a "modern corporate system" (*xiandai qiye zhidu*)—one that could be understood as meaning only that which existed in the industrialized West—proponents of these reforms were, like those earlier nineteenth-century reformers discussed in chapter 3, seeking to understand and capture what they understood as the Promethean power of the West. The idea was not to offer an alternative to, or otherwise outdo, the West. Quite the contrary, it was to figure out institutionally what made the West so head-spinningly powerful—so modern, in essence—and then incorporate that solution into China. The immediate aim was neither to outdo nor even catch up to the West. Rather, it was simply to replicate the West as closely as possible, if only to realize a fraction of its vitality while lifting China from the depths of its postsocialist morass.

All of this would need to be done in the face of considerable political sensitivities. For the proponents of corporatization—whether they happened to be in academia, government, or the firms themselves—this would be an uphill process encumbered by all manner of red lines that had yet to be tested: prohibitions against overt privatization, continued dominance of the party over managerial appointments, myriad regulatory claims by innumerable ministries and agencies, strict limits on the degree of overseas involvement, and on and on. The process, however, would march on inexorably in no small part because everybody, no matter how much they sought to impede or otherwise bend the process to suit their needs, could embrace the idea that in the end, China would somehow emerge more modern, more in possession of at least some modicum of the power and status enjoyed by the advanced industrial West.

It was into this intellectual tide that CNOOC and roughly 1,200 of its state-owned peers were swept. Together, they traveled a common path in the 1990s that would result for all of them in public listing on stock exchanges.

As in other firms, the process began in CNOOC with a kind of segregation of assets. Everything associated with the firm's main business focus, the exploration and production (E&P) of offshore oil and natural gas, was brought together and placed in a stand-alone company, CNOOC Ltd.[15] This company was then officially registered (and headquartered) in Hong Kong in 1999. The rest of the original CNOOC's operations— oil field services, construction, petrochemicals, finance, engineering support, and so forth—were placed in a series of mainland registered subsidiaries, all of which, including CNOOC Ltd., were placed under the authority of an umbrella organization, CNOOC (which, for reasons of clarity, will hereafter be termed the CNOOC Group). As indicated by figure 7.1, original CNOOC essentially became a holding company, and Hong Kong-registered CNOOC Ltd. is its most important and valuable commercial part. The situation has obtained all the way through the present. In 2008, the CNOOC Group as a whole had 57,000 employees and annual profits of RMB 67.8 billion. More than RMB 44 billion of those profits (65 percent) were generated by CNOOC Ltd. alone, though the firm accounted for only about 6 percent of the group's total employment.[16] There is little doubt that CNOOC Ltd. is in fact the jewel in the crown, the core asset of the broader CNOOC Group.

In many respects, achieving such segregation was precisely the point of the restructuring efforts surrounding corporatization. Once isolated from ancillary operations and all the other organizational baggage inherited from the socialist past, the core business—upstream E&P—could potentially be whipped into shape as a modern, globally oriented corporation. Meanwhile, it would continue to be owned by something more closely resembling a traditional state-owned enterprise, the CNOOC Group. Thus, a link to the state could be maintained, and any hint of selling off assets owned by the nation avoided.

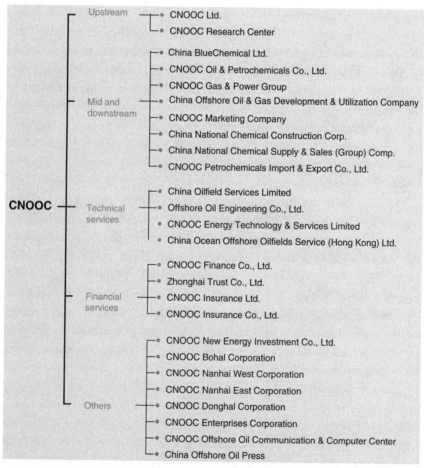

FIGURE 7.1 CNOOC Organizational Structure, 2009
Source: CNOOC company Web site, http://en.cnooc.com.cn/

Having achieved this division, CNOOC in 2001 then entered the next phase of corporatization: the public listing of its core business. Thus, Hong Kong-registered CNOOC Ltd. in February 2001 issued shares on both the New York and Hong Kong Stock Exchanges. That CNOOC was listed overseas rather than just domestically is important. For most of the roughly 1,200 SOEs that were divided up and corporatized in the 1990s, the process culminated with public listing only on China's two domestic exchanges, Shanghai and Shenzhen. For a smaller subset of the truly elite, however—that is, the three oil and gas majors, financial firms like the Bank of China and the China Construction Bank, energy giants like Huaneng, and telecommunications giants like China Mobile—listing of the corporatized arm would take place on overseas exchanges, namely, New York and Hong Kong.

By pushing reforms in this direction, policy architects, whether intentionally or not, shifted the emphasis from institutional emulation (the borrowing of Western-style corporate governance structures) to overt institutional outsourcing (the shifting of regulatory authority to overseas actors and legal systems). For the most elite firms, therefore, it was not simply that their listed arms would take on the appearance of Western-style corporations while remaining domiciled within China and subject to Chinese domestic rules. Instead, though still majority owned by domestic parent firms (which were themselves directly owned by the Chinese government), these corporatized entities would be formally registered and listed overseas. As a direct consequence, they were thrust into a thoroughly alien regulatory environment replete with all manner of rules, requirements, and intermediaries (i.e., law firms, investment advisory firms, accounting firms, etc.) that neither had historical precedent in China nor answered to any authority in Beijing. This was, and continues to be, a remarkable development.

Although skeptical observers, including this author at various points in the past, may have believed that such overseas-listed firms remained thoroughly Chinese—that is, unaffected by the overseas listing process—for the firms themselves, and especially for their senior management, the whole experience was exhilarating, bewildering, and decidedly intimidating. As I have come to understand, the experience remains so today. As we see in this chapter, not just the listing process but the ongoing challenge of managing a publicly listed firm on a global stock exchange continues for Chinese enterprise leaders to represent a daunting, often wild climb up the learning curve.

Before we delve further into this, some additional details about the relationship among the government, the parent company, and the listed corporate subsidiary are in order. In CNOOC's case, which is typical in many ways, the CNOOC Group, as a central (*zhongyang*) state-owned enterprise, falls under the formal jurisdiction of the central government's State-Owned Asset Supervision and Administration Commission (SASAC). As is discussed later, a number of governmental agencies claim regulatory authority over CNOOC's operations, but at least in formal jurisdictional terms, SASAC represents the state in its 100 percent ownership claim over the CNOOC Group. As indicated by figure 7.2, taken directly from the CNOOC Group's Web site, the company has a senior management team, the top six officials of which concurrently hold party positions and together comprise the Party Leadership Committee. The president of the CNOOC Group serves simultaneously as the company's party secretary.

Fu Chengyu	President, Party Leadership Group Secretary (also Chairman of the Board of Directors and CEO of CNOOC Ltd.)
Zhou Shouwei	Vice President, Vice Party Leadership Group Secretary (also a nonexecutive director of CNOOC Ltd.)
Cao Xinghe	Vice President, Party Leadership Group Member (also a nonexecutive director of CNOOC Ltd.)
Wu Zhenfang	Vice President, Party Leadership Group Member (also a nonexecutive director of CNOOC Ltd.)
Wu Guangqi	Chief Compiance Officer, Party Leadership Group Member (also Compliance Officer and an executive director of CNOOC Ltd.)
Lu Bo	Assistant President, Party Leadership Group Member
Wu Mengfei	Chief Financial Officer
Zheng Changbo	Assistant President
Yang Hua	Assistant President (President and CFO, as well as an executive director, of CNOOC Ltd.)
Liu Jian	Assistant President
Yuan Guangyu	Assistant President (and Executive Vice President of CNOOC Ltd)
Wang Jiaxiang	Assistant President
Li Fanrong	Assistant President

FIGURE 7.2 The CNOOC Group Senior Management Hierarchy, 2009
Source: CNOOC company Web site, http://en.cnooc.com.cn; CNOOC Ltd. company Web site, www.cnoocltd.com

The CNOOC Group, then, holds a controlling ownership stake (64.41 percent of all shares) in the publicly listed CNOOC Ltd. subsidiary. This sort of "one-third privatization" is typical for corporatized Chinese SOEs.[17] One-third of the shares float (i.e., are made available for purchase on the open market), and two-thirds remain in the hands of either the state itself or state-related commercial entities. For CNOOC Ltd., it is the latter case. Two-thirds of its shares are controlled by a parent corporation that is itself 100 percent owned by the state. Worth noting is the managerial overlap between the parent and the listed subsidiary. The president and party secretary of the parent corporation is also the chairman and CEO of the publicly listed subsidiary, a situation that makes sense given that the listed subsidiary constitutes the core business and main profit center of the entire group. Put simply, it is in its Hong Kong-registered subsidiary that the real action of CNOOC takes place. After all, CNOOC Ltd. is the part of the group that by its founding charter has exclusive rights to the upstream oil and gas E&P business. As such, it is where the power, money, status, and prestige all reside. It is, in essence, the flagship.

Precisely this kind of outcome was the point of the overall corporatization reform program. The nation's most valuable assets would be ensconced within a new institutional setting that was not only based on an overseas model but also effectively administered and bound by overseas rules. It was hoped that as a result, the assets and their surrounding corporate organization would be catapulted into the era of modernity and thrust forward to the leading edge of all that might be humanly possible in China. At the same time, the firms, though domiciled and listed overseas, would presumably be anything but foreign. Instead, in their inherent Chineseness, they would signify the ability of the nation to join the club of advanced countries, advanced companies, and advanced societies. In their absorption of foreign structures and practices, challenging and fraught though that process might be, they would ideally capture that Promethean energy that had so long graced the West and eluded China.

The Challenge of Overseas Listing:
A Chinese Manager's Perspective

For managers in a firm like CNOOC Ltd., listing on a leading global stock exchange—whether that of Hong Kong or New York—poses a series of daunting challenges. First, there are the listing requirements of the stock exchange itself. Take Hong Kong's listing rules, for example.[18] Firm's applying to issue shares, among other things, must appoint a board of directors, all of whom are subject to review by the exchange. At least three members of the board must be independent nonexecutive directors.[19] That is, at least three members of the board, subject to the exchange's review, must be complete outsiders, entirely free of prior relationships with the company's management and majority owner. In CNOOC Ltd.'s case, the board in the first few years after the company's listing would be composed of eight members, four of whom, the executive directors, were the top four managers of the company, and four of whom, the independent nonexecutive directors, came from outside.[20] Among those outsiders was a former Swiss ambassador to China, a vice chairman of Goldman Sachs Asia, and a former CEO of Shell's global chemical business, all highly experienced individuals with professional reputations to protect. Neither their own professional interests nor the rules of the Hong Kong Stock Exchange would permit them simply to be toadies of the company's senior management. And indeed, it is fair to say that CNOOC's management, quite cognizant of both its own limited experience and the magnitude of the challenges it faced moving forward, was looking for outsiders who could provide real guidance rather than just an unqualified yes.

The Hong Kong Exchange also required that listed issuers establish an audit committee chaired by an independent nonexecutive director with an appropriate accounting or financial management background. Typically, audit committees worldwide are in charge of ensuring that a company meets the reporting and financial disclosure requirements of the stock exchange upon which it is listed, as well as any additional requirements of higher level regulatory agencies (e.g., the Securities and Exchange Commission in the case of the New York Stock Exchange). Running such a committee is a weighty task that requires expertise not just in internal corporate financial management, but also business-government relations and standard regulatory practice. It is easy to see why CNOOC Ltd. leaders, unversed in such matters, reached out to a seasoned and highly senior Goldman Sachs executive to fill the role. The company in a very short period of time was being forced to wade into very complicated regulatory and disclosure requirements.

On that score, the Hong Kong Exchange, like its global counterparts, requires that applicants for listing provide extensive documentation regarding their financial condition, prior business history, personnel structure and financial stakes of all insiders, plans for use of the proceeds of the initial public offering, and a variety of other matters, several of which are quite technical. Partly in consequence, applicants are generally required to appoint an independent sponsor to prepare all this information and related documentation. Furthermore, they are generally required to appoint an independent compliance adviser, licensed by the exchange, to ensure that financial disclosure requirements are met during the firm's initial year of operation after listing. For a firm like CNOOC that is simultaneously listed on a secondary exchange—in this case, the New York Stock Exchange—numerous additional reporting requirements of the U.S. Securities and Exchange Commission must also be met. Annual audited financial reports must be issued and made public, and major business transactions—including pending ones that are starting to leak out into the press (and therefore, that might influence share prices)—must be publicly disclosed.

The point is that the listing requirements force the firm into a position in which it not only has to disclose information but also has to become reliant on a series of external, expert advisory services to do so: compliance advisers, accounting firms, legal counsel, investment banking advisers, and others. For a firm like CNOOC that never engaged in this world before, public listing is like getting thrown into a whirling torrent of rules and regulations that carry all manner of risk to the company but at the same time can be managed only through tremendous reliance on outsiders. It is easy to see how company leaders under such circumstances could feel challenged, if not totally overwhelmed and vulnerable.

The reliance on outsiders stems from more than just the nature of the listing rules. An initial public offering (IPO) for any company represents a high-stakes endeavor involving not only financial risk but also great transactional complexity. Inevitably, major questions arise about where, when, and at what target share price the initial offering should be attempted. What are the shares likely to be worth in the eyes of potential buyers on the market? Pricing them too low could entail squandering the company's value, effectively giving away to private purchasers assets that rightfully belong to the people of China. Pricing them too high, on the other hand, could lead to a bust, an undersubscription of the initial offering, and an embarrassment to the company. For any firm contemplating an IPO, these are questions that naturally lead to the role of the investment banker. For good reason, investment bankers are brought in both for the accumulated experience they offer through basic advisory services and the risk mitigation they provide through underwriting. In other words, investment bankers—particularly the leading, big-name global firms—offer a series of potential lifelines for Chinese companies wholly new to the IPO game.

The banker can hold the client's hand in terms of pricing advice and market timing. The banker, in cooperation with legal advisers, can also walk the client through the regulatory process and ensure that all the rules are followed. And by underwriting the IPO, the banker ensures that the underlying securities will be sold at the very least at a minimum, baseline price.

Of course, from the Chinese manager's perspective, the investment banker, while critical, is also somewhat suspect. Bankers—particularly those hailing from high-status, top-tier firms—offer unparalleled expertise and assurances that nothing will go wrong, a major deal for a manager bearing on his or her shoulders custodial responsibility over important national assets. When a major Chinese SOE like CNOOC, Bank of China, or China Mobile goes public, it is big news both internationally and within China. No manager wants to screw this up. And having a firm like Goldman Sachs or J. P. Morgan handling everything seems as good a way as any to ensure that precisely such a screw up is avoided. At the same time, Chinese managers understand that the bankers are going to exact whopping fees for their advisory services, fees that are astronomically high from the perspective of those accustomed to the traditional compensation levels of Chinese state industry. Moreover, managers understand that given the way underwriting deals are structured, bankers, in exchange for mitigating risk, are going to exact huge premiums if the IPO ends up oversubscribed, a not uncommon occurrence for overseas listings of major Chinese firms. And throughout the process, the bankers—holding all the cards in terms of information, expertise, and access—are going to be in control, driving things along while the manager scrambles to climb the learning curve in this, his or her first major global business deal.

For CNOOC in particular, the initial interaction with the investment banking community was not an entirely happy one. In a deal handled and underwritten by Salomon Smith Barney, CNOOC Ltd. first attempted to go public in Hong Kong in the fall of 1999. The IPO, however, in what amounted to a significant public embarrassment for all parties involved, got canceled at the last minute after the offering price was substantially slashed. Whether anybody in particular was to blame is not the issue here. One could reasonably argue that the Hong Kong market simply pitched downward, catching the bank and its corporate client unaware. Moving forward with the IPO in a market that had suddenly turned bearish would have been ill advised. The more important point, though, is that for CNOOC managers, the failed flotation represented a major setback. Unquestionably, some felt strongly, whether fairly or not, that they had been misinformed and misserved by their investment bankers. At the very least, they were reminded of their own lack of experience in the global business game and their resultant vulnerability to intermediaries possessing greater expertise and professing greater wisdom. It was a lesson, in effect, about power—who in reality had it and who did not.

Partly as a result of these power disparities, the company shifted its human resources strategy, bringing into the senior management ranks people with the kind of experience and background that permitted them to deal on an equal footing with global partners, whether investment bankers or otherwise. Thus, in what amounted to another key consequence of overseas listing, the company had to absorb within its own ranks a series of "insider-outsiders"; people who though they were Chinese, had not in their adult professional lives ever been part of the Chinese system. As the traditional Chinese saying rather crassly puts it, "You have to attack poison with poison" (*yi du gong du*).

Not long after the failed flotation in 1999, the then-chairman of CNOOC Ltd. recruited as his new senior vice president and chief financial officer an individual who, though ethnically Chinese, had spent his entire career in the United States, not surprisingly in both the energy industry and investment banking. This individual also had a U.S.-acquired PhD and MBA degree, the latter at MIT. Indeed, it was through this individual, whom I had initially met in the classroom, that I became involved with CNOOC. Just as they brought him in to better manage their integration with the broader global business community, so too did he bring into the process still more distant outsiders, whether as members of the international advisory board or members of the board of directors itself (as independent nonexecutive directors).

In a way, one can discern close parallels between what commercial organizations like CNOOC and governmental agencies like the People's Bank of China (the Chinese government's central bank) were doing on the personnel front. Because of institutional outsourcing (overseas listing in the case of the former and the challenge of facilitating currency convertibility for global producers in the case of the latter), both organizations had to bring into their senior ranks people who just years earlier would likely have been completely anathema. In CNOOC's case, they hired a U.S.-trained MBA who had spent his entire professional career in elite American corporations. In the central bank's case, they brought in U.S.- or European-trained economists to serve key regulatory roles. Until recently, the vice governor of China's central bank was a U.S.-trained economics PhD who, prior to returning to China, had been a tenured economics professor at Indiana University. This individual now has been promoted to head the State Administration for Foreign Exchange, the agency in charge of handling China's foreign reserves. Similarly, the deputy chief executive officer of the Shanghai Stock Exchange, until recently, was a Stanford-trained economics PhD. He has since become the director of Shanghai municipality's investment office.

There are now many cases like this, and they no longer seem remarkable today. And that, in some sense, is the point. These individuals, at least as I have come to know them, are not revolutionaries bent on making trouble or overtly subverting the system. Indeed, part of the reason they are in the system at all is that the country's senior leadership, starting with then-Premier Zhu Rongji in 1999, has repeatedly and publicly reaffirmed their importance to China's overall modernization mission.[21] At least in the commercial sector, given that they are compensated at globally competitive levels, patriotism alone need not explain their return.[22] That said, again at least in my own experience, these individuals, to a person, are deeply committed to the modernization of their nation. Their particular feelings toward the government are difficult to discern, for that is not something they generally discuss. Indisputable, though, is their deep loyalty to the goal of modernizing China and their deep commitment to the idea of working within the existing system today to realize a far better system tomorrow.

The interesting point, though, is that as outsiders, at least in a sense, they inevitably embody different perspectives and different approaches from those who grew up entirely within the Chinese system. Whether for a company like CNOOC or agencies like the Chinese central bank or Shanghai Stock Exchange, it is easy to see why as their global interactions deepen, they need to bring in insider-outsiders to manage such interactions. Important to recognize, though, is that by incorporating such individuals, the organizations themselves undergo change.

Such change happens in part because the role insider-outsiders play ends up deepening over time. CNOOC Ltd. is a case in point. The company, in what at the time was an exceptional move for an SOE, brought in a U.S.-trained CFO in part to ensure that its second IPO effort would end more satisfactorily than its first. That second effort, underwritten by Merrill Lynch, Credit Suisse First Boston, and Bank of China International, went off smoothly in 2001. The need for insider-outsiders, though, hardly receded after that point. Indeed, once CNOOC Ltd. listed, it was effectively thrust onto the global business community's radar screen. The company not only had a Hong Kong address, but its financial performance, its cash reserves, its operating assets, and its geographical scope of operations were all now matters of public information. Regardless of its own strategic ambitions or those of its home government, the company now became a major target for other people's ambitions. Countless individuals—some seeking to have their firms acquired by CNOOC; others seeking to sell to CNOOC selected corporate assets, such as a particular oil or natural gas field in a given global location; some proposing to coinvest with CNOOC on domestic Chinese projects; others trying to encourage CNOOC to move into new business areas—all came knocking on the door. CNOOC, after all, presumably had ambitions to grow and plenty of cash on hand. It was a perfect target for deal making.

I witnessed some of this at arm's length. Some, though, I experienced first hand. Although completely uninvolved in CNOOC's corporate governance structure or its internal operations, I was listed in company press releases and regulatory filings as a member of the international advisory board. As a result, on at least several occasions during my nine years of membership on the IAB, I was approached by a variety of global commercial actors seeking to get proposed deals put in front of CNOOC's senior management. That they were coming to me was in some sense comical, given my distance from the actual operations of the company. Nonetheless, the situation provides a sense of the volume of the offers coming in and the degree of buzz surrounding a publicly listed Chinese energy company, whether CNOOC or any other. Potential deal makers want to get in the door, and they will try any avenue possible.

When so many people like this come knocking, investment bankers again get thrust into a central position, this time in their corporate advisory role. The bankers are presumed to have the most expertise on asset valuation and negotiating tactics. They will provide critical advice on how an offer should be structured (i.e., all cash, all stock, some combination of the two, etc.) and how it should be financed. In many cases, they provide the actual financing. And throughout the process, they manage the deal, ensuring that regulatory compliance is maintained, that relevant stakeholders (including overseas governments and legislators) are notified and lobbied, and that the company's own investors are kept appropriately abreast of what is going on.

In many cases, precisely because they play this role so often and in so many different business domains, investment bankers become key nodes in information networks that extend around the globe. They are often the first to hear when an asset—an oil field in Indonesia, for example—is coming up for sale, when a company is in financial distress and is looking to be taken over, or when somebody is seeking partners for joint development of an energy project. Thus, while by necessity brought in when potential deal makers come knocking, the investment bankers themselves, once they are in the room, start pouring in additional deals and opportunities. From the perspective of managers at a firm like CNOOC, the sheer tempo of it all is exhilarating, mind bending, and stress inducing. And all the while, these managers know that the intermediaries upon whom they rely have their own independent interests that are not always entirely consonant with those of the company. Yet again, that ramps up the need for insider-outsiders, people within the managerial ranks who can sort through these proposed deals, figure out just whose interests they really serve, and then come up with strategies for moving forward with them. It is a stressful, high-stakes business rife with dueling interests, myriad judgment calls, and frequent differences of opinion both within the company and beyond. And finally on this front, it is worth remembering that in the case of overseas listed Chinese SOEs, they are totally new at this game. This can make life difficult for everybody involved: the traditional SOE managers, the newly recruited insider-outsiders, and the various intermediaries and advisory firms playing key roles on the outside.

The challenges do not end there, though, for company managers in these new settings. Registered and listed overseas, their companies become subject to intense media and investor scrutiny. At CNOOC Ltd., managers had to learn to deal not just with the press conferences following each quarter's board of directors meeting, but also the almost day-to-day inquiries that flowed in from reporters, many of whom were following up on leaks and rumors about company operations or pending business transactions. CNOOC Ltd. also had to deal with some particularly attentive minority investors in Hong Kong who in very public ways sought to scrutinize and police the operations of the company. Some of this scrutiny was carried out through online blogs, which were then picked up by the media.[23] In one case lasting through 2004 and 2005, a Hong Kong investor, after carefully examining the company's 2002 and 2003 annual reports, determined that the company was depositing funds in a finance company owned by the CNOOC parent organization. The transactions were noted in the annual report. Nonetheless, the investor's accusation, made very publicly online, was that regardless of the fact that the deposits were acknowledged in the annual reports, they were "connected-party" transactions which, by the rules of the Hong Kong Stock Exchange, should have been allowed to proceed only with formal review and approval by the company's independent shareholders (through the independent nonexecutive directors). The accusation was that such a review and approval process never occurred.

Whether company managers intentionally engaged in wrongdoing or simply received bad advice from their Hong Kong-based legal advisers is impossible for me to say. What is clear, though, is that as a result of scrutiny initiated by aggressive investors, the Hong Kong Stock Exchange in October 2005 formally censured CNOOC on this matter for breaching the company's listing agreement and the exchange's listing rules.[24] The censure represented the culmination of a minor media brouhaha that had been going on for more than a year. How important the censure was in its own right is a matter of debate. It certainly indicated, though, that CNOOC would be held accountable to the exchange on which it was listed. More important, this event influenced how CNOOC would later have to proceed in its takeover bid for Unocal. In essence, the censure provided early indication of a crucial reality surrounding institutional outsourcing. Despite the 64.4 percent ownership stake enjoyed by the CNOOC Group—and by the extension, the Chinese government—over CNOOC Ltd., now that this company was publicly listed in Hong Kong, its fate would be subject to a variety of countervailing forces, some of them decidedly non-Chinese in nature.

And as if that were not enough, CNOOC Ltd. managers, running a state-owned company in a strategic, geopolitically sensitive industry, also have to deal with their home government. I have no way of knowing whether agencies of the Chinese government issue specific directives to CNOOC managers on how the company should be run, on what overall strategic directions it should take, and on what specific deals it should sign. I do not believe any outsider could say with certainty whether such interventions do or do not take place. I never witnessed or was told of interventions like that during my decade-long period of interaction with the company. But then again, I would not likely have been informed of such sensitive matters had they been going on.

What I have in fact witnessed, though, suggests that the main form of interaction between CNOOC Ltd. and the Chinese government—and indeed, the main reason CNOOC managers find governmental relations difficult—has less to do with rigid top-down control than with mixed signals, ambiguity, and even outright silence. It is indisputable that the chairman of CNOOC Ltd., who is also the president of the CNOOC Group, concurrently holds a party position, party secretary of the group in fact. In other words, he in formal terms holds rank in the party-state hierarchy. Yet, his problem and that of his management team seem not to be that the government demands they jump in response to specific orders and directives. Instead, the problem appears to be the opposite.

China, in a manner perhaps matched only by the United States, is one of the few major energy-consuming nations yet to articulate a clear national energy policy. The Chinese government at various times, and often simultaneously, has voiced a variety of different energy-related objectives: assurance of supply, much of which comes from overseas; maintenance of low prices for energy consumers; reduction of dependence on overseas energy sources; increasing reliance on renewable energy; pollution reduction; and use of energy deals to support China's "going-out" strategy and overall image as a positive force in global affairs. As this abbreviated list suggests, most of the goals are difficult to reconcile, and some are thoroughly contradictory.

That is not entirely surprising because in China, authority over energy-related issues is spread across numerous ministries and agencies, some of which have completely antithetical interests. Roughly comparable issues exist in the United States as well, but at least in the United States, there is a Department of Energy. No such organization exists in China. To paraphrase Henry Kissinger's famous lament about Europe, there is simply no single telephone number that somebody in CNOOC or any other organization can call to reach the person or agency in charge of energy matters in China. If you absolutely had to point to one, it would probably be the central government's National Development and Reform Commission (NDRC, or in Chinese, *Fagaiwei*), for that body has final approval-granting authority for major infrastructure projects and energy deals. The NDRC's Energy Bureau, however, is tiny, staffed by fewer than a hundred people. Talented though they may be, they simply have no means of effectively monitoring, let alone directing, the countless transactions that take place across China's vast energy sector, which is arguably dominated much more by the coal industry than by petroleum.

At the same time, talented people with technical backgrounds in energy-related areas have for the most part long since left the regulatory agencies and moved over to the three national oil companies. In some respects, the talent flow stems from policy design. Two of the three national oil majors (CNOOC is the exception) were carved directly out of the former Ministry of Petroleum Industry (now defunct) and thus took with them virtually all the ministerial staff with operational expertise. In other respects, the talent flow simply reflects economics. It is at the company level, not the government, that talented young people can make real money and get involved in real decision making. People today in China can choose where they work. Those with the kind of engineering, management, or finance backgrounds suited to energy-related employment generally do not go to the NDRC, the State-Owned Assets Supervision and Administration Commission, or the Ministry of Foreign Affairs. Instead, they go to the companies.

That, of course, is both good and bad for managers at a firm like CNOOC Ltd. On the plus side, they can attract extremely talented employees. Moreover, they enjoy substantial informational advantages over their governmental bosses and regulators. They understand their own business, whereas their government generally does not. Probably because of that, the government appears to take a relatively hands-off approach to dealing with energy companies. In the case of CNOOC's global expansion efforts in the mid-2000s, including during the time of the Unocal takeover attempt, it appears that CNOOC had general approval from the NDRC to pursue international deals, but it also appears that the company was under no specific orders to pursue particular deals. That is, although the company was granted a general "ticket" (the term CNOOC managers actually used) to do global deals, it was not told specifically what to do and, as a result, did not feel compelled to consult or otherwise report upward in any great detail on what it actually was doing. The company basically operated with a great degree of managerial leeway.

The downside, though, is that while direct authority relations were murky, company managers had to deal with a plethora of competing and contradictory governmental voices. Certain agencies or specific leaders were publicly advocating that SOEs become world-class companies—that is, do global deals and achieve commercial success. Other leaders and agencies were urging that energy companies find ways to reduce China's reliance on overseas resources. Still other leaders were pushing companies to supply cleaner fuels like natural gas, which, given China's limited supplies, almost by definition has to come from abroad. And then there were powerful regional governments, such as that of Shanghai, which were at once connected to senior leaders but were eager to partner in their own right with companies like CNOOC in the development of the natural gas business. Did they represent the center? Were they acting only in their local capacity? It was hard to say and, for everyone involved, better not to inquire too deeply.

Meanwhile, though the government was speaking with many different voices, it was not—at least from the perspective of company managers—doing what overseas governments do with respect to their own domestically based energy firms: providing diplomatic support and intergovernmental lobbying for international energy deals. In other words, as it slowly began to ink deals in places like Indonesia and Australia in the years immediately after its public listing, CNOOC felt that it was in some senses operating naked, devoid of the kind of governmental support that truly global companies routinely perceive. Ironically enough, for all the American concern about Chinese mercantilism in energy-related areas, Chinese energy executives, if anything, felt that their own government was effectively absent without leave when it came to supporting global deals. In fact, these executives felt that their investment bankers, all from the highest stature global firms, had far better access to the powers that be in Beijing than they themselves had.

In what must have been maddening to CNOOC executives, foreign investment bankers on at least some occasions became critical for lobbying the executives' own home government. In 2006, when Henry Paulson, the former chairman of Goldman Sachs, was undergoing U.S. Senate confirmation for his appointment as Secretary of the Treasury, the American media made some issue of the roughly seventy trips he had taken to China while at the helm of Goldman. The implication was that he had somehow been doing the Chinese government's bidding. Executives at state-owned firms like CNOOC knew otherwise. Perhaps bitterly for some, they recognized that Paulson was doing exactly what he should have been doing: advocating on behalf of his company's business interests and doing it through the kind of access to Beijing's inner halls of power that they, even as managers and party officials in key state-owned firms, could never hope to enjoy.

What Are the Managers of Overseas-Listed Firms Trying to Do?

Swamped with new regulatory demands, thrust into relationships with difficult-to-comprehend financial intermediaries, barraged by commercial offers from every corner of the globe, and only on occasion provided hints of guidance from above, much of it contradictory and incoherent, what really do managers in an overseas-listed SOE like CNOOC end up trying to do? What are their objectives? What do they try to accomplish as they chart out company strategy? What in their minds is considered a successful outcome?

Given that we are discussing state-owned firms, we might expect these managers to pursue different objectives from what we would find in normal commercial organizations. That is, we might expect them to seek political objectives like obedience to governmental directives, maximization of national security interests, expansion of national power to new parts of the globe, or acquisition of nationally vital, strategic technologies. Whether managers in a firm like CNOOC Ltd. ever pursue such goals is difficult to say. That is not the sort of information an outsider such as myself would likely be told. Nonetheless, to the extent CNOOC managers were responding to political goals, they were doing so awfully quietly and extremely indirectly. Although I cannot entirely discount the possibility that CNOOC Ltd. was being used as an arm of the Chinese state, what I can say for certain is that the things I did witness over the years pointed to a very different story indeed.

In concrete terms, managers over the years appeared to be trying to accomplish several objectives. First, with every quarterly report, they wanted to show the kind of performance results that would gain favor with global investors and boost the company's share price. In other words, managers were determined to achieve increasing revenues and profitability. Medium-size companies like CNOOC, or even global giants like Exxon-Mobil or BP, cannot single-handedly affect the global price of oil and gas. They are essentially price takers for their basic upstream product. Thus, particularly for a company like CNOOC focused on upstream exploration and production of oil and gas (as opposed, for example, to downstream production of refined products or petrochemicals), there are really only two basic ways to increase revenues and profitability. The company either has to expand its oil and gas reserves, presumably through new discoveries or the purchase of already-discovered fields from other companies, or it has to find ways to produce existing resources at lower cost. For CNOOC, as with any other oil and gas company, both avenues are pursued aggressively. As oil and gas prices plummeted in 2008, cost cutting on the production side received particular emphasis. So, even as revenues declined on a year-on-year basis, the company was determined to show that through cost-cutting measures and other production efficiencies, the bleeding was far less serious at CNOOC than at other firms.

Second and related, managers want to show that they are outperforming similarly sized and similarly positioned (i.e., upstream- rather than downstream-focused) companies in the global oil and gas business. For CNOOC, the relevant comparison set is not Exxon-Mobil, BP, or Shell, and certainly not the real giants of the oil and gas world, Middle Eastern producers like Saudi Aramco or the National Iranian Oil Company. Instead, the appropriate comparisons are with firms like Apache, Burlington, Devon, Anadarko, and Occidental, which are relatively unknown to the general public but closely watched by the analyst and investor community. In its internal discussions and external investor presentations, CNOOC consistently compares itself to such firms, organizations it assiduously seeks to duplicate in terms of managerial sophistication and exceed in terms of commercial performance.

Third, though not stated publicly, the goal of outperforming China's other two national oil companies is ever present. The degree of rivalry among these firms is intense and heartfelt, at least from the CNOOC viewpoint. The company is by far the smallest of China's three state-owned oil and gas majors. Its business domain, due primarily to historical circumstances, is also the most narrowly circumscribed. In many respects, it is, or least views itself as, a kind of orphaned stepchild, a firm that because it is small in size and devoid of high-powered connections, has always had to work harder to gain success. The company has enjoyed many successes over the past several years, but often the biggest smiles appear on managers' faces when they can show that they did well while PetroChina (the listed arm of the China National Petroleum Company) and Sinopec (China Petroleum and Chemical Corporation) lagged.

CNOOC managers, in the spirit of competition, relish even those victories they acknowledge came less from their own efforts than from structural circumstances in the market. In 2007, for example, when global oil prices skyrocketed, CNOOC did relatively well because its business is concentrated in upstream production. PetroChina and Sinopec, however, were hurt because, though they are involved heavily upstream, substantial portions of their business also involve downstream production and the sale of refined products on the Chinese domestic market. Prices for such products in China are capped by Beijing. Thus, when the global price of crude oil—the feedstock for refined products—surges, companies selling downstream products in China get clobbered. Their costs go up, but they are prohibited from raising prices to compensate. CNOOC managers hardly went into mourning when they saw all this transpiring in their peer organizations. Thus, while we can only speculate about the orders that might or might not flow from the government to the state firm, we can say with certainty that the state firms compete bitterly among themselves.

That then leads to a fourth managerial objective, the goal of expanding into new business areas. This is particularly true for CNOOC, whose oil reserves are substantially smaller than those of its two domestic counterparts. Moreover, given the way that the Chinese government divided up the industry years ago, CNOOC has effectively been prohibited from engaging in onshore oil production in China. In the upstream E&P business, therefore, it either has to drill offshore within China's territorial waters or go abroad entirely. On the oil side of things, therefore, it has been put in the position of perpetually having to play catch up with its larger domestic counterparts.

In the China market, though, the natural gas business, at least historically, received relatively little attention from traditional state players, the Ministry of Petroleum Industry and its subsequent corporate manifestations, PetroChina (CNPC) and Sinopec. As a result, that side of the industry remained small and underdeveloped, a situation that would represent for CNOOC by the late 1990s and early 2000s a prime opportunity. The company, shut out in so many ways from competing against its domestic peers in the oil business, could do an end run around them by rushing forward and developing the natural gas side both upstream and down. Furthermore, given the eagerness with which important regional governments, such as that of Shanghai, wanted to get into this business—both for financial and environmental reasons (natural gas is a far cleaner fuel than is the coal traditionally burned in China)—CNOOC could push into this area without appearing somehow to diverge from official governmental interests (or at least the interests of some parts of the Chinese government). At the center, the policy on gas was vague at best, and at the regional level, especially among the country's wealthiest coastal provinces, there was considerable enthusiasm. Thus, the natural gas business offered CNOOC the possibility of moving into an area for which there were few established rules and doing so in a way that could be justified as responsibly loyal. The point is important because the natural gas business, arguably far more than oil, motivated CNOOC's subsequent interest in Unocal.

And finally, in terms of concrete managerial objectives, a fifth element crops up that is hardly unique to China or this particular company. CNOOC managers—if not to a person, at least generally—want to do deals. It is not that they want to plunge into reckless or commercially nonsensical deals. But like aggressive managers anywhere, they want to keep things moving. They want to score successes of the kind that will gain notoriety, boost their own and their company's stature, and effectively put the company on the map. As at any company, not all senior managers at CNOOC share the same preference for risk, and not all agree completely on every deal. But generally speaking, they are determined to do the things that will keep the company growing and eager to raise the bar on what they as managers are capable of pulling off. Aggressive and entrepreneurial for the most part, they want to keep upping the challenge for themselves and their employees. In some ways, perhaps, as for many businesspeople, it is a matter of ego. In other ways, it is simply a matter of responsible leadership under highly competitive conditions. The bottom line is that managers in CNOOC, despite the apparent absence of clear orders from above, are determined to keep pressing forward and determined to keep exploring the bounds of the possible in a highly volatile and highly dynamic global business. Over the years, they have proven their willingness to try many new things. They have never been willing, however, to simply mark time as custodians of dead or dying assets.

Overarching all these concrete objectives is an aim more abstract yet ever present. Managers at CNOOC Ltd. want themselves and their company to be viewed as world class. It is not so much that they want to be viewed as world class within China. Rather, they want to be viewed as world class by the global business community, namely, their peers in North America and Europe. That is the club they want to join. They do not want to outdo it. They simply want to be in it. In other words, in the comparisons they draw to firms like Apache, Anadarko, or Occidental, only part of the issue is that they want to come out ahead performance-wise. Equally or more important is that they want to be recognized as part of this club, a member of a group of world-class firms. My sense from years of observation is that regardless of what the Chinese government may or may not be telling them, managers at CNOOC are not first and foremost focused on locking up global assets or somehow winning at all costs. They are, of course, as already stated, committed to expanding the company. Yet, they are even more deeply committed to doing so in a particular fashion that they perceive is the one employed by leading commercial companies in globally competitive markets. That mode includes all the attributes and accoutrements of modern business: public listing on a major global exchange, autonomous management accountable to private investors, deal making brokered and financed by top-flight investment bankers, a positive public image fostered through extensive interactions with the analyst community and the media, and ultimately, financial success.

Because their company has been listed overseas—that is, because they are on the receiving end of institutional outsourcing—CNOOC Ltd.

managers have to abide by certain overseas, essentially global, rules and practices. In some respects, they are forced to play our game. In a deeper sense, though, they volunteer, and volunteer assiduously, to play, for by doing so, they enhance their status and sense of self-worth. Building the company is important. Getting the company to perform in a way outsiders deem world class is even more so. It is an issue that gets wrapped up in the managers' own identity and sense of self. Managers at CNOOC are not trying to best the West. *They are trying to be the West*. And from their perspective, they are attempting all this in the face of an extremely steep managerial learning curve, considerable global volatility in their particular industry, and a home government that is—at least relative to what their global peers experience—unresponsive to their needs.

In many ways, the actions and ambitions of CNOOC managers today reflect the very same desires of Chinese reformers a hundred years prior. By embracing the practices, structures, and rules of the advanced West, they are hoping not to beat the West but rather to join it. And by joining it, they can make as part of their own identity, and be recognized by others as possessing, that which has eluded their nation for centuries: modernity.

The Unocal Acquisition Attempt

With these background factors in mind, we can now examine the deal that captured so much global attention in 2005, the attempted takeover of Unocal. The version popularized in the West is that CNOOC, at the eleventh hour, jumped in and tried to break up a marriage between Chevron and Unocal. Moreover, as the version goes, CNOOC was able to come in with a grandiose offer—a US$18.5 billion all-cash bid, US$1.5 billion higher than Chevron's part-cash, part-stock offer—precisely because the Chinese firm had preferential financing from its own government. Presumably, the Chinese government, through a commercial entity it fully controlled, was seeking—whether malignly or not—to lock up a bunch of global oil assets, including ones located in North America. China, the thinking went, had a growing appetite for oil, which its government, blessed with newfound wealth, was more than willing to feed. Thus, CNOOC was seen as somehow competing unfairly. It was intruding in areas it should not have been, it had come in at the last minute out of nowhere, it was a mysteriously nontransparent state entity, and it was throwing around money it had accessed on thoroughly noncommercial terms. Hence, a political uproar erupted in the United States, Congress began throwing up regulatory impediments to the deal's passage, Chevron came in with a counteroffer, and CNOOC withdrew from the field of play. A Chinese mercantilist foray onto American territory was effectively rebuffed. End of story, or was it?

As I have said before, I cannot speak to whether actors within the Chinese government were somehow driving CNOOC's actions from behind the scenes. I saw no evidence of this, but that does not rule out its having happened. As far as I can tell, claims by some observers that the Chinese government played an active role in this deal, whether accurate or not, are based purely on conjecture.[25] I have yet to this day seen any evidence of the Chinese government's active involvement. The rich evidence that does exist—all of it available publicly precisely because CNOOC, Unocal, and Chevron are (or were, in Unocal's case) all listed companies bound by extensive disclosure requirements—tells a different story. Perhaps there exist secrets of which I am not aware that are behind CNOOC's bid for Unocal. What interests me, however, and what I recount here, are not the secrets but rather the publicly available information. That information alone describes a picture starkly different from what got fixed in the public's eye.

Prior to bidding for Unocal, CNOOC Ltd. since its IPO in 2001 had been cautiously and incrementally building its international operations. At the start, the company had essentially no international operations at all. With the guidance and support of its investment bankers, CNOOC in 2003 acquired for US$275 million a 12.5 percent stake from BP in a liquefied natural gas (LNG) production joint venture in Indonesia (the Tangguh LNG Project).[26] The venture was intended to supply LNG to a terminal under construction in Fujian, China, an infrastructure project in which CNOOC also had an equity stake. Later that year, again with the support of its primary banking advisers, including Goldman Sachs, the company acquired for US$348 million a production stake and a portion of the reserves in another natural gas project, this one on Australia's North West Shelf. The deal would ultimately grow to US$567 million. The idea here was to supply North West Shelf LNG to a terminal project in Guangdong, China, which CNOOC was also involved in developing as an equity partner.[27] The transaction, at the time Australia's largest export deal in history, was lauded by then-Australian Prime Minister John Howard and received highly favorable press coverage in the region. The story was presented as a case of a Chinese company benevolently feeling its way internationally and an opportunity for countries in the region, especially natural resource exporters like Australia, to cash in on growing Chinese demand. The company in 2004 also acquired a small, US$7.75 million interest in a production-sharing contract in Morocco and one in Myanmar as well.

The overall point is that throughout this period, CNOOC Ltd. was testing the waters globally, primarily in the upstream natural gas business. It was doing these deals openly and with global partners and was receiving positive press attention and favorable investor reaction in the process. And in line with its upstream investments abroad, the company, primarily through the vehicle of its parent, was strengthening its position in the downstream natural gas business (i.e., LNG terminals, gasification facilities, pipelines, etc.) within China.[28] Things for CNOOC at the beginning of 2005 were looking good. The company was on a growth trajectory, it had developed a pioneering position in China's emerging LNG market, and it was enjoying a string of solid, modestly scaled successes.

In that context, CNOOC began contemplating a larger acquisition that would transform it into what its managers deemed a truly global, truly world-class organization. The search hardly took place in secret. Its culmination, CNOOC's formal purchase bid for Unocal, came as anything but a bolt out of the blue for a variety of the multinational players involved. Indeed, many of them had participated in and deeply influenced the offer's evolution. For all we know, Chinese government officials may have been involved in one way or another. The CNOOC offer, however, did not miraculously appear from the inner sanctums of the Chinese party-state. Instead, it traveled a complicated, multistaged route that, in an era of outsourced institutions, says far more about Beijing's irrelevance than its mercantilist potency.

As it searched for a potential acquisition target, CNOOC Ltd. did what most corporations do. It secured the advisory services of two major investment banks, Goldman Sachs and J. P. Morgan. As modern market players, CNOOC, Goldman Sachs, and J. P. Morgan did exactly what they were supposed to do. CNOOC was looking for an acquisition that could sustain the company's growth (presumably by adding new oil and gas reserves), transform the firm from an Asian regional to a truly international company, elevate and globalize the firm's internal management, and possibly add technological and managerial expertise for deeper water drilling. As in any good firm, top managers had a variety of views about what such an acquisition should look like, how large it should be, and how it should be financed. Up to this point in time,

CNOOC had moved very cautiously on the global front, sticking to deals that were small relative to the size of the firm as a whole. At this next stage, however, major deals were being contemplated. As it happened, CNOOC in one fell swoop jumped from paying roughly half a billion dollars for a stake in Australia's North West Shelf LNG project to offering US$18.5 billion, roughly equivalent to CNOOC's entire market capitalization at the time, for an American oil and gas company. Needless to say, not everybody in CNOOC was equally comfortable with the magnitude of this step forward.

The discussion, though, was not happening exclusively within CNOOC's managerial ranks. As noted, the acquisition search was being supported in an overall sense, and in a completely above-board manner, by Goldman Sachs and J. P. Morgan. Specific legal, accounting, and human resources-related support was provided by a variety of other international advisory firms. Again, there is nothing untoward about this. This is what investment bankers and others engaged in corporate advisory services are supposed to do. They provide clients with advice on deals, connect clients to appropriate professional advisers (i.e., international law firms, accounting firms, public relations and lobbying firms, etc.), carry out valuation of potential deals, perform due diligence, and among other things, provide advice on how to structure deals financially. For all that, they are rewarded handsomely. In this particular case, CNOOC's management, the company's investment bankers, and an assemblage of more specialized global advisory firms involved in the process together narrowed down the acquisition search to twenty-seven potential targets, all small to medium-size energy companies from across the advanced industrial world. Over a period of months, that group was narrowed down to fourteen firms, then seven, and then one, Unocal.

Dueling Suitors: Chronology of a Competitive Bidding Process

In the months running from late 2004 through the announcement of CNOOC's Unocal bid in April 2005, it was not just CNOOC's bankers who knew about the company's intentions. The reality is that throughout this period, as documented by its own filings with the SEC—all of which are publicly available—Unocal had been actively courting a number of potential buyers, Chevron and CNOOC among them. Unocal was looking to be taken over, and by keeping several potential buyers in play simultaneously, its management was quite understandably and appropriately trying to maximize the price Unocal shareholders would ultimately receive in the transaction. The time line, at least according to what Unocal reported to the SEC in its Form DEFM 14A—filed on July 1, 2005—is fascinating. It is worth summarizing at least briefly to provide a sense of how these kinds of takeover transactions unfold.

According to Unocal management, conversations with CNOOC Ltd. began in December 2004, when CNOOC Ltd.'s chairman contacted Unocal's chairman to express potential interest in an acquisition.[29] Who exactly contacted whom—in other words, whether the discussion was initiated by CNOOC Ltd. or Unocal—is a matter of some dispute among the people involved, but all seem to agree that discussions began in late 2004. Again according to the account Unocal provided the SEC, conversations with CNOOC continued for several weeks, during the course of which rumors of the matter began appearing in the Western press. Then, in early January 2005, the chairman of Chevron entered the scene, contacting the Unocal chairman to inquire whether they might discuss a "strategic transaction," a takeover. Less than a week later, a third firm, a non-U.S. energy company, also contacted Unocal to express interest.[30] Unocal was clearly in play as a takeover target, and three suitors were actively circling.

In early February, Chevron proposed that negotiations with Unocal be conducted on an exclusive basis, but Unocal demurred. Instead, Unocal proposed a period of due diligence, protected by a confidentiality agreement, during which the two companies could exchange information about a possible transaction. The confidentiality agreement was executed in mid-February. On February 26, the chairman of Chevron, having already been granted a go-ahead by his board, delivered a written proposal to Unocal for an all-stock merger. The day before, February 25, the chairman of Unocal had spoken with the chairman of CNOOC Ltd., who, like Chevron, wanted to proceed with a due diligence review. A confidentiality agreement was then signed between CNOOC and Unocal, and the due diligence review commenced. On March 1, the Unocal board declined Chevron's offer, and the senior management of Unocal then contacted both CNOOC Ltd. and the other non-U.S. suitor, requesting preliminary proposals by March 7. Chevron appeared out, and the other two players were in.

Over the next few weeks, Unocal's attention would turn to CNOOC Ltd. On March 7, CNOOC Ltd. presented a written proposal, subject to a variety of due diligence conditions and approvals, for an all-cash acquisition of Unocal at a price of between US$59 and US$62 per share. The acquisition was to be financed through bank debt and cash on hand. Included in the proposal were letters from the financing sources expressing their willingness to provide acquisition funds for CNOOC. Meanwhile, Unocal continued its negotiations with the second non-U.S. bidder and also informed Chevron management that it would be willing to entertain a higher bid by them as well. All of the bidders were informed that they should present their best offers by March 30, at which point the Unocal board would meet and make decisions about moving forward. On March 29, Chevron delivered a new offer, still an all-stock proposal, but at a higher price than the last. Unocal management was behaving exactly as could be expected. It was stoking up competitive bidding so as to maximize shareholder value.

At this point, however, CNOOC Ltd. begged off. On the same day Chevron issued its improved offer, CNOOC Ltd.'s chairman informed Unocal's that, though CNOOC was still interested in a deal, a new offer would not be forthcoming for several weeks. This delay is important, and we return to it shortly. Meanwhile, although CNOOC was temporarily out, the third suitor came in with a proposed all-cash bid of US$58 per share. After meeting, the Unocal board instructed management to reject the third potential acquirer's bid, inform Chevron that its bid would have to be substantially changed to move forward, and request a "definitive" proposal from CNOOC by April 2. Clearly, Unocal wanted to keep CNOOC in the mix, even as CNOOC had earlier indicated it would still need several weeks to produce a new offer. On the morning of April 2, CNOOC Ltd.'s chairman informed Unocal that his company would not be able to make a definitive offer at that time but expressed hope that CNOOC would be considered if Unocal opted not to move ahead with a transaction in April. That same day, Chevron came in with a revised offer, a combined stock and cash proposal valued at roughly US$16.5 billion. On the evening of April 3, the Unocal board met and approved the merger agreement with Chevron. The agreement was signed and announced the following day.

For the general public, unaware of the competitive bidding that had been unfolding for months, it was really only at this point in April that the story began. From their perspective, Chevron and Unocal had inked a friendly takeover agreement. Then, on June 22, CNOOC Ltd. entered the picture out of nowhere with a hostile takeover bid, an all-cash offer of US$67 per share.[31] The CNOOC proposal, as indicated by the company's filings with the SEC, was to be financed as follows: bridge loans from J. P. Morgan and Goldman Sachs in the amount of US$3 billion, bridge loans from the Industrial and Commercial Bank of China in the amount of US$6 billion, a long-term loan from the company's majority shareholder (the CNOOC Group) in the amount of US$4.5 billion, a bridge loan from that same majority shareholder in the amount of US$2.5 billion, and US$3 billion of CNOOC Ltd.'s own cash resources.[32]

As we know, over the ensuing weeks as Unocal considered the offers, a political furor erupted in the United States. Both Chevron and CNOOC—as well as their various advisory firms—conducted dueling public relations campaigns, Congress expressed inclinations toward blocking the CNOOC bid, and Chevron came in with a still higher bid. Then, in a public announcement dated August 2, 2005, CNOOC Ltd. withdrew its proposed offer, and Chevron's acquisition of Unocal proceeded apace.

In the aftermath of this whole episode, there was no small amount of finger pointing and "he said, she said" accusations among the many different parties involved. The dividing lines were hardly limited to just Chevron and CNOOC. From the principals to their assemblages of advisory firms, lots of players were involved, and not all were happy with the others' performance. Those disputes, however, will neither be aired nor resolved here.

More important and worth noting is the degree to which the chronology just described departs from the popular image of a shadily run Chinese state entity popping up out of the shadows and making a hostile bid for U.S. energy assets. The reality is far more interesting. A publicly listed Chinese company (or technically speaking, a publicly listed Hong Kong company), in concert with a team of investment bankers, lawyers, and other advisory specialists, had engaged in an extended negotiation with a publicly listed U.S. company. The U.S. company had not just been aware of the Chinese company's interest but had actively egged it on, soliciting bids and counterbids and cooperating with the Chinese firm's due diligence efforts. Understandably, the U.S. company, clearly seeking to be taken over and at the highest price possible, had been doing the same with at least two other potential acquirers. Meanwhile, at various points in the process, both the U.S. and Chinese firms had been in contact with American regulators about the ongoing negotiations. Many, many people—whether in global investment banking circles, the global energy industry, the Hong Kong regulatory community, or the U.S. government—were either fully or partly aware of what was going on. Indeed, the global media had started reporting on CNOOC's interactions with Unocal as early as January 2005.

That all of these parties were aware of what was happening was in no small part due to the fact that CNOOC Ltd., despite being majority state owned, was listed in Hong Kong and was behaving in accordance with the demands of modern commerce. Throughout its endeavors, it was working hand in hand with global advisory services, particularly investment banks. Indeed, some critics who felt the Unocal takeover attempt was ill advised would quietly complain, whether fairly or not, that CNOOC Ltd. management let itself be swayed by the blandishments of bankers, people whose main financial interest lay in getting a deal done.

Whether such criticism is fair or not is beyond the scope of this analysis. What the criticism points to, though, is the fact that CNOOC Ltd. managers were operating in entirely new waters. Having never before attempted a deal of this size before, they themselves acknowledged the magnitude of the intellectual and organizational challenge involved. They were scrambling up a very steep learning curve and, as a result, had to accept a high degree of dependence on global players for whom deals like this were relatively routine. Needless to say, the interests of those advisory partners, though not antithetical to CNOOC's, were not wholly consonant either. Thus, apart from Chevron and Unocal, even just on the CNOOC side, numerous players were involved, and numerous interests were placed in contention. Because the deal failed—and failed due to political theatrics that at least some observers argue should have been anticipated in advance—the various players on the CNOOC side to this day do not exactly see eye to eye on who is to blame. What is clear, though, is that the situation differs markedly from the image burned into the public's mind, an image of Chinese state officials hidden away in secret chambers plotting their next gambit for global domination. At least for CNOOC managers, whipsawed by the political eruption they inadvertently ignited in the United States, the globe had dominated them rather than vice versa.

The Delay in CNOOC's Bidding Process

One of the most important and least understood aspects of CNOOC's Unocal bid involves the delay that took place between the Chinese company's initial expression of interest (in late 2004) and the delivery of its formal bid (in June 2005). Here is where the significance of CNOOC Ltd.'s registration and listing in Hong Kong becomes most apparent. There exist any number of theories as to why CNOOC Ltd. sought to acquire Unocal, everything from good business sense on the part of company management to geopolitical ambition on the part of China's national leadership. In some respects, no amount of evidence will ever be able to definitively prove one theory over another. The interesting point, though, is that regardless of who was pushing the deal or why, other countervailing forces—distinctly non-Chinese forces—dictated the pace and timing of the CNOOC offer. In so doing, they substantially dictated the ultimate outcome: Chevron's acquisition of Unocal.

As noted earlier, CNOOC Ltd., to finance its Unocal bid, had support from three banks; two were global, and one was Chinese. The loans that were being extended, though, and the cash that CNOOC Ltd. had available on hand were not together enough to make a serious run at Unocal. To make up the very substantial difference—amounting to roughly 40 percent of the complete deal—CNOOC Ltd. intended to borrow US$7 billion from its parent company, the CNOOC Group. As indicated earlier, CNOOC Ltd. is more than just a normal subsidiary. It alone accounts for the bulk of the parent company's revenue, and its own chairman and that of the parent are the same individual. What the proposal amounted to, then, was an effort to fund the company's publicly listed arm through financial infusions from its wholly state-owned other arm.

Critics in the United States, including some in Congress, objected vociferously to what they viewed as a violation of fair competition. In their view, here was a firm that was being given free access to the virtually limitless financial resources of the Chinese government. Armed with such cash, CNOOC Ltd. would be bidding on non-commercial terms and could therefore outbid pretty much anybody. It could thus gobble up scarce American energy assets at will, and no commercial entity could stop it. From Congress's perspective, this was all the more reason to threaten to block the deal, never mind that Unocal shareholders would benefit enormously from the bidding up of the value of their holdings.

Whether preferential financing in a corporate acquisition constitutes a restraint of trade or any other sort of violation of international agreements is a matter of debate. It is also largely irrelevant to what really counts in this story. That CNOOC Ltd. had access to funds from its state-owned parent obviously permitted it to offer a far higher price for Unocal than would have been possible otherwise. Yet—and this is the crucial point—precisely because it chose to rely on those funds, CNOOC Ltd. was cast into a regulatory morass made unavoidable because of the company's public listing in Hong Kong.

According to rule 14.33 of the Hong Kong Stock Exchange's Listing Rules, a listed issuer (a company listed on the exchange) is bound to do certain things when it engages in a "major" or "very substantial" acquisition.[33] It must, among other things, notify the exchange in advance, inform shareholders, and subject the acquisition to shareholder approval.[34] For CNOOC Ltd., getting shareholder approval presumably would not be a problem. After all, the majority shareholder is the firm's state-owned parent.

The complication, though, is that additional rules kick in when connected-party transactions are involved—that is, cases in which the listed issuer receives financing from one of its own substantial shareholders.[35] Such "connected transactions," according to the exchange's listing rules, must receive the approval in writing not just of the shareholders but of the *independent* shareholders.[36] The point is that the exchange has a large body of protections for minority shareholder rights in precisely these kinds of situations. Specifically, the rules (rule 13.39) call for the issuer to establish an independent board committee, composed only of independent nonexecutive directors, to advise shareholders on whether the proposed connected transaction is reasonable and worthy of approval.[37] As part of that process, the issuer and its independent nonexecutive directors are required to appoint an independent financial adviser approved by the exchange to make a separate written assessment of the proposed transaction. This assessment is then delivered to the independent shareholders separate from the independent nonexecutive directors' own recommendation.

As noted earlier, CNOOC Ltd. in 2004 had already gotten into trouble with the exchange for violating this rule with regard to funds being moved from the listed firm to its nonlisted parent. The transactions had been declared in annual reports but were not subject to independent shareholder review and approval. While formal censure by the exchange would come in the fall of 2005, well after the Unocal affair had concluded, the issue had been roiling within the company and in the broader investment community since at least the summer of 2004. It had received considerable attention among CNOOC managers and directors. It was, in short, a big deal at the time. Therefore, as the bidding process for Unocal unfolded in early 2005, neither CNOOC Ltd.'s management nor its board of directors were inclined to incur any further violations of the listing rules, particularly on this very issue. This was especially true of the independent nonexecutive directors. Regardless of any personal feeling they may have had about the Unocal bid, whether positive or negative, as soon as the bid involved financing from CNOOC Ltd.'s state-owned parent, those four independent directors came under legal obligation to convene a review. Furthermore, they were legally obligated to hire an outside consultancy, an independent financial adviser, to conduct a separate review.

That review process was in fact initiated in the spring of 2005 and explains why the CNOOC chairman told Unocal in late March that several more weeks would be needed before a formal proposal could be delivered. As CNOOC Ltd. noted in its SEC filings, the independent advisory firm brought in for the purpose was N. M. Rothschild & Sons (Hong Kong) Ltd.[38] Both the independent non-executive directors' committee and the independent financial adviser apparently concluded that the proposed transaction was reasonable, and they recommended approval. The review process, however, took roughly six weeks. Again, that explains in large part why the chairman of CNOOC Ltd., despite the urgings of Unocal, could not deliver a definitive bid earlier in the game. Because of the nature of the funding upon which he was relying, he and his firm, regardless of their preferences, were bound by regulatory mechanisms far more cumbersome than anything Chevron faced. Hence, though CNOOC initially was deeply involved in the bidding, it had to back off during the review process, permitting Chevron a prime opportunity to conclude a deal. After that point, CNOOC could reenter the process only as a hostile bidder, and a litany of relatively predictable problems ensued.

What is ironic about this is that the very thing so many outsiders believed gave CNOOC Ltd. an unfair advantage—its access to non-commercial, ostensibly state-backed financing—was actually the single most important factor in impeding the company's progress with Unocal. In other words, it was only because of the connected-party aspect of the financing that CNOOC Ltd., precisely because it is bound by Hong Kong rules, became subject to independent share-holder approval mechanisms and a lengthy review process. No matter what the Chinese government intended CNOOC Ltd. to do (to the extent it had clear intentions at all), no matter how large the size of the CNOOC Group's controlling interest in CNOOC Ltd., and no matter what the personal opinions of the company's independent non-executive directors, the legal requirements of the Hong Kong Stock Exchange would reign supreme. Hence, CNOOC Ltd. would have to proceed at a pace dictated by nothing else but the Hong Kong Stock Exchange's rules. And Chevron, as a result, would be granted a golden opportunity to spoil CNOOC's deal of the century.

Conclusion

Whether or not the Unocal deal made good business sense for CNOOC Ltd. is hard to say. In many respects, the company was more interested in Unocal's Asian-based natural gas assets than anything else. Indeed, when political opposition mounted in the United States, CNOOC was more than willing to forgo purchasing Unocal's North American-based oil assets, and instead just focus on acquiring the firm's Asia-based assets. As CNOOC Ltd. openly documented in its presentations to investors, Unocal's Indonesia-based gas reserves were ideally suited to be exported, as LNG, to the four terminals then under development along China's Southeast Coast (in Guangdong, Fujian, Zhejiang, and Shanghai, respectively).[39] That said, the question of whether Unocal was worth what CNOOC was offering is today moot. So too, in many ways, is the question of whether Chinese officials were using this deal to further their geostrategic ambitions. If the question is not moot, it is at least unanswerable.

The important point is that regardless of what CNOOC managers—and even possibly Chinese government officials—were trying to do, their actions were not exclusively, or even primarily, dictating where CNOOC would ultimately end up. This is a remarkable outcome. After all, we are talking about a strategic industry and a firm in that industry that is owned by the Chinese state.

The American public viewed CNOOC's Unocal bid as a Chinese governmental quest for American energy assets. In at least one way, they were not far off. The bid did represent a quest, but not one necessarily by the Chinese government and not one for energy assets per se. Instead, this quest—this quest for modernity—extends across the entire Chinese nation. It is a quest that has resulted in firms like CNOOC, absolutely critical national organizations, getting listed on global stock exchanges. It is a quest that has forced into the Chinese mix a variety of global players—everything and everyone from global investment banks to U.S.-trained business professionals and economists. Moreover, it has created situations in which these external players end up exerting tremendous influence on domestic affairs. It is a quest that has subjected key Chinese organizations to external rules that in many ways trump things like ownership and state control, even in the most traditionally state-dominated industries. Thus, it is a quest that has subjected China's traditional political hierarchy to a series of new, countervailing forces, many of which emanate from well beyond China's borders.

Yet, it is by no means clear that such forces should be—or are— viewed in China as impediments to national aspirations or threats to national sovereignty. Indeed, it is often quite the opposite. Even as they restrict the reach of the state and exert influence deep within the Chinese system, these countervailing forces are not just tolerated but quietly welcomed. Present as a result of purposive policy efforts— purposive efforts, in other words, to place key Chinese organizations in a modern institutional context—they signify a certain coming of age for the nation and its people. Institutional outsourcing may cause numerous headaches for companies like CNOOC and its governmental overseers at home. More profoundly, though, that such headaches exist—that domestic companies have become so enmeshed in modern global commerce—suggests an achievement by China of something it has been seeking for well over a century: presence among the community of advanced industrial societies. As demonstrated by the CNOOC experience, playing by global rules, in terms of the details on the ground, is fraught with uncertainty and risk. Yet, as an endeavor, regardless of the outcome in any particular transaction, playing by the rules of the West becomes the avenue toward a truly modern identity and truly modern status. Ironically enough, in surrounding itself and abiding by rules from abroad—not slavishly necessarily, but as an equal of the world's most advanced players—China can persuade itself and those with whom it deals that after a century of trying, it truly has stood up.

EIGHT

Self-Obsolescing Authoritarianism

I F YOU VISIT Taiwan today—in addition to seeing towering new buildings, stunning public parks, and state-of-the-art mass transit systems in the island's major urban centers—you will witness a thriving democracy.[1] You will be in a place that in 1991 held its first free and fair elections for the National Assembly, what at the time was effectively the Republic of China's Parliament. You will also be in a place that in 1994 amended its constitution so as to make the presidency a popularly elected position. In 1996, the first presidential election took place, marking the first time in modern Chinese history that ordinary citizens were granted the opportunity to select their national leader. In 2000, in another first, the main opposition party, the Democratic Progressive Party (DPP), captured the presidency in a closely matched multiparty election. A true transition of power ensued, and the system remained intact. And in the 2008 elections, yet another transition occurred as Taiwan's traditional ruling party, the Kuomintang (KMT), recaptured its hold on the presidency.

The democracy that exists in Taiwan today is by no means perfect. It is in the best of times rough and tumble and on occasion seemingly wild. More than once recently, it has been tarnished by scandals and corruption at the highest levels of power. For all those problems, though, it is a democracy indisputably characterized by a free and highly vocal press, an informed and engaged citizenry, rich and contentious public debate, and through it all, an impressive degree of institutional stability. Elections come and go, the parties hurl accusations at one another, the media froths with rumor and innuendo, but in the end, citizens go out to vote, power gets transferred, the government performs its basic functions, and the island, its people, and its economy keep chugging along. And should you visit Taiwan today, all of that will be completely evident, staring you in the face as if it had been going on for decades and maybe even centuries.

On that same visit, though, you could choose to scratch a bit under the surface and see things that will remind you of just how extraordinary Taiwan's contemporary "ordinary" really is. You could, for example, if you happen to be in Taipei visiting the Presidential Office or the Parliament building, walk just a few blocks to the West, enter the city's Peace Park (Heping Gongyuan), and visit the Taipei 228 Memorial Museum (Taibei Er Er Ba Jinian Guan). That museum marks an event, the "February 28 (1947) Incident," that for nearly fifty years after its occurrence was treated as officially taboo by Taiwan's KMT-ruled authoritarian regime, the same KMT, by the way, that holds power today under decidedly different conditions. The February 28 Incident involved the rounding up, and in many cases summary execution, of local Taiwanese dissenters to KMT rule, rule which had been imposed at the end of World War II with Taiwan's reversion to Chinese control after fifty years of Japanese colonial administration (from 1895 to 1945). Coming over from the mainland, the KMT government and its military forces were viewed as outsiders by many local Taiwanese. Many locals, in turn, in the immediate aftermath of World War II and the intensification of China's own Civil War, were viewed by the KMT as Japanese collaborators and communist sympathizers. Even today, the feelings are raw, and the interpretations of what exactly happened in 1947 are highly divergent. The history—discussion of which was banned prior to the 1990s—is now debated vociferously across various constituencies in Taiwan, some with familial and historical linkages to the traditional KMT and others with local ties in Taiwan going back centuries. Everybody agrees that violence erupted, that a governmental reimposition of order occurred (some term it a "White Terror"), and that many local people—probably in the range of 10,000–20,000 individuals—were killed.

During the KMT's nearly five decades of authoritarian rule on Taiwan, the incident was not just completely denied but prohibited as a topic of public discussion. For years, anybody who dared bring up the event, let alone argue for an official apology or compensation for victims, risked being thrown in prison or even worse. Discussion of the incident was treated by the regime as outright sedition, a crime that under Taiwan's martial law conditions at the time was punishable by death.

Hardly a mild form of benevolent authoritarianism, KMT rule on Taiwan for much of its history amounted to a tough, war-hardened, and absolutely merciless regime determined to impose an iron grip over the island it considered only its temporary home. With the dawning of democracy, it was with good reason considered extraordinary when then-President Lee Teng-hui in 1995 issued a formal apology for the February 28 Incident. That was the first time the event was publicly acknowledged on the island by a head of state. It is all the more extraordinary today that the event, though still debated within Taiwanese society, is memorialized in a major public museum in the heart of the island's political center. Normal today. Unthinkable less than twenty years ago.

And if you are visiting Taiwan today, you can easily make your way to the city of Taidong on the southeastern coast and from there take a ferry to the roughly twenty square mile outcropping of volcanic rock known as Green Island (Ludao). Today, Green Island, surrounded by gloriously vibrant coral reefs, is a combination diver's paradise and honeymoon getaway. Prior to the 1990s, though, one would not normally have been permitted to visit that island. Even mentioning it in Taiwan was a risky endeavor. Between 1951 and 1987, Green Island was a gulag, the site of a succession of harsh, desperately isolated political prisons. It was, in effect, a dumping ground for enemies of the ruling KMT.

On Green Island today, you can visit those prison camps, preserved by the state as a human rights museum and memorial park. You can walk the grounds of the New Life Correction Center, which from 1951 through the late 1960s held roughly 2,000 prisoners at any given time, some of whom, particularly at the time of the Korean War, were tattooed with the slogan, "Oppose the Communists, Resist the Russians."[2] You can continuing walking along the rocky shores where prisoners for decades had engaged in forced labor, and you will come upon the prison blocs and isolation cells of the Green Island Reform and Reeducation Prison. It is a place better known in the annals of Taiwanese political history as Oasis Villa (Luzhou Shanzhuang), the name given it by the dissidents—democracy advocates, Taiwan independence seekers, suspected communists, human rights activists, and numerous other enemies of the state—who were housed there from 1972 to 1987. Political prisoners were still being delivered there in the last year of its operation, a time only slightly more removed from the present than the Tiananmen crackdown is on the mainland. Twenty years ago, give or take.

Along the interior walls of the Oasis Villa prison yard, you can still clearly see slogans, faded a bit now in the tropical sun, that in their ferocity and belligerence, if not their particular object of scorn, could easily be confused for ones that appeared on the mainland during the height of Maoism. "Steadfastly oppose communism (*Jianding fan gong*)!" "Wipe out communism, and recover the country (*Mie gong fu guo*)!" "Love your hometown, and love your country (*Ai xiang ai guo*)!"

And what kinds of activities were getting people thrown into such prisons well into the 1970s and 1980s? A paramount example involves the 1979 Kaohsiung Incident. In that year, protests broke out in Taiwan's main southern city, Kaohsiung, in the days surrounding International Human Rights Day. The government cracked down by arresting and charging with sedition eight of the rally's organizers, intellectuals associated with what at the time was an increasingly popular and politically free-thinking new journal, *Meilidao* (Beautiful Island, or "Formosa").[3] The eight activists—one of whom, Annette Hsiu-lien Lu, would twenty-one years later become Taiwan's vice president under decidedly different conditions—were tried in military courts and handed sentences of between twelve years and life. A second group of thirty-three individuals were tried by civilian courts and given sentences of two to six years. In addition, a group of members of the Presbyterian Church in Taiwan, an organization associated with the opposition, went on trial for hiding protest organizers. The general secretary of the church, Reverend Kao Chun-ming, received a seven-year sentence.

The most gruesome treatment was reserved for political activist Lin Yi-hsiung, a man who twenty years later would run Democratic Progressive Party (DPP) candidate Chen Shui-bian's successful campaign for Taiwan's presidency. Immediately after the 1979 Kaohsiung protests, Lin was arrested and severely beaten while in police custody. While under detention, he was visited by his mother, who had been in contact with Amnesty International. The day after her visit, she and Lin's twin seven-year old daughters were stabbed to death in the family home. An older daughter was badly wounded. Despite the home's being under round-the-clock police surveillance at the time, the government denied any knowledge of the crime.[4] Lin himself remained in prison through 1984, at which point he was paroled and sent to the United States.

The point of this discussion is to emphasize how the Taiwan we see today as a thriving, modern democracy was as recently as two decades ago a brutally repressive, one-party authoritarian regime. All the way through the end of the1980s, it would have been perfectly reasonable to conclude that this regime would never cede power willingly. Time and again, even in the 1980s, overt challenges from within were met with an unyielding iron fist.

Undoubtedly in the late 1970s and 1980s—with the death of Chiang Kai-shek and the ascendancy of his son, Chiang Ching-kuo—observers would have witnessed a number of evolutionary changes under way. They would have seen the ruling KMT subtly shift the source of its legitimacy from ideological claims rooted in the past to forward-looking commitments to deliver economic development to Taiwan. They would have seen the promises to liberate the mainland recede into the background and with them the insistence on maintaining a war footing within Taiwan. The government would stop talking about the mainland and instead talk about things like the Ten Great Construction Projects (*Shi da jian she*), a modernization program that would transform the island's physical infrastructure.

The KMT, which for so long had based its rule on an existential commitment to defeat communism and recover the mainland, now finally appeared ready to acknowledge that Taiwan would be the extent of its domain. As such, the party would strive to build a constituency for long-term survival. It would devote unprecedented attention and energy to economic development. It would tolerate and even encourage deepening commercial interaction with global producers. It would, in fact, try to embrace the local Taiwanese business community. Meanwhile, as the economy boomed, citizens came to understand that to do well in life, they no longer needed to rely on political connections or other kinds of privileged access but could instead depend on their own hard work and entrepreneurial talents. An engineering degree, particularly from an overseas institution, became a better guarantor of success than the right family name, the right connections in the army, or the right sinecure in the party-state bureaucracy. Life as a whole became increasingly depoliticized as indoctrination classes were tempered down in the schools and martial law strictures gradually eased.

In the midst of all these changes, the KMT now had to work harder to attract members and maintain relevance as something more than just power ruling from on high. Seeking to broaden and reconstitute its based, the KMT opened itself up to previously excluded groups, particularly local Taiwanese, including people from the business community and the politically suspect Presbyterian Church. One of those local Taiwanese, Lee Teng-hui, would ultimately succeed Chiang Ching-kuo at the helm of the KMT and serve as Taiwan's last president under nondemocratic rule.

Observers would have seen all these changes happening, but they would likely have doubted that anything resembling true democracy would come anytime soon. Who would have thought, even in the 1980s, that Taiwan would democratize? Between the brutality with which overt dissenters were treated and the massive security apparatus maintained by the state right up to the end, there was plenty of evidence to suggest that the reforms under way were aimed not at promoting democracy but avoiding it. That is, it would have made perfect sense all the way through the end of the 1980s to believe that the KMT, by combining an economically liberal velvet glove with a politically recalcitrant iron fist, was setting Taiwan up for single-party rule into perpetuity. And then, in what now seems like the blink of an eye, it would all be gone by the mid-1990s.

Interestingly, the mode of rule would disappear but not the party. The KMT would keep on going, albeit over time as a transformed organization. And though it would fall out of power for a time, it would return with renewed vigor, but this time on the basis of solid electoral victories. Thus, it would resume its place at the top of the political system but in a completely new fashion and on the basis of a completely new form of rule. In its return, it would be led by a kind of insider-outsider, an individual not with a military background or a long history of service in the party's ranks but instead a person with law degrees from New York University and Harvard and years of experience in the United States. This individual, Ma Ying-jeou, was somebody who, not unlike the skilled engineers who were trickling back to Taiwan from Silicon Valley to start high-tech firms, returned home not to play a traditional "apparatchik" role within the KMT's party ranks but instead to serve as a professional bureaucrat, a civil servant.[5] By 1993, the U.S.-trained legal expert was appointed justice minister by then-President Lee Teng-hui.

Taiwan is obviously not mainland China. The former is a nation (though one not generally recognized in formal diplomatic terms internationally) of slightly more than 22 million people with a per capita income in 2008 of just under US$32,000.[6] The latter is a nation of more than 1.3 billion people with a per capita income in 2008 of US$2,770.[7] These two entities are at totally different stages of economic development, and they have evolved at least since the late nineteenth century along different historical paths. To some extent, their people today share different identities. For all these reasons, one must be careful about drawing off-the-cuff, flip comparisons.

That said, in their modern political origins, mainland China and Taiwan share an intimately close bond.[8] The KMT and CCP (Chinese Communist Party), bitter enemies for much of the twentieth century, emerged from the same crucible of revolution. Both were born as Leninist organizations with the self-appointed task of rescuing China and remaking it into a modern nation. Both married the party to the gun and made violence, coercion, and a crusading impulse key aspects of their governance style. Both became wrapped up in the messianic visions of their respective charismatic leaders. Partly as a result, both came to view their own survival as one in the same with that of the Chinese nation. The party—the organization—in each case became an end unto itself. No price could be considered too high and no struggle too bitter to save the party, for in the party's salvation lay the nation's. And in fact, for both the KMT and CCP during much of their history, the struggle—whether against each other, against the imperialists pressing in from abroad, or against the innumerable enemies, real or perceived, from within their own ranks—truly was about salvation, an almost religious, spiritual deliverance from China's century of weakness and humiliation. It is easy to understand how authoritarianism—and a particularly intense, harsh form of authoritarianism at that—could have emerged for both parties as their common approach to governance.

Once the fervor of revolution had waned and the founding fathers had departed the scene (Chiang Kai-shek died in 1975, and Mao Zedong one year later), both the KMT and CCP would cling steadfastly to authoritarian rule, but they would have to find new ways to justify and legitimize their hold on power. Both would do so under postcharismatic, reformist leaders, Chiang Ching-kuo in the KMT's case and Deng Xiaoping in the CCP's. As it turned out, the approaches adopted by these men, each a hardened party infighter in his own right, would end up roughly similar. In the KMT's case, partly due to Taiwan's smaller size and the nature of the KMT's particular ideology, things would move faster. The overall path, however, was not so different across the two. Both the KMT and CCP would begin to emphasize economic development over ideological purity. Both would increasingly justify their rule in terms of tangible deliverables rather than historical right. At the same time, neither would brook dissent, and both on numerous occasions would demonstrate their willingness to crush political opponents.

And both parties, as their rule became grounded in performance rather than destiny, had to support change. Both had to absorb trained professionals into their ranks as governance tasks became increasingly complex and specialized in nature. To enable the kind of growth outcomes they were promising, both had to pursue policy ends that would have been heretical just years earlier: the encouragement of nonstate-related entrepreneurship, the opening up to international business, the espousal of rule of law, and the absorption of international standards.

To some extent, both parties became prisoners of their rhetoric. In promising economic development, they had to tolerate the accumulation of wealth—and by extension, unprecedented political autonomy—on the part of previously suppressed and still-mistrusted societal constituencies. Moreover, to continue delivering development, they truly did have to build a kind of rule of law that, if it did not completely apply to state insiders, at least had to be made to stick consistently in day-to-day commercial and societal affairs.

And of course, opponents—most, though not all, essentially still loyal to the system—began using these new legal instruments to press their cause. Resistance, though still dangerous and dicey, became arguably rightful rather than definitively counterrevolutionary.[9] In both Taiwan and mainland China, in lagged fashion chronologically, citizens, though remaining for the most part obedient and loyal, began developing an independent political identity infused with notions of rights and entitlements. They may not have fought for the right to participate, whether through voting or other mechanisms, but they came to see themselves as something other than just subjects.

In no small part due to all these developments, both the KMT and CCP not only had to accelerate their policy reform efforts, but they also had to keep on broadening their membership. In the 1980s, the KMT, under Chiang Ching-kuo's encouragement, dramatically increased its recruitment of native Taiwanese, who presumably had no personal or ideological commitment to "One China" (the notion of Taiwan and mainland China being a single nation) or even the sanctity of KMT rule itself. Perhaps not surprisingly, one of these recruits, Lee Teng-hui, would later be vilified by traditional KMT stalwarts when as president he ostensibly—at least in their view—sold out KMT interests by furthering democratization and encouraging pro-Taiwan independence sentiments. And in the CCP's case, the party, too, would increasingly be opened up to outsiders, technocrats, educated professionals, and perhaps most interesting of all, by the late 1990s, private entrepreneurs (capitalists!). By the 2000s, college students were flocking to join the party not because of what it represented politically but instead because membership in it, at least on one's résumé, was useful for landing jobs in the commercial sector, including in leading foreign firms. The party for many ambitious citizens had become the establishment, nothing more and nothing less. Joining the party, whatever one actually believed and however much one could have cared less if it dropped off the face of the Earth tomorrow, was a good way to get ahead.

That brings us to the themes we have discussed in previous chapters. We have considered a number of images of contemporary China: the globalist converger that in a period of deep national crisis, reconstituted its identity through linkage to the international economy; the capitalist facilitator that opened up its domestic industry to global firms and allowed them, in the context of unprecedented technological possibilities, to fit China into a new structure of global production; and the institutional outsourcer that even in its most strategically sensitive industries bound key domestic players to overseas legal institutions and foreign sources of authority. We even saw to some extent how the Chinese government, by absorbing insider-outsiders while at the same time ramping up commitments to deliver ostensibly modern conditions like rule of law and governmental accountability, repeatedly doubled down its bets, promising ever more rather than backpedaling in retreat. And last but not least, in this concluding chapter, we have arrived at the notion of self-obsolescing authoritarianism.

Of course, in China's case, the country is still under authoritarian rule. Arguments about whether Chinese authoritarianism is on the wane or, conversely, girding itself for the long haul through newly flexible adaptive measures, must by definition be speculative.[10]

In Taiwan's case, we need not speculate. The KMT's variety of authoritarianism was, in fact, self-obsolescing. Moreover, even as it breathed its last, we would have been hard pressed, as we are with China today, to identify it as a true case of democratization. Simultaneously fighting enemies while pursuing reform to its very end, KMT-style authoritarianism up to its last days could easily have been described as adaptive, setting itself up for either long-term survival or defeat at the hands of societal upheaval.

As it would happen, neither outcome would obtain in Taiwan. The authoritarianism obsolesced but not the organizations or individuals who perpetrated it. Rather, they adapted to a new form of governance:

democracy. The system changed, and over time, though we wou. not likely have quite understood what was happening, a revolution in governance occurred. That revolution involved no mounting of the barricades per se, no dismantling of the old party organizations, and no formal settling of scores. In the end, though, even as the KMT rose back again to rule, everyone would acknowledge that a systemic revolution had taken place. Just visit the Taipei 228 Museum or the Green Island Human Rights Memorial and Museum if you are not sure.

It is in that sense that the comparison to mainland China becomes so interesting. Again we can only speculate, but the argument here is that given the kind of institutional outsourcing that has already taken place, Chinese authoritarianism is currently self-obsolescing in ways that roughly mirror what transpired two decades earlier in Taiwan.

Some things, of course, we do not have to speculate on, for they have already happened. As discussed at the very start of this book, the China of today in political terms barely resembles the China of twenty years ago. Institutional outsourcing in its economic dimensions has moved hand in hand with changes on the political front. The demise of the work-unit system of economic and political control, once so central to authoritarian rule, could not conceivably have occurred in the absence of China's opening to the West and, more specifically, China's allowing overseas commercial firms to lead the way in restructuring the domestic manufacturing sector. That restructuring process, then, upped the need for new rules and institutions, and the government itself would have little choice but to promulgate a rule of law agenda. Foreign competition also squeezed domestic incumbents in heavy industry, increasing the need for the kind of reforms that led to overseas listing. And all of those changes led to the arrival on the scene of new players—domestic entrepreneurs, technocrats, insider-outsiders, and financially independent ordinary citizens—all of whom were armed with unprecedented access to information, and all of whom had to be integrated into the existing political order. Many of those new players, often through the workplace, are now linked to overseas employers, overseas partners, overseas regulatory standards, and overseas ideas. All of that must be integrated politically in China. The process is clearly under way now. How long it will take and what kind of system it will ultimately lead to are questions that only the future can answer.

In Taiwan, we know how things ended up. The transformation, tightly linked with the island's commercial integration with the world, took decades. China is obviously starting from a much poorer position economically and faces a variety of unique complicating factors that

ig the change process. At the same time, China is also inte-
lly under historically unprecedented technological con-
ruably increase the pace with which change now takes
ed in chapter 4, factors like digitization and its impact
ion management have broadened the range of production
ues now possible in places like China. Digitization has also deepened the connections between those activities and activities going on
in other global locales. Truly global production chains have been made
possible but with them have come increasingly complex and demanding
managerial tasks. The managerial challenge, then, provides key openings for foreign firms and foreign-educated individuals to play absolutely critical, formative roles in China's ongoing transformation. In
areas like advanced R&D, overseas actors and the forces of globalization they represent now substantially shape the evolution and deployment of human talent within China. At the same time, because some
of the world's most sophisticated production activities now take place
in China, and take place in coordinated fashion with activities overseas,
the need for seamless information flow across China's borders grows by
the day. Things like the Internet may still seem politically threatening,
and the government may still engage in ham-handed efforts to exert
control. Yet, given the developmental path China is currently on, the
Internet and the information flows surrounding it enjoy a status now
more as indispensable commercial enablers than counterrevolutionary
threats.[11] Thus, that which is threatening also happens to be that which
is central to the government's achievement of its developmental goals.
The enemy of the state has become the friend of the state.

For some Americans, this kind of image is comforting. It suggests
that the seeds of destruction have been planted at the heart of the
Chinese system. Elements of this image have a basis in reality. In previous chapters, we have discussed how institutional outsourcing has
been associated with the rise of countervailing forces that exist apart
from, and to some extent in opposition to, state authority. Similarly, we
have considered how China's global integration has given rise to new
social groups neither necessarily loyal to nor beholden to the existing
political hierarchy. And we have considered how state goals, such as the
promotion of indigenous innovation, have been twisted and reshaped
by the realities of China's position in global production. All of these
observations convey a certain reality about China today, a reality of
growing contestation, growing challenges to the existing order, and a
state that appears increasingly trapped by the rhetoric it espouses and
the promises it extends.

All of that is true. All of it is part of the reality of contemporary China. Yet, it is not the full extent of the reality. As was also discussed in previous chapters, for all the internal problems, contradictions, and challenges that China's current path of international integration presents, that path is one of China's own choosing. China today is playing our game, and in playing our game, it is inducing stress on its existing political and social order. Yet, this is not just, or even primarily, a story of an authoritarian regime unwittingly planting the seeds of its destruction. It is not even the story of a regime unwittingly pursuing economic policies that benefit outsiders more than insiders. This is not primarily about the Chinese government selling out to foreigners or relinquishing key aspects of sovereignty, though as we have pointed out, key aspects of sovereignty have yielded in interesting ways.

Rather, this is a story of China purposively pursuing a particular path of international integration and doing so as part of its core modernization mission. In China, national identity has for at least a century been fused with the quest for modernity. What is so noteworthy now is that in recent years, that quest for modernity has been fused with an image of the global order that is decidedly our own. China today, after nearly a century of upheaval, is recapturing its identity and sense of self-worth not by lashing out but instead by attaching itself to an existing global order, our order. In the process, of course, some difficult to manage things have found their way into China's door and, indeed, deep into Chinese society. Yet, those difficult to manage things—the new players, the new rules, the newly emboldened citizens—are in many ways China's own. They are part and parcel of the system China has embraced. Thus, even as foreigners push to have rules enforced and citizens push for rights, so too, strangely enough, does the government in many cases. The outsiders push, and increasingly now, the government pushes along with them. Still in some cases, as occurred in Taiwan, the government lashes out and crushes what it views as an overt challenge. Equally or more often, it embraces or attempts to co-opt the new forces that have arisen.

This happens in no small part because the government and the new social constituencies it is attempting to manage are allied in a common effort. As we saw earlier in Taiwan and now in mainland China, despite the persistence of egregious abuses of power and gross injustices, state and society become increasingly invested in a common change process. Yes, that process threatens the existing order. But the existing order itself increasingly comes to be seen, even by the ruling party-state, as an obstacle to modernity. That is, it becomes an embarrassment, an insult to the nation's identity. China today—societally, not just governmentally—is playing our game and playing it willingly. It is not just opening itself up to us as investors or economic actors. Rather, it is absorbing our notions of governance and taking them as its own. Hence, the government's program of rule of law, political accountability, and increasing popular participation become something more than cynical rhetoric. They become an aspiration, an expression of values and intentions. Certainly, in some respects, we can argue that the Chinese government, in pursuing its chosen mode of international integration, has become a prisoner of its rhetoric. More interesting, however, we can also argue that the government has become a believer of its rhetoric, an advocate.

Thinking speculatively, I have no reason to believe the Chinese Communist Party will disappear anytime soon. I have no reason to believe it will be challenged on the barricades by an organized opposition. What I do believe, however, is that like the KMT, it will rule in a manner far different twenty years hence from the way it rules today, just as the way it rules today is far different from how it operated twenty years past. In that sense, like Taiwan in the not too distant past, China today, precisely because of the way it has evolved both economically and politically, can be understood as experiencing self-obsolescing authoritarianism. The ruling organization may not, and perhaps need not, yield the throne. However, the way that throne is being employed—the manner, in effect, by which the country is being governed—is undergoing rapid change for all the reasons discussed in previous chapters. Self-obsolescing authoritarianism, as evidenced by the Taiwan case, need not be about a governmental overthrow or a collapse of order. It may, in fact, end up being about traditional players learning, accepting, and even embracing new ways of governing. That is, it may very well amount to a revolution in behavior rather than a contest between dueling claimants.

As Americans, many of us like to think of politics in terms of contestation. This is a reasonable perspective that travels across many different places, including China. Yet, in China—as in Taiwan—there is another perspective that is far less familiar to us: the politics of collective mission and communal self-realization. China's purposive effort to play our game fits into that category of communal self-realization. So too, increasingly these days, does the goal of moving beyond authoritarianism. Conveniently for the CCP, as the examples of the KMT on Taiwan and, until just recently, the nearly fifty years of unbroken single-party rule in Japan demonstrate, the end of authoritarianism need not mean the end of the party. Nor must it mean the end of single-party rule. However, that rule must be founded on new principles of legitimacy and exercised through new modes of behavior, all goals that the CCP now embraces as part of its modernization mission. Authoritarianism today in China is obsolescing. Only time will tell whether the ruling party, as it did on Taiwan, will permit the gerund to become a final, definitive adjective. Only time will tell, that is, whether the process will be permitted to reach its natural, peaceful denouement.

Those are issues for the future. In terms of the present, however, we as Americans and citizens of the West more broadly face choices. With respect to China now, we face a situation that we could have only dreamed about thirty years ago. China societally, as discussed throughout these chapters, has chosen to develop by tying itself to us and trying to become like us. While neither blindly imitative nor insensitive to its own sovereignty, China has in remarkable ways exposed itself—indeed, tied itself—to a variety of external influences, particularly ones emanating from our own system. The country has in essence linked its domestic transformation process—its destiny—to a global system that we designed and that we dominate. In the process, China has increasingly absorbed—and even embraced as its own—values, practices, and aspirations that have in their origins our own.

It would be both arrogant and foolish to believe that somehow the West has arrived, and China is still in a state of becoming. No nation, economy, or political system is entirely static. None has reached the "end of history."[12] All are continually evolving. Yet, unlike most of the West, China is purposively changing, purposively seeking to become something else. More precisely, it is purposively seeking to converge toward us—our way of conducting business, our way of managing an economy, or way of innovating, and even our way of governing. Our present reality is for many Chinese, including many deep within the party-state establishment, their hope for the future.

That is remarkable on two fronts. First, it has led to a situation in which China is pursuing its modernization mission in ways that complement the Western world's greatest societal strengths. As discussed previously, many of the production activities going on in China now foster unprecedented degrees of specialization in American and other overseas firms. America's greatest strength resides not in its military or, as so glaringly demonstrated by its recent financial troubles, its banks. Rather, the nation's greatest strength lies in its innovative capacity, its ability to produce new technologies, new products, and new ways of doing things. Many of the forces that have delivered manufacturing activities to China have at the same time opened up wide-ranging opportunities for innovation in the United States. They have essentially played to our strengths. This is not necessarily about who is winning and who is losing. It is about multiple nations, including the United States and China, together climbing the ladder of economic growth, together benefiting immensely from globalization, and together fostering one another's continued modernization.

There is something else remarkable about China's chosen path toward convergence. The United State today has real conflicts—over scarce resources, the environment, trade practices, appropriate defense posture, and a variety of other areas.—with numerous countries, Japan and the nations of Western Europe among them. Some of those conflicts are intense, neither easily ignored nor clearly resolvable. However, for a number of nations—again, Japan and the nations of Western Europe most particularly—we do not seriously envision any of these conflicts ever escalating to war. Japan, for example, is today the world's third largest consumer of oil, behind only the United States and China. We frequently disagree with the diplomatic approaches Japan takes to ensure its energy security. We also in some sense compete with Japan over the same scarce global resources. We do not, however, seriously envision fighting Japan for the last drop of oil or facing down Japan's Navy in a contest over global sea lines of communication. It is simply unthinkable. We do not contemplate such fights presumably because with Japan, we share certain values, certain investments in a common system, and a certain shared common fate as partners in the existing global order.

In many areas, we have comparable, if not more serious, disputes with China. The differences again range across trade, the environment, defense modernization, competition for scarce resources, and a number of other areas. With respect to China, though, we have in recent times in some domains (i.e., energy competition, military expansion, etc.) been inclined to view these disputes as precursors to armed conflict. That is, some in the United States have been inclined to think, at least conceptually, in terms of a fight with China over something like dwindling oil supplies. In short, we have been inclined to think of China as an adversary not on an issue-by-issue basis but existentially.

One of the points of this book is that precisely because of the development path China is now pursuing, its time as an existential adversary has drawn to a close. The conflicts, on an issue-by-issue basis, have not disappeared, and they will not likely disappear in the near future. In some areas—trade and financial relations, for example—they will probably intensify. Yet, although the issues of dispute persist, the conditions under which they are conducted have changed radically. Because of the developmental choices China has made and the kind of influence we exert as a result, we now enjoy a position with respect to China that we could have only dreamed of decades ago. China, by linking its national destiny to the existing global order and by defining so many of its aspirations in terms similar to our own, is now neither necessarily an ally nor a friend. What it is, however, whether or not we choose to describe it as such, is a partner, an entity that shares with us an increasingly common set of values, practices, and outlooks. Most transparently, it shares with us an interest in sustaining the global system it has joined.

At least eight successive U.S. presidential administrations, from Nixon to Obama, have sought to integrate China into the global economy and make it a stakeholder in the existing international order. In choosing to play our game, China has effectively accepted that role and done so mostly on our terms. That is an extraordinary outcome that bodes well for the many differences and disputes that separate our nations. It is particularly important now, given that in certain pressing areas of global concern—climate change paramount among them—no solution is possible without the cooperation of both the United States and China.

For Americans, the challenge now is to recognize the opportunities that China's particular style of global integration represents. Of course, Americans today, particularly as we climb out of a financial crisis, face urgent economic problems. Frankly, even in the best of times over the past decade, middle-class Americans have not had it easy. Wages have failed to keep up with economic growth. Income disparities have deepened. Employment, in ways, ironically, not so different from what has occurred in China, has become euphemistically flexible: uncertain, temporary, and often devoid of benefits. Health-care costs have skyrocketed. And in many cases, jobs in manufacturing and traditional industry have disappeared, most recently with the demise of the U.S. auto industry. All of these things have happened, and many Americans have suffered as a result.

It would be a great mistake, however, to look abroad for sources of blame. The United States today accounts for almost 25 percent of total global economic output. China, despite all its growth in recent years, accounts for 6 percent. China is not the source of America's economic problems. As the dominant force in the global economy,

America to a greater extent than any other country is the determinant of its own fate. Many of the problems we face today are of our own making—ones related to political choices we have made, personal consumption patterns we have engaged in, regulatory lapses we have tolerated, and ideological blinders we have willingly borne. None of these problems, however, is insurmountable. And none can seriously threaten the single asset that we as a nation possess in unsurpassed quantity: our capacity for innovation and entrepreneurship. It is neither intellectually sound nor pragmatically useful to point the finger of blame abroad, whether at China or anybody else. The seeds for our renewal reside within.

What we can do, however, is craft a situation in which, through our own renewal, we foster positive change in others and growing stability across the global system. That China today, the fastest growing economy in the world, is playing our game marks an incredible opportunity for everybody. China today is doing what we in the United States and the advanced industrial West more broadly have for decades hoped it would do. It has invested itself in our global system, our game basically. Consequently, now more than ever, we must move boldly and responsibly to renew rather than abandon our own investment in that game. We need not, and in fact should not, embrace the Chinese government and all that it does. We must, however, embrace the change process in which China is engaged. It is in our interest. It is in China's interest. And it is in the world's interest.

Notes

Chapter 1

1. See Andrew G. Walder, *Communist Neo-Traditionalism: Work and Authority in Chinese Industry* (Berkeley: University of California Press, 1988); Mark W. Frazier, *The Making of the Chinese Industrial Workplace: State, Revolution, and Labor Management* (New York: Cambridge University Press, 2002); Hsiao-Po Lu, Elizabeth J. Perry, and Xiaobo Lu, eds., *Danwei: The Changing Chinese Workplace in Historical and Comparative Perspectives* (Armonk, N.Y.: M. E. Sharpe, 1997).

2. For a discussion of the institutional logic of command planning, see Justin Yifu Lin, Fang Cai, and Zhou Li, *The China Miracle: Development Strategy and Economic Reform* (Hong Kong: Chinese University Press, 2003).

3. Data in this paragraph are drawn from National Bureau of Statistics of the People's Republic of China, *China Statistical Yearbook* (Beijing: China Statistics Press, various years). Data acquired online through *All China Data Center,* http://chinadataonline.org/.

4. On allocation of health-care provision, see China Development Research Foundation, *Zhongguo renlei fazhan baogao 2005 [China Human Development Report 2005]*, United Nations Development Programme, 2005.

5. See, for example, David B. Audretsch, Max C. Keilbach, and Erik E. Lehmann, *Entrepreneurship and Economic Growth* (New York: Oxford University Press, 2006).

6. These figures for 2008 are based on *World Bank* calculations employing both Atlas and Purchasing Power Parity methodology. See World Bank, "World Development Indicators" database, revised October 7, 2009.

7. For an interesting discussion of the U.S. case, see Michael J. Piore and Sean Safford, "Changing Regimes of Workplace Governance, Shifting Axes of Social Mobilization and the Challenge to Industrial Relations Theory," *Industrial Relations*, 45, no. 3 (2006), pp. 299–325.

8. From 1996 to 2003, the number of state-owned firms in China shrank from 114,000 to 34,000, and in the process, approximately 40-million state-sector jobs disappeared. Ross Garnault, Ligang Song, Stoyan Tenev, and Yang Yao, *China's Ownership Transformation* (Washington, D.C.: World Bank, 2005), p. xi. For a detailed discussion on Chinese unemployment data, see John Giles, Albert Park, and Fang Cai, *How Has Economic Restructuring Affected China's Urban Workers?* William Davidson Institute Working Paper 628, October 2003.

9. In 1995, 98 million Chinese were employed in manufacturing. By 2002, the number was down to 83 million, even as the size of the working-age population ballooned. National Bureau of Statistics, *China Statistical Yearbook 2008*; and *All China Data Center*, "China Data Online."

10. National Bureau of Statistics, *China Statistical Yearbook 2008*; and *All China Data Center*, "China Data Online."

11. *The People's Daily*, "China's Floating Population Tops 140 Million," July 27, 2005.

12. See David Blumenthal and William Hsiao, "Privatization and Its Discontents: The Evolving Chinese Health Care System," *The New England Journal of Medicine*, 353, no. 11 (September 15, 2005), pp. 1165–1170.

13. See, for example, Hu Jintao, *Hold High the Great Banner of Socialism with Chinese Characteristics and Strive for New Victories in Building a Moderately Prosperous Society in All Respects*, Report to the Seventeenth National Congress of the Communist Party of China, October 15, 2007.

14. Mary E. Gallagher, "'Use the Law as Your Weapon!' Institutional Change and Legal Mobilization in China," in Neil Diamant, Stanley Lubman, and Kevin O'Brien, eds., *Engaging Chinese Law* (Stanford, Cal.: Stanford University Press, 2005).

15. For a deeper discussion of the phenomenon, see: Kevin O'Brien and Liangjiang Li, *Rightful Resistance in Rural China* (Cambridge: Cambridge University Press, 2006); Andrew C. Mertha, *China's Water Warriors: Citizen Action and Policy Change* (Ithaca, N.Y.: Cornell University Press, 2008); Ian Johnson, *Wild Grass: Three Portraits of Change in Modern China* (New York: Vintage, 2005).

16. Lily L. Tsai, *Accountability Without Democracy* (New York: Cambridge University Press, 2007).

17. For the report that has gained the most attention, published in book form, see Tianyong Zhou, Wang Changjiang, and Wang Anling, *Gongjian: Shiqida hou Zhongguo zhengzhi tizhi gaige yanjiu baogao [Storming the Fortress: Research Report on China's Political System Reform after the Seventeenth Party Congress]* (Urumqi: Xinjiang shengchan jianshe chubanshe, 2007).

18. I have observed this over the past two years in China. Brad Setser of the Council on Foreign Relations has also noted this in his online blog *Follow the Money*. See Brad Setser, "Does the China Investment Corporation Have a Coherent Investment Strategy?" *Follow the Money* (online blog), Council on Foreign Relations, December 30, 2007.

19. Michael Wines, Keith Bradsher, and Mark Landler, "China's Leader Says He Is 'Worried' over U.S. Treasuries," *The New York Times*, March 13, 2009.

20. The economists Wu Jinglian and Qian Yingyi have also characterized this period as marking a fundamental break from the past. See Yingyi Qian and Jinglian Wu, *China's Transition to a Market Economy: How Far Across the River?* Paper prepared for the Conference on Policy Reform in China, Center for Research on Economic Development and Policy Reform, Stanford University, 1999, revised May 2000. Qian and Wu date the start of the turning point at November 1993 Third Plenum of the Chinese Communist Party's Fourteenth Congress.

21. For a more trade-oriented view of globalization, see Martin Wolf, *Why Globalization Works* (New Haven, Conn.: Yale University Press, 2005); Jagdish Bhagwati, *In Defense of Globalization* (New York: Oxford University Press, 2007).

22. For comparable perspectives, see Suzanne Berger, *How We Compete* (New York: Doubleday, 2005); Gary Gereffi and Miguel Korzeniewicz, eds., *Commodity Chains and Global Capitalism* (Westport, Conn.: Praeger, 1993); Timothy J. Sturgeon, "Modular Production Networks," *Industrial and Corporate Change*, 11, no. 3 (2002), pp. 451–496; Peter Nolan, Jin Zhang, and Chunhang Liu, "The Global Business Revolution, the Cascade Effect, and the Challenge for Firms," *Cambridge Journal of Economics*, 32 (August 2007), pp. 29–47.

23. The "flat" world image is taken from Thomas Friedman's elegant writings about globalization. See Thomas L. Friedman, *The World Is Flat* (New York: Farrar, Straus and Giroux, 2005).

Chapter 2

1. Other scholars have also noted the impact that both external and internal crises in the late 1980s and early 1990s have had on Chinese reform. For example, see Dali Yang, *Remaking the Chinese Leviathan: Market Transition and the Politics of Governance in China* (Stanford, Calif.: Stanford University Press, 2004).

2. Thomas L. Friedman, *The World Is Flat* (New York: Farrar, Straus and Giroux, 2005).

3. Peter Nolan, Jin Zhang, and Chunhang Liu, "The Global Business Revolution, the Cascade Effect, and the Challenge for Firms," *Cambridge Journal of Economics*, 32 (August 2007), pp. 29–47; Timothy J. Sturgeon, *What Really Goes on in Silicon Valley? Spatial Clustering and Dispersal in Modular Production*, MIT Industrial Performance Center Working Paper 03–001, April 2003.

4. This idea of a natural sequence running from proper institutional establishment to increased trade and then finally to growth is presented in sophisticated form in Jeffrey D. Sachs and Andrew M. Warner, *Economic Convergence and Economic Policies*, NBER Working Paper 5039, February 1995. See also John Williamson, "What Washington Means by Policy Reform," in John Williamson, ed., *Latin American Adjustment: How Much Has Happened?* (Washington, D.C.: Institute for International Economics, 1990).

5. This form is comparable to what in Japan's case is referred to as *gaiatsu*, a term translated literally as "foreign pressure" but often taken to mean foreign pressure purposely used by domestic leaders to justify their own reform efforts. See Michael

L. Beeman, *Public Policy and Economic Competition in Japan* (London: Routledge, 2002), especially chapter 8, "Gaiatsu as a Source of Policy Change."

6. For a wonderful description of global supply chains in the apparel industry—one written well before the term *globalization* entered common parlance—see James Lardner, "Annals of Business: The Sweater Trade," *The New Yorker*, January 18, 1988.

7. It should be noted that to the extent jobs have moved to China, they have generally done so from Southeast Asia. Those jobs generally left the United States decades ago. See Guillaume Gaulier, Francoise Lemoine, and Deniz Unal-Kesenci, *China's Integration in East Asia: Production Sharing, FDI and High-Tech Trade*, CEPPI Working Paper 2005–2009, Paris, 2005.

8. For a description of socialism's double airlock system, see Barry Naughton, *The Chinese Economy* (Cambridge, Mass.: MIT Press, 2007), pp. 380–381.

9. Nicholas R. Lardy, *Integrating China into the Global Economy* (Washington, D.C.: Brookings Institution Press, 2002), p. 22.

10. For a more detailed discussion of this aspect, see Edward S. Steinfeld, "The Capitalist Embrace: China Ten Years After the Asian Financial Crisis," in Andrew MacIntyre, T. J. Pempel, and John Ravenhill, eds., *Crisis as Catalyst: Asia's Dynamic Political Economy* (Ithaca, N.Y.: Cornell University Press, 2008), pp. 183–205.

11. Naughton, 2007, p. 380; Gang Yi, "Renminbi Exchange Rates and Relevant Institutional Factors," *The Cato Journal*, March 22, 2008.

12. Yi, 2008.

13. For example, Yi Gang, the current vice governor of China's central bank (The People's Bank of China) and the head of the State Administration of Foreign Exchange (SAFE), is a U.S.-trained economist who prior to returning to China, was a tenured faculty member at Indiana University. As an academic, he authored the book *Money, Banking, and Financial Markets in China* (Boulder, Colo.: Westview, 1994). Examples of similar individuals are now too numerous to mention.

14. One could argue that a rough parallel would be the situation in the 1950s when many Chinese were sent to the Soviet Union for training and then returned to build command planning in China. In the 1990s and 2000s, however, the individuals who were returning had initially gone abroad at the objection of the powers that be. The objection stemmed from the fact that places like the United States were viewed as an ideological threat. Now, what had been an ideological threat became an institutional necessity, and individuals who had previously been held off at arm's length became crucial to lure back.

15. Stephen Green, *The Privatisation Two Step at China's Listed Firms*, China Project Working Paper 3, Chatham House, 2004.

16. Edward S. Steinfeld, *Forging Reform in China* (New York: Cambridge University Press, 1998).

17. For example, in December 2009, the Chinese courts sentenced outspoken human rights activist Liu Xiaobo to an eleven-year prison term. His crime—"inciting subversion of state power"—stemmed from his circulation of the "Charter 08" petition calling for greater freedom of expression and democracy in China.

18. For an alternative argument that the party has effectively co-opted these groups, see Kellee S. Tsai, *Capitalism Without Democracy* (Ithaca, N.Y.: Cornell University Press, 2007).

19. For more detail in several of these areas, see Elizabeth C. Economy, *The River Runs Black* (New York: Council on Foreign Relations, 2005); Yan Sun, *Corruption and Market in Contemporary China* (Ithaca, N.Y.: Cornell University Press, 2004); William Hurst, *The Chinese Worker After Socialism* (New York: Cambridge University Press, 2009).

20. Kevin O'Brien and Liangjiang Li, *Rightful Resistance in Rural China* (Cambridge: Cambridge University Press, 2006); Andrew C. Mertha, *China's Water Warriors: Citizen Action and Policy Change* (Ithaca, N.Y.: Cornell University Press, 2008).

21. To put it more accurately, they were liberal relative to the standards that existed at the start of China's reform era. In those days, to be liberal effectively meant to be supportive of market reform. To be conservative was to be opposed to reform. By the 1990s and 2000s, the spectrum had shifted such that everybody was for market reform, for markets were the accepted reality. Divisions along the political spectrum, then, would play out along questions of how different aspects of reform should be prioritized and how aggressively the state should exert its regulatory powers.

22. David Shambaugh, in his excellent book *China's Communist Party: Atrophy and Adaptation* (Berkeley: University of California Press, 2009), makes a comparable argument that the party has engaged in dynamic adaptation, but he is somewhat more circumspect in terms of the degree to which this constitutes either the adoption of liberal political principles or the chipping away of authoritarian rule.

23. The phrase also frequently appears as "linking up with the international track" (*yu guoji jiegui*). For an extensive analysis of the use of this phrase, see Hongying Wang, "'Linking Up with the International Track': What's in a Slogan," *The China Quarterly*, 189 (March 2007), pp. 1–23.

24. See Jintao Hu, *Gaoju Zhongguo tese shehui zhuyi weida qizhi, wei duoqu quanmian jianshe xiaokang shehui xin shengli er fendou [Hold High the Great Banner of Socialism with Chinese Characteristics and Strive for New Victories in Building a Moderately Prosperous Society in all Respects]*, Report to the Seventeenth National Congress of the Communist Party of China, October 15, 2007.

25. For this perspective in general, see Alice Amsden, *The Rise of 'the Rest'* (New York: Oxford University Press, 2001); Alice Amsden, *Asia's Next Giant* (New York: Oxford University Press, 1989); Robert Wade, *Governing the Market* (Princeton, N.J.: Princeton University Press, 1990).

26. For example, see Peter H. Nolan, *China's Rise, Russia's Fall: Politics, Economics and Planning in the Transition from Stalinism* (London: Palgrave Macmillan, 1995); Jean C. Oi, *Rural China Takes Off: Institutional Foundations of Economic Reform* (Berkeley: University of California Press, 1999).

27. This view within China is termed the "neoauthoritarian" perspective (*xin quanwei zhuyi*). See Liu Jun and Li Lin, eds, *Xin quanwei zhuyi: dui gaige lilun gangling de lunzheng [Neoauthoritarianism: A Debate on the Theories of China's Reform]* (Beijing: Jingji Xueyuan Chubanshe, 1989). Singapore's Lee Kuan Yew has

frequently been associated with this view. See "Political, Economic Reforms 'Need Not Go Hand in Hand'; Citing Tiananmen Incident, Minister Lee Points out That China Wouldn't Be Better off Today if Students Had Toppled Govt.," *The Straits Times* (Singapore), August 17, 2004. For an excellent overall analysis of the intellectual cross-currents in China, see Joseph Fewsmith, *China Since Tiananmen: The Politics of Transition*, second edition (New York: Cambridge University Press, 2008).

28. Aristotle, *The Politics*, Carnes Lord, trans. (Chicago: University of Chicago Press, 1984), book III, chapters 7–8, pp. 95–97. Alexander Hamilton, James Madison, and John Jay, *The Federalist Papers*, Penguin Classics edition (New York: Penguin, 1987). In the *Federalist*'s case, needless to say, the solution to tyranny of the majority was not authoritarianism but rather representative government and checks and balances.

29. Ted C. Fishman, *China, Inc.: How the Rise of the Next Superpower Challenges America and the World* (New York: Scribner, 2006).

30. John J. Mearsheimer, *The Tragedy of Great Power Politics* (New York: W. W. Norton, 2003); U.S.–China Economic and Security Review Commission, *2008 Report to Congress* (Washington, D.C.: U.S. Government Printing Office, 2008).

31. The mercantilist interpretation is hinted at in recent claims that excessive Chinese savings lie behind America's domestic credit problems. See Ben S. Bernanke, *The Global Saving Glut and the U.S. Current Account Deficit*. Speech delivered for the Sandridge Lecture at the Virginia Association of Economists, Richmond, March 10, 2005. In terms of the connection between China's national security establishment and technological innovation, see Evan Feigenbaum, *China's Techno-Warriors: National Security and Strategic Competition from the Nuclear Age to the Information Age* (Stanford, Cal.: Stanford University Press, 2003).

32. See Yasheng Huang, *Selling China: Foreign Direct Investment During the Reform Era* (New York: Cambridge University Press, 2003); Yasheng Huang, *Capitalism with Chinese Characteristics: Entrepreneurship and the State* (New York: Cambridge University Press, 2008); Wing Thye Woo, "The Real Reasons for China's Growth," *The China Journal*, no. 41 (January 1999), pp. 115–137.

33. The argument is derived from Samuel P. Huntington's *Political Order in Changing Societies* (New Haven, Conn.: Yale University Press, 1968). Huntington's point is not necessarily that democratization must occur but that political order must be maintained whether through coercion or inclusion. In the Chinese context, the argument is made most eloquently by Minxin Pei in his *China's Trapped Transition: The Limits of Developmental Autocracy* (Cambridge, Mass.: Harvard University Press, 2008).

34. Nolan, Zhang, and Liu, 2008, p. 43.

35. The idea here is that a variety of formal institutional constructs are possible and indeed are observable across different successful countries. At the same time, in practice, the institutions—the rules by which the economy operates, whether they are formal or not—must ultimately be compatible with the operation of global markets. That is, institutions can take many forms across nations, but to

the extent these nations participate deeply in global production, their institutions functionally must harmonize with those of global leaders. This view bears similarities to the institutional arguments of Dani Rodrik in his *One Economics, Many Recipes: Globalization, Institutions, and Economic Growth* (Princeton, N.J.: Princeton University Press, 2008).

36. Though by no means necessarily applauding these changes, Marc Blecher documents the degree to which this rhetoric has been internalized by everyday workers in China, even those who have been most hurt by this modernization process. See Marc J. Blecher, "Hegemony and Workers' Politics in China," *The China Quarterly*, no. 170 (June 2002), pp. 283–303.

37. In some respects, this view of the party corresponds to that of several authors who have written about adaptive authoritarianism. For excellent works employing this perspective, see Shambaugh, 2009; Arthur Kroeber, "Rising China and the Liberal West," *China Economic Quarterly* (March 2008), pp. 29–44; Andrew J. Nathan, "Beijing's Authoritarian Acrobatics," *The Wall Street Journal*, June 4, 2009. These works tend to emphasize the adaptive resilience of the party. The institutional outsourcing perspective, however, emphasizes that global production creates forces of change that not only swamp the party but also change its internal composition. Hence, it may be adaptive, but it is adapting in ways that are leading to its obsolescence.

38. Benjamin I. Schwartz, *In Search of Wealth and Power: Yen Fu and the West* (Cambridge, Mass.: Harvard University Press, 1990), p. 20.

39. Schwartz, 1990, p. 19.

40. I am grateful to Professor Anthony Saich of Harvard University's Kennedy School of Government for this phraseology.

Chapter 3

1. This concept of national self-definition through a quest for modernity is best articulated by Jonathan Spence in *The Search for Modern China* (New York: W. W. Norton, 1999).

2. Much has been written about the 1989 movement by observers and participants alike. One of the most insightful works is Craig Calhoun's *Neither Gods nor Emperors* (Berkeley: University of California Press, 1997).

3. Interview, Nanjing, China, August 1991.

4. Yingyi Qian and Jinglian Wu, *China's Transition to a Market Economy: How Far Across the River*. Paper prepared for the Conference on Policy Reform in China, Center for Research on Economic Development and Policy Reform, Stanford University, 1999, revised May 2000, p. 13.

5. Interview, Cambridge, Mass., May 1999.

6. Francis Fukuyama, *The End of History and the Last Man* (New York: Penguin, 1992).

7. John Williamson, "What Washington Means by Policy Reform," in John Williamson, ed., *Latin American Adjustment: How Much Has Happened?* (Washington, D.C.: Institute for International Economics, 1990).

8. Benjamin I. Schwartz, *In Search of Wealth and Power: Yen Fu and the West* (Cambridge, Mass.: Harvard University Press, 1990), p. 238.

9. Schwartz uses the term "Promethean explosion of might" to explain how the West broadly appeared to Chinese intellectuals at the end of the nineteenth century. See Schwartz, 1990, p. 151.

10. See Edward S. Steinfeld, *Forging Reform in China* (New York: Cambridge University Press, 1998); Nicholas R. Lardy, *China's Unfinished Economic Revolution* (Washington, D.C.: Brookings, 1998).

11. On this issue, see Dali Yang, *Remaking the Chinese Leviathan: Market Transition and the Politics of Governance in China* (Stanford, Cal.: Stanford University Press, 2004).

12. Jiang Zemin, *Jiakuai gaige kaifang he xiandaihua jianshe bufa duoqu you Zhongguo tese shehuizhuyi shiye de geng da shengli* [Speed up the pace of reform, the open door, and modernization construction in order to strive for even greater victories for the cause of Socialism with Chinese characteristics], Report to the Fourteenth Party Congress, October 12, 1992; Qian and Wu, 2000, p. 8.

13. Politburo of the Communist Party of China, *Guanyu jianli shehuizhuyi shichang jingji tizhi ruogan wenti de jueding* [Decision on various questions regarding the establishment of a socialist market economic structure], November 11, 1993; Qian and Wu, 2000, p. 10.

14. Ross Garnault, Ligang Song, Stoyan Tenev, and Yang Yao, *China's Ownership Transformation* (Washington, D.C.: World Bank, 2005), p. xi.

15. Qian and Wu, 2000, p. 11.

16. In 1985, formally state-owned industry (*quanmin suoyouzhi qiye*) accounted for 65 percent of China's industrial output value. At the end of the 1980s, the number still hovered at approximately 60 percent. By 1999, that number was down to 28 percent. By 2007, though ownership in China had become more diverse and the definition of what exactly constituted a state firm more difficult to pin down, the figure had declined to roughly 13 percent (and that number includes not just formal SOEs but also majority state-owned publicly listed firms and majority state-owned joint ventures). Data from China Statistical Yearbook, various years, through All China Data Center, *China Data Online*.

17. Moving forward in time, one could still see evidence of the complex mixture of attitudes. In surveys conducted for the *2008 Pew Global Attitudes Project*, 86 percent of Chinese respondents reported satisfaction with their country's general direction, the highest level among twenty-four nations polled that year. At the same time, though, contentment with family life, incomes, and jobs was far lower, hovering at some of the lowest levels found for any of the nations surveyed. See Pew Global Attitudes Project, *The 2008 Pew Global Attitudes Survey in China*, Pew Research Center, 2008, pp. 1–2, www.pewglobal.org.

18. On the enterprise reform side, see, for example, Jinglian Wu, *Xiandai gongsi yu qiye gaige [The Modern Company and Enterprise Reform]* (Tianjin, China: Tianjin People's Publishing House, 1994).

19. Marc J. Blecher, "Hegemony and Workers' Politics in China," *The China Quarterly*, 170 (June 2002), pp. 283–303.

20. For an excellent analysis of the phenomenon, see Kevin O'Brien and Liangjiang Li, *Rightful Resistance in Rural China* (Cambridge: Cambridge University Press, 2006).

21. Gang Fan, "Haiyao doushao nian cai neng dida he dui an?" [How Many Years Are Needed to Arrive at the River's Other Side?], *Nanfang Zhoumo* [*Southern Weekend*] (August 27, 2008).

22. Qian and Wu, 2000, p. 13.

23. This discussion draws largely from Schwartz, 1990, pp. 10–16.

24. Schwartz, 1990, p. 72.

25. Schwartz, 1990, p. 72.

26. Schwartz, 1990, p. 54.

27. Mao Zedong was, of course, a socialist. Yet, his deepening fears in the late 1950s that China's socialist revolution was grinding to a halt, and fears in particular that the ruling party was becoming a bastion of stasis and caution (and thus, counterrevolution), led him to incite popular campaigns against the very core of the party-state. The Cultural Revolution (1966–1976) marked the height of these campaigns. For Mao and his most radical followers, such campaigns undoubtedly represented efforts to save socialism. As many Chinese, including those who participated in these movements, would come to understand, the Maoist campaigns, beyond wreaking social havoc across the nation, nearly obliterated the legitimacy of the socialist party-state.

28. Ah Q is the main character in the what is arguably the most famous story in modern Chinese literature, "The True Story Ah Q" (*Ah Q Zheng Zhuan*). Penned by arguably the most famous writer in modern Chinese history, Lu Xun (1881–1936), the story lays out a bitingly sarcastic and cynical depiction of Chinese society. The character Ah Q himself is held out as the prototypical common man, the equivalent of Joe Six-pack for Americans. Foolish, craven, vain, and intractably stubborn, Ah Q has virtually no redeeming qualities. He is the embodiment of spiritual sickness, the essence of what many early twentieth-century Chinese intellectuals believed to be the heart of China's national problem. Even today, Chinese citizens will occasionally criticize one another for displaying an "Ah Q mentality" (*Ah Q sixiang*). See Lu Xun, "Preface" and "The True Story of Ah Q," in *Selected Stories of Lu Hsun* (Beijing: Foreign Languages Press, 1978), pp. 1–6, 65–112.

Chapter 4

1. For a wonderful account of the reform experience in China's South, see Ezra F. Vogel, *One Step Ahead in China: Guangdong Under Reform* (Cambridge, Mass.: Harvard University Press, 1989).

2. National Bureau of Statistics, *China Statistical Yearbook 2008* (Beijing: China Statistics Press, 2008); All China Data Center, *China Data Online*.

3. Mary Amiti and Caroline Freund, *An Anatomy of China's Export Growth*, Policy Research Working Paper 4628, World Bank, January 2008, p. 2.

4. United States Trade Representative (USTR), *U.S.–China Trade Facts*, June 5, 2009 update, http://www.ustr.gov/countries-regions/china.

5. The International Monetary Fund defines FDI as a category of international investment in which the investor seeks a long-term relationship with, and substantial managerial influence over, an enterprise resident in another country. The IMF treats a 10 percent ownership stake as the minimum threshold for investment to be considered FDI. The Chinese government used a 25 percent ownership stake as the minimum threshold. See International Monetary Fund, *Balance of Payments Manual*, fifth edition, 1993, p. 86; Nirupam Bajpai and Nandita Dasgupta, *What Constitutes Foreign Direct Investment? Comparison of India and China*, Center on Globalization and Sustainable Development Working Paper 1, Columbia University Earth Institute, January 2004; Yasheng Huang, *Selling China: Foreign Direct Investment During the Reform Era* (New York: Cambridge University Press, 2005).

6. All China Data Center, *China Data Online*.

7. See Amiti and Freund, 2008, p. 21.

8. Dani Rodrik estimates that the sophistication of China's export bundle is that which one would expect of a country three times richer than China in per capita terms. Dani Rodrik, *What's So Special About China's Exports?* NBER Working Paper 11947, January 2006, p. 4.

9. Denis Fred Simon and Cong Cao, *China's Emerging Technological Edge* (New York: Cambridge University Press, 2009), p. 105.

10. Simon and Cao, 2009, p. 119.

11. For an excellent overview of various approaches to understanding growth, see William Easterly, *The Elusive Quest for Growth: Economists' Adventures and Misadventures in the Tropics* (Cambridge, Mass.: MIT Press, 2002).

12. Lant Pritchett, "Divergence, Big Time," *Journal of Economic Perspectives*, 11, no. 3 (Summer 1997), pp. 3–17; William Easterly and Ross Levine, "It's Not Factor Accumulation: Stylized Facts and Growth Models," *The World Bank Economic Review*, 15, no. 2 (2001), pp. 177–219.

13. Jeffrey D. Sachs and Andrew M. Warner, *Economic Convergence and Economic Policies*, NBER Working Paper 5039, February 1995.

14. Andrei Shleifer and Robert Vishny, *The Grabbing Hand: Government Pathologies and Their Cures* (Cambridge, Mass.: Harvard University Press, 1999); Robert Bates, *Markets and States in Tropical Africa* (Berkeley: University of California Press, 1981).

15. Joseph E. Stiglitz, *Wither Reform? Ten Years of Transition*. Paper prepared for World Bank Annual Conference on Development Economics, Washington, D.C., April 1999.

16. Robert D. Putnam, *Making Democracy Work: Civic Traditions in Modern Italy* (Princeton, N.J.: Princeton University Press, 1993); Gregory Clark, *A Farewell to Alms: A Brief Economic History of the World* (Princeton, N.J.: Princeton University Press, 2007).

17. Paul Krugman, *Geography and Trade* (Cambridge, Mass.: MIT Press, 1992).

18. See Alice H. Amsden, *The Rise of the Rest: Challenges to the West from Late-Industrializing Economies* (New York: Oxford University Press, 2003).

19. In fact, Japan and Germany by the late nineteenth century were already in the club of wealthy nations. South Korea and Taiwan, however, truly shifted from poor to rich in the late twentieth century.

20. Takahiro Fujimoto, *Architecture, Capability, and Competitiveness of Firms and Industries*. Paper prepared for the Saint-Gobain Centre for Economic Research Conference "Organizational Innovation Within Firms," November 2002, p. 3.

21. For an explanation along these lines, see Amsden, 2003.

22. Alfred D. Chandler and Takashi Hikino, "The Large Industrial Enterprise and the Dynamics of Modern Growth," in Alfred D. Chandler et al., eds., *Big Business and the Wealth of Nations* (New York: Cambridge University Press, 1997).

23. Fujimoto, 2002, makes this argument for automobile production.

24. Chandler and Hikino, 1997.

25. See Michael A. Cusumano, *The Japanese Automobile Industry: Technology and Management at Nissan and Toyota* (Cambridge, Mass.: Harvard Asian Monographs, 1986); Michael A. Cusumano and Kentaro Nobeoka, *Thinking Beyond Lean* (New York: Simon and Schuster, 2008).

26. For an excellent description of this process in South Korea, see Alice Amsden, *Asia's Next Giant: South Korea and Late Industrialization* (New York: Oxford University Press, 1992).

27. General Administration of Customs of the People's Republic of China, *2008.12 jinchukou qiye xingzhi zong zhi*, January 22, 2009, http://www.customs.gov.cn/publish/porta10/tab1/info156574.htm.

28. Organisation for Economic Cooperation and Development (in cooperation with the Ministry of Science and Technology, China), *OECD Reviews of Innovation Policy: China, Synthesis Report*, 2007, p. 15.

29. National Bureau of Statistics, *China Trade and External Economic Statistical Yearbook 2007* (Beijing: China Statistics Press, 2007), p. 596.

30. National Bureau of Statistics, *China Trade and External Economic Statistical Yearbook 2007* (Beijing: China Statistics Press, 2007), p. 617. See also Amiti and Freund, 2008, p. 22.

31. Greg Linden, Kenneth L. Kraemer, and Jason Dedrick, *Who Captures Value in a Global Innovation System? The Case of Apple's iPod*, Personal Computing Industry Center, University of California, Irvine, June 2007.

32. Linden, Kraemer, and Dedrick, 2007, p. 6.

33. Interviews, Cambridge, Mass., September 2006.

34. My understanding of modularity, particularly in the electronics industry, has been influenced immeasurably by two sources: the work of Suzanne Berger (see especially, *How We Compete*) and the ongoing research of Charles Sodini, Tayo Akinwande, and Douglas Fuller of the Massachusetts Institute of Technology. On modularization, see also Carliss Y. Baldwin and Kim B. Clark, *Design Rules: The Power of Modularity*. Vol. 1 (Cambridge, Mass.: MIT Press, 2000); Masa Aoki and Hirokazu Takizawa, "Modularity: Its Relevance to Industrial Architecture. Paper presented to Conference on Innovation within Firms, Saint-Gobain Centre for Economic Research, Paris, 2002.

35. An extensive discussion of this history is available through IBM's online archives. See *IBM Archives: Valuable Resources on IBM's History* 2009, http://www-03.ibm.com/ibm/history/index.html.

36. For a more detailed discussion, see Edward S. Steinfeld, "China's Shallow Integration: Networked Production and the New Challenges for Late Industrialization," *World Development*, 32, no. 11), 2004: pp. 1971–1987. The survey, funded by and done in conjunction with the World Bank, involved 1,500 "higher tech" firms drawn from the following cities: Beijing, Shanghai, Chengdu, Guangzhou, and Tianjin. There were 995 manufacturing firms in the sample.

37. United States Trade Representative (USTR), *U.S.–China Trade Facts*, June 5, 2009 update, http://www.ustr.gov/countries-regions/china.

38. See U.S.–China Business Council, *US Exports to China by State 2000–2007*, Research Report, 2008, http://www.uschina.org/public/exports/state_exports_2007.html.

39. Federal Foreign Office, Germany, *China*, online report, April 2009, http://www.auswaertiges-amt.de/diplo/en/Laenderinformationen/01-Laender/China.html#t4.

40. See Yasheng Huang, *Selling China: Foreign Direct Investment During the Reform Era* (New York: Cambridge University Press, 2005).

41. See Hao Zhang, "Wo'erma Zhongguo fouren zai Hua caigou suojian si cheng" ["Wal-Mart China Denies Forty Percent Contraction in China Sourcing"], *Caijing* August 7, 2007; James T. Areddy, "China's Export Machine Threatened by Rising Costs," *The Wall Street Journal*, June 30, 2008; Gordon Fairclough, "Wal-Mart Sneezes, China Catches Cold," *The Wall Street Journal*, May 29, 2007.

42. The US$18 billion figure comes from Fairclough, 2007, and is repeated by Zhang, 2007.

43. Fairclough, 2007.

44. "Global Supermarket Makes It in China," *Renmin Huabao*, November 2007.

45. Zhang, 2007.

46. Anecdotal evidence suggests that some commodity supplies when caught in this bind cut costs by cutting labor, safety, or environmental standards. For example, see Jane Spencer and Juliet Ye, "Toxic Factories Take Toll on China's Labor Force," *The Wall Street Journal*, January 15, 2008.

47. Presentation by Stan Shih to visiting MIT researchers, Taipei, Taiwan, January 1998. The smile curve has now been replicated in a variety of publications and venues. Wikipedia's version is a typical example, http://en.wikipedia.org/wiki/Smiling_Curve.

48. For interesting perspectives on the maturation of Taiwanese high tech producers, see Douglas B. Fuller, "Globalization for Nation-Building: Taiwan's Industrial and Technology Policies for the High-Technology Sectors," *Journal of Interdisciplinary Economics*, vol. 18, no. 2/3, 2007, pp. 203–224; Douglas B. Fuller, "The Cross-Strait Economic Relationship's Impact on Development in Taiwan and China," *Asian Survey*, 48, no. 2 (2008), pp. 239–264.

49. Interview, Foxconn senior managers, Cambridge, Mass., February 2009.

50. Data from company Web site, www.asus.com.

51. Timothy J. Sturgeon, *What Really Goes on in Silicon Valley? Spatial Clustering and Dispersal in Modular Production*, MIT Industrial Performance Center Working Paper 03–001, April 2003.

52. This pattern of each point in the deverticalized supply chain becoming dominated by just a handful of highly scaled-up firms applies not just to electronics. It can be observed in a variety of industries, including aerospace, automotives, and food and beverages. For a detailed discussion of this, see Peter H. Nolan, Jin Zhang, and Chunhang Liu, "The Global Business Revolution, the Cascade Effect, and the Challenge for Firms," *Cambridge Journal of Economics*, 32 (August 2007), pp. 29–47.

53. AnnaLee Saxenian, *The New Argonauts: Regional Advantage in a Global Economy* (Cambridge, Mass.: Harvard University Press, 2007).

54. For an excellent discussion of this product's evolution, see Clive Thompson, "The Netbook Effect: How Cheap Little Laptops Hit the Big Time," *Wired Magazine*, Issue 17.03 (February 23, 2009).

55. Thompson, 2009.

56. Thompson, 2009.

57. I thank Doug Steinfeld of AG Mednet for guiding me through these issues.

58. Data from the IT industry market intelligence firm Interactive Data Corporation (IDC). See *PC Market Growth Evaporates in Fourth Quarter as Financial Crisis Hits Home*, IDC press release, January 14, 2009, http://www.idc.com/getdoc.jsp?containerId=prUS21627609.

59. This point is made by Ge Dongsheng and Takahiro Fujimoto in "The Architectural Attributes of Components and the Transaction Patterns of Detail Design Drawings: A Case Study of China's Motorcycle Industry," *International Journal of Automotive Technology and Management*, 5, no. 1 (2005), pp. 46–70.

60. For more detailed discussion, see Edward S. Steinfeld, "Chinese Enterprise Development and the Challenge of Global Integration," background paper for World Bank Study, *Innovative East Asia*, November 2002. Also available in somewhat abbreviated form in Edward S. Steinfeld, "Chinese Enterprise Development and the Challenge of Global Integration," in Shahid Yusfu, M. Anjum Altaf, and Kaoru Nabeshima, eds., *Global Production Networking and Technological Change in East Asia* (Washington, D.C.: World Bank, 2004), pp. 255–296. See also Ge and Fujimoto, 2005.

61. I conducted interviews at Lifan, Zongshen, and Jialing in 1999, a period of intensive growth in the sector in Chongqing. Now, the city accounts for 25 percent of all motorcycle production in China and claims some 959 separate firms engaged in transportation-related production. Output and enterprise data from *Chongqing Statistical Yearbook 2008* via *China Data Online*.

62. Ge and Fujimoto, 2005.

63. Ge and Fujimoto, 2005, discuss this process elegantly. I was also able to witness this process under way even in the late 1990s in firms like Lifan and Zongshen.

64. Todd Zaun and Karby Leggett, "Road Warriors: Motorcycle Makers from Japan Discover Piracy Made in China," *The Wall Street Journal*, July 25, 2001; Sadanand

Dhume, "Road Warriors: In Indonesia, Chinese Motorcycle Manufacturers Are Challenging the Japanese for a Slice of the Market," *The Far Eastern Economic Review* (December 27, 2001).

65. Interview, major European automotive design consultancy that does contract work for Chinese assemblers, 2007.

66. Jeffrey T. Macher and David C. Mowery, eds., *Innovation in Global Industries: U.S. Firms Competing in a New World* (Washington, D.C.: National Academies Press, 2009), p. 11.

67. Clayton M. Christensen, *The Innovator's Dilemma* (Cambridge, Mass.: Harvard University Press, 1997). The point is also discussed with relevance to China in Steinfeld, 2004. See also Carliss Y. Baldwin and Kim B. Clark, *Design Rules: The Power of Modularity* (Cambridge, Mass.: MIT Press, 2000); Masahiko Aoki and Hirokazu Takizawa, *Modularity: Its Relevance to Industrial Architecture.* Paper prepared for the Conference on Innovation within Firms, Saint-Gobain Centre for Economic Research, Paris, November 2002.

68. Michael Kanellos, "IBM's Racetrack Memory Seeks 100x Boost in Density," *CNET News*, April 10, 2008, http://news.cnet.com/8301-10784_3-9915449-7.html?tag=mncol; John Markoff, "Reshaping the Architecture of Memory," *The New York Times*, September 11, 2007.

69. For a discussion along similar lines, see Saul Hansell, "How Apple Keeps Its Value," *The New York Times*, October 23, 2007.

70. See Charles H. Fine, *Clockspeed: Winning Industry Control in the Age of Temporary Advantage* (Reading, Mass.: Perseus, 1998).

Chapter 5

1. Dani Rodrik, *One Economics, Many Recipes: Globalization, Institutions, and Economic Growth* (Princeton, N.J.: Princeton University Press, 2008).

2. Yasheng Huang, *Capitalism with Chinese Characteristics: Entrepreneurship and the State* (New York: Cambridge University Press, 2008).

3. Data from State Statistical Bureau, *China Statistical Yearbook 1990* (Beijing: State Statistical Press, 1990), p. 412.

4. See National Bureau of Statistics, *China Statistical Yearbook 2008* (Beijing: China Statistics Press, 2008).

5. See Yasheng Huang, *Selling China: Foreign Direct Investment During the Reform Era* (New York: Cambridge University Press, 2003).

6. Janos Kornai, "What the Change of System from Socialism to Capitalism Does and Does Not Mean," *Journal of Economic Perspectives*, 14, no. 1 (2000), pp. 27–42.

7. This point is made by Mary Gallagher in her book *Contagious Capitalism: Globalization and the Politics of Labor in China* (Princeton, N.J.: Princeton University Press, 2007).

8. A variety of excellent scholarly works have been written on the topic. See, for example, Stanley Lubman, *Bird in a Cage: Legal Reform in China After Mao* (Stanford, Cal.: Stanford University Press, 2000); Randall Peerenboom, *China's Long March Toward Rule of Law* (New York: Cambridge University Press, 2002);

C. Stephen Hsu, ed., *Understanding China's Legal System: Essays in Honor of Jerome A. Cohen* (New York: New York University Press, 2003).

9. Mary Gallagher makes a similar argument in her work on labor relations in China. See Gallagher, 2007.

10. Ministry of Foreign Trade and Economic Cooperation of the People's Republic of China, *China—Labor Law, 1994*, 1994. Available in English online through lexmercatoria.com, http://www.jus.uio.no/lm/china.labor.law.1994/sisu_manifest.html. For the most recent revision, see Zhonghua Renmin Gongheguo Renli Ziyuan he Shehui Baozhang Bu [Ministry of Human Resources and Social Security of the People's Republic of China], *Zhonghua Renmin Gongheguo Gongwu Yuanfa (Labor Law of the People's Republic of China]*, April 27, 2005. Available in Chinese at http://www.mohrss.gov.cn/Desktop.aspx?PATH=/sy/ztzl/gwyf/gwyfqw.

11. Interviews, Wenzhou, 2003.

12. Interviews, Shanghai, 1999; Wenzhou, Hangzhou, Ningbo, 2003.

13. Although in many firms using migrant workers from other (primarily rural) regions, the labor force often enters through deals brokered by quasi-official employment agencies from their home localities. Many of the foreign-owned manufacturing operations in South China operate in this fashion.

14. Mary E. Gallagher, "'Use the Law as Your Weapon!' Institutional Change and Legal Mobilization in China," in Neil Diamant, Stanley Lubman, and Kevin O'Brien, eds., *Engaging Chinese Law* (Stanford, Cal.: Stanford University Press, 2005).

15. National Bureau of Statistics, 2008.

16. For a description of the double airlock system, see Nicholas R. Lardy, "Chinese Foreign Trade," *The China Quarterly*, no. 131 (September 1992), pp. 691–720.

17. Gang Yi, "Renminbi Exchange Rates and Relevant Institutional Factors," *The Cato Journal* (March 22, 2008), p. 188.

18. As Alice Amsden points out, a key feature of South Korean developmental strategy involved the government's maintenance of multiple prices for foreign exchange. See Alice Amsden, *Asia's Next Giant: South Korea and Late Industrialization* (New York: Oxford University Press, 1992).

19. In fact, the situation would be more complicated than that because falling dollar values would also reduce input costs for China-based manufacturers, who—as discussed earlier—are highly dependent on imported, high-end componentry.

20. Yi, 2008, pp. 194–195.

21. For an extensive and more technical discussion of this process, see Brad Stetser and Arpana Pandey, *China's $1.5 Trillion Bet: Understanding China's External Portfolio*, Council on Foreign Relations Center for Geoeconomic Studies Working Paper, May 2009, pp. 364–395; Wayne M. Morrison and Marc Labonte, *China's Holding of U.S. Securities: Implications for the U.S. Economy*, Congressional Research Service, January 9, 2008.

22. Setser and Pandey, 2009, p. 1.

23. Yi, 2008, pp. 195–196.

Chapter 6

1. Organisation for Economic Co-Operation and Development, *OECD Reviews of Innovation Policy: China* (Paris: OECD Publishing, 2008), p. 49.

2. OECD, 2008, p. 49.

3. OECD, 2008, p. 49.

4. Magnus Karlsson, ed., *The Internationalization of Corporate R&D: Leveraging the Changing Geography of Innovation* (Stockholm: Swedish Institute for Growth Policy Studies, 2006), p. 231.

5. Data from Table 4.8 in Denis Fred Simon and Cong Cao, *China's Emerging Technological Edge* (New York: Cambridge University Press, 2009), pp. 146–147.

6. Karlsson, 2006, p. 231.

7. Company information from www.huawei.com. For interesting discussions of Huawei, see Arthur Kroeber, "China's Push to Innovate in Information Technology," in Linda Jakobson, ed., *Innovation with Chinese Characteristics* (London: Palgrave, 2007) pp. 37–70; Dieter Ernst, *A New Geography of Knowledge? Asia's Role in Global Innovation Networks,* (Honolulu, HI: East-West Center, 2009), pp. 30–31.

8. Company information from www.lenovo.com.

9. Google in 2010 captured headlines when it announced that it services (Gmail, primarily) had been the victim of cyber attacks originating from China, and that in response it would no longer accept Chinese governmental content restrictions (censorship, basically) on the company's Chinese language search engine (google. cn). The story was generally presented as Google versus China. It is worth noting, though, that despite the tense relationship between Google and the Chinese government, and despite Google's complaints about China-based hackers, Google has also been able to integrate a China-based R&D center into the company's broader R&D efforts worldwide.

10. Simon and Cao, p. 32.

11. For the commission's charter, see http://www.uscc.gov/about/charter.php.

12. U.S.–China Economic and Security Review Commission (USCC), *2008 Report to Congress* (Washington, D.C.: U.S. Government Printing Office, 2008), p. 82, www.uscc.gov.

13. USCC, 2008, p. 70.

14. USCC, 2008, p. 70.

15. USCC, 2008, p. 82.

16. USCC, 2008, p. 73.

17. USCC, 2008, p. 82.

18. OECD, 2008, p. 46. See also, Simon and Cao, 2009, p. 164.

19. Organisation for Economic Co-Operation and Development, *Main Science and Technology Indicators,* Vol. 2009/2 (Paris: OECD Publishing, 2010), pp. 24–25. See also Linda Jakobson, "China Aims High in Science and Technology," in Linda Jakobson, ed., *Innovation with Chinese Characteristics* (London: Palgrave, 2007), p. 12.

20. OECD, 2008, p. 49.

21. "Chuangxin Zhongguo lu zai hefang?" ["Where Is the Path to an Innovative China?"], *Caijing*, September 4, 2007.

22. Simon and Cao, 2009, pp. 158–165.

23. *Caijing*, 2007.

24. This point has been made in several public settings by Xue Lan, professor and associate executive dean, Tsinghua University School of Public Policy and Management. See *Caijing*, 2007.

25. Questions about the appropriate level of innovation for a given country at a given level of development, although interesting, are totally unresolved in the literature. Assessments of innovation policy, whether for developing or advanced industrial nations, often jump quickly to the conclusion that innovation is somehow lacking and then offer prescriptive suggestions about how the situation can be improved.

26. In addition to my own work on Chinese enterprise development, I have benefited enormously from participation in collaborative research endeavors at MIT. Elements of this chapter draw on field interviews conducted by me and my colleagues (Richard Lester and Edward Cunningham, in particular) in the MIT Industrial Performance Center's China Energy Group. To an even greater degree, this chapter draws on enterprise-level interviews conducted in both Europe and China in 2007 by a team of colleagues from the MIT Political Science Department and MIT Sloan School of Management. In addition to me, that team included Suzanne Berger, Yasheng Huang, and Rachel Wellhausen. Funding for that particular project in 2007 was generously provided by the Essonne Development Agency (l'Agence pour l'Economie en Essonne) of the government of France.

27. For a general discussion, see Karlsson, 2006, pp. 27–29; United Nations Conference on Trade and Development (UNCTAD), *World Investment Report 2005: Transnational Corporations and the Internationalization of R&D* (New York and Geneva: United Nations, 2005).

28. UNCTAD, 2005, pp. 105–106.

29. Ernst, 2009, p. 11.

30. UNCTAD, 2005, p. 119.

31. UNCTAD, 2005, p. 119.

32. This three-way categorization, frequently used by people carrying out R&D at the corporate level, was expressed most clearly to me during an interview with a research director at a major global telecommunications firm (interview, telecommunications company A, Europe, 2007). The view travels across a number of industries, but the reader should be aware that the respondent raised it in the context of telecommunications equipment provision. For a slightly different scholarly take that employs four rather than three categories, see Ernst, 2009, pp. 4–7.

33. Interviews, Institute of Nuclear and New Energy Technology, Tsinghua University, July 2006; Chinergy (the joint venture between Tsinghua University and the China Nuclear Engineering and Construction Corporation charged with building the HTR demonstration reactor in Shandong), July 2006.

34. This kind of R&D often combines what Richard Lester and Michael Piore term "analytical" and "interpretive" approaches to innovation. The analytical approach, through a hierarchical distribution of tasks, seeks to meet a specific need such as an existing demand in the marketplace. The interpretive approach is much looser, often involving interactions with multiple stakeholders (including consumers), and an effort to provide consumers with projects they could never on their own imagine but which enable them to live more closely to their ultimate aspirations. See Richard K. Lester and Michael J. Piore, *Innovation—The Missing Dimension* (Cambridge, Mass.: Harvard University Press, 2004).

35. Interview, multinational electronics and mission-critical systems provider A, Europe, 2007.

36. Interview, multinational telecommunications company B, Cambridge, 1999.

37. Interview, multinational automotive component and subsystem provider, Europe, 2007.

38. Interview, multinational cosmetics company, China, 2007.

39. Interviews, multinational pharmaceutical A, Europe, 2007; multinational pharmaceutical B, China, 2007; multinational pharmaceutical C, China, 2007.

40. See "New Medicine for China," *Caijing*, January 12, 2008; David Blumenthal and William Hsiao, "Privatization and Its Discontents—The Evolving Chinese Health Care System," *The New England Journal of Medicine*, 353, no. 11 (September 2005), pp. 1165–1170; Andrew Browne, "Costly Cure: In China, Preventive Medicine Pits Doctor Against System, *The Wall Street Journal*, January 16, 2007.

41. Interview, multinational medical device manufacturer, Cambridge, 2000; multinational pharmaceutical B, China, 2007; multinational pharmaceutical C, China, 2007.

42. Interview, multinational pharmaceutical B, China, 2007.

43. This point was underscored to the author in an interview with an R&D director at a major multinational telecommunications equipment provider (multinational telecommunications company C), Europe, 2007.

44. This discussion draws on interviews with telecommunications equipment providers network operators in Europe and China, 2007.

45. Interview, multinational telecommunications equipment provider C, Europe, 2007.

46. Interview, European aerospace company A, Europe, 2007.

47. Interview, multinational telecommunications company C, Europe, 2007.

48. Interview, multinational telecommunications company C, Europe, 2007.

49. Interview, multinational telecommunications company A, China, 2007.

50. Interview, multinational pharmaceutical B, China, 2007.

51. Interview, multinational electronics and mission-critical systems provider A, Europe, 2007; multinational electronics and mission-critical systems provider A, China, 2007.

52. This is an interesting example of how IBM has moved out of the production of boxes—that is, personal computers, desktop computers, and so on—and into the creation of highly specialized software applications for corporate customers. IBM,

like its competitors, wants its proprietary products to be the ones enabling global business operations.

53. Interview, multinational telecommunications company C, China, 2007.

54. Simon and Cao, 2009, p. 290.

55. Interview, multinational business software developer, China, 2007. Another respondent, a multinational mobile phone handset maker with operations in a second-tier Chinese city, noted that it can attract only local talent and could never hope to attract somebody from Tsinghua or Shanghai Jiaotong.

56. Interview, S&T policy expert, Tsinghua University, 2008.

57. Interview, multinational telecommunications company C, China, 2007.

58. To some extent, this mirrors the situation in global production more generally. For example, IBM has ceded box making—in this case, computer production—to Lenovo, but IBM has scrambled forward into high-end software solutions.

59. In network security systems, for example, Huawei has partnered with Symantec. Huawei provides the physical equipment—routers, in this case—but Symantec provides the network security software.

60. Interview, Europe, 2007.

61. Data from International Atomic Energy Agency, http://www.iaea.or.at/programmes/a2/.

62. For more extensive discussion of this expansion, see Edward S. Steinfeld, Richard Lester, and Edward A. Cunningham, "Greener Plants, Grayer Skies: A Report from the Front Lines of China's Energy Sector," *Energy Policy*, 37, no. 5 (May 2009), pp. 1809–1824; Edward S. Steinfeld and Richard K. Lester, "China's Real Energy Crisis," *Harvard Asia Pacific Review*, 9, no. 1 (Winter 2007). Daniel Rosen and Tevor Houser, "China Energy: A Guide for the Perplexed," *China Balance Sheet* (Washington, D.C.: Center for Strategic and International Studies and the Peterson Institute for International Economics, May 2007).

63. For detailed statistics on power generation in China, see Guojia Dianli Xinxi Wang [State Power Information Network], *Quanguo dianli tongji shuju [National Electric Power Statistical Data]*, http://www.sp.com.cn/dlsc/dltj/.

64. In interviews in 2006 with officials from the Chinese central government's National Development and Reform Commission (NDRC), Energy Research Institute (ERI), this author was told of the forty-GW goal. In 2008, NDRC Vice Minister Zhang Guobao was widely reported as saying that, given the pace of new construction, the actual level may end up at sixty GW. China today has eleven plants in operation and fourteen under construction.

65. This discussion is based on interviews conducted in 2005 and 2006 with officials and analysts at the Chinese government's Energy Research Institute and Development Reform Commission and Tsinghua University's Institute of Nuclear and New Energy Technology.

66. Interviews, Beijing, 2006.

67. Interview, global energy company A, Europe, 2007.

68. Interview, global energy company A, Europe, 2007.

69. In other words, power might have to be generated in locales geologically suited for underground injection of carbon. For more extensive discussion of these issues, see *MIT Study on the Future of Coal: Options for a Carbon-Constrained World*, Massachusetts Institute of Technology, 2007, http://web.mit.edu/coal/.

70. This discussion draws on the author and his colleagues' extensive quantitative and qualitative field research. See Steinfeld, Lester, and Cunningham, 2009, pp. 1809–1824.

71. For a provocative discussion of the interaction between competitive markets and such protected spaces, see Lester and Piore, 2004.

72. Professor Erica Fuchs of Carnegie Mellon University, in her pioneering work on the geography of product design, makes a similar point about the offshoring of manufacturing. See Erica Fuchs et al., "Strategic Materials Selection in the Automotive Body: Economic Opportunities for Polymer Composite Design," *Composite Science and Technology*, 68, no. 9 (2008), pp. 1989–2002.

73. Interview, multinational telecommunications company A, China, 2007.

74. For an exception and a somewhat different view on the matter, see Keith Bradsher, "China Builds High Wall to Guard Energy Industry," *The New York Times*, July 13, 2009.

Chapter 7

1. Unocal's management accepted Chevron's bid in early April. The Unocal board of directors endorsed the bid, but at the time CNOOC extended its own offer in June, Unocal shareholders had still not yet voted on whether to accept Chevron's earlier bid. Thus, even though Unocal management appears to have courted the CNOOC counteroffer, because the offer was never endorsed by the Unocal board of directors, it technically amounted to a hostile takeover attempt.

2. See United States Department of Energy, Energy Information Administration, *A Primer on Gasoline Prices*, May 2006, http://www.eia.doe.gov/pub/oil_gas/ petroleum/analysis_publications/primer_on_gasoline_prices/html/petbro.html.

3. *Zhongguo Nengyuan Tongji Nianjian 2007 [China Energy Statistics Yearbook 2007]*, Table 5–7 Fen hangye yuanyou xiaofei zongliang [Consumption of Crude Oil and Its Main Varieties by Sector].

4. See, for example, James A. Dorn, *U.S.–China Relations in the Wake of CNOOC*, Policy Analysis 553, CATO Institute, November 2, 2005.

5. Steve Lohr, "Unocal Bid Denounced at Hearing," *The New York Times*, July 14, 2005.

6. Lohr, 2005.

7. United States House of Representatives, H. Res. 344, June 30, 2005.

8. CNOOC is formally listed on the Hong Kong Stock Exchange, and its shares— typical for foreign firms colisted on the New York Stock Exchange (NYSE)—are available for purchase in the United States as American despository shares (ADSs). When bought on the NYSE, the Hong Kong-listed common stock is held by an American bank in a custodial account on behalf of the investor, who is then issued American depository receipts (ADRs) to reflect the asset holding.

9. The honorarium was US$5,000, a sum that remained constant throughout my time on the board.

10. For an extensive and excellent analysis of reform in China's oil industry, see Jin Zhang, *Catch-Up and Competitiveness in China: The Case of Large Firms in the Oil Industry* (London: RoutledgeCurzon, 2004).

11. The policy, to the extent it could be considered as such, emerged in 1993 and 1994 and was termed "grasping the large and releasing the small" (*zhua da fang xiao*).

12. These 150 central SOEs are defined as such because, at least officially, they are under the direct supervision of the central government's State-Owned Assets Supervision and Administration Commission, an agency established in 2003. For more information, see www.sasac.gov.cn.

13. Geoff Dyer and Richard McGregor, "China's Champions, Why State Ownership Is No Longer Proving a Dead Hand," *The Financial Times*, March 17, 2008, p. 7.

14. The clearest contemporary account of this effort, published just as the reforms were gaining steam, was written in 1993 by economist Jinglian Wu, an extremely influential scholar and governmental policy adviser in China. See Jinglian Wu, *Dazhongxing qiye gaige: jianli xiandai qiye zhidu [Large and Medium-Size Enterprise Reform: Establishing a Modern Enterprise System]* (Tianjin: Tianjin Renmin Chubanshe, 1993).

15. In the terminology of the global oil and gas industry, exploration and production (E&P) pertains to the activity of getting the resource out of the ground. It is the upstream part of the supply chain. Once extracted, those resources then need to be transformed into refined products. Refining is generally understood as midstream in the overall supply chain. Then, those refined products need to be marketed to final consumers. Marketing and distribution, including the ownership of things like gas (petroleum) stations, are considered the downstream part of the oil industry. At various points in time, depending in part on the global price of crude oil, some parts of the overall supply chain may be far more profitable than others. Though CNOOC is concentrated primarily in upstream E&P it has moved into midstream activities like refining in recent years.

16. According to CNOOC Ltd.'s 2008 annual report, the firm had 3,584 employees (compared to the CNOOC Group's 57,000). See CNOOC Limited, *A Clear Vision of the Future*, Annual Report 2008, www.cnoocltd.com.

17. See Stephen Green, *The Privatisation Two-Step at China's Listed Firms*, Chatham House, China Project Working Paper 3, 2004.

18. The Hong Kong Stock Exchange publishes its listing rules in a two-volume book available online. See Hong Kong Stock Exchange, *Rules Governing the Listing of Securities on the Stock Exchange of Hong Kong Limited*, Update no. 92, September 2009, http://www.hkex.com.hk/rule/listrules/vol11_1.htm. This book will hereafter be termed HKSE, 2009.

19. HKSE, chapter 3 ("General: Authorized Representatives and Directors"), 2009, p. 3.

20. By 2008, the board of directors had grown to twelve members: three executive directors (senior CNOOC managers), four nonexecutive directors (affiliates of CNOOC or its supervisory agencies), and five independent nonexecutive directors.

21. Zhu Rongji, in an April 1999 speech at MIT, explicitly called on China's "best and brightest," its young people studying and working in the United States, to return home to take up important positions. Moreover, he promised that they would be compensated at globally competitive levels.

22. CNOOC Ltd. is a good example. According to the company's public filing with the U.S. Securities and Exchange Commission in 2004, the period just prior to the takeover bid for Unocal, CNOOC Ltd.'s top five executives received salaries ranging from just over US$1,000,000 to US$350,000. See CNOOC Ltd., Form 20-F, filed June 22, 2005. Note: SEC filings are public and available free online through the agency's Electronic Data Gathering, Analysis, and Retrieval System (EDGAR). See http://www.sec.gov/edgar/aboutedgar.htm.

23. See, for example, the Web site of Hong Kong resident David Webb, http://www.webb-site.com/pages/aboutus.asp.

24. The Stock Exchange of Hong Kong, "The Listing Committee of the Stock Exchange of Hong Kong Limited censures CNOOC Limited (the Company) for breaching paragraph 2 of the then Listing Agreement and the then Rule 14.26(6) of the Exchange Listing Rules," October 6, 2005.

25. These accounts cite truisms—that is, that CNOOC Ltd. is the subsidiary of a wholly state-owned firm or that the chairman of CNOOC Ltd. is also the party secretary of the CNOOC Group—and then make the intellectual leap of assuming those truisms prove Chinese governmental involvement in the firm's commercial activities.

26. CNOOC Ltd., SEC Form 20-F, June 22, 2005.

27. CNOOC Ltd., SEC Form 20-F, June 22, 2005.

28. In a January 13, 2005 press release—also reported to the SEC as a Form 6-K on the same date ("Report of Foreign Private Issuer Pursuant to Rule 13a-16 or 15d-16 of the Securities Exchange Act of 1934)—CNOOC Ltd. announced that CNOOC Gas & Power Ltd., a wholly owned subsidiary of the CNOOC Group (CNOOC Ltd.'s parent company), had entered an agreement with China's Shenergy Group to codevelop an LNG terminal in Shanghai. Shenergy, listed on the Shanghai Stock Exchange, is a majority state-owned energy infrastructure investment company with strong ties to the Shanghai provincial government.

29. The chronology presented here, unless otherwise noted, is drawn directly from Unocal's SEC filing Form DEFM 14A, July 1, 2005. The chronology, therefore, represents Unocal's account of how its acquisition by Chevron unfolded.

30. This firm was subsequently identified in the U.S. press as Eni, the partially state-owned Italian energy company.

31. In its SEC Form DEFM 14A, Unocal notes that CNOOC's chairman communicated to a senior Unocal executive on June 1 that a takeover proposal would be forthcoming in the next few days.

32. CNOOC Ltd., SEC Form 6-K, June 23, 2005.

33. A "major" acquisition is defined as one worth between 25 percent and 100 percent of the listed issuer's total assets. A "very substantial" acquisition is worth more than

100 percent of the issuer's total assets. CNOOC's acquisition of Unocal would be just on the border between the two. See HKSE, chapter 14, 2009, p. 9.

34. HKSE, chapter 14, 2009, p. 9.
35. See HKSE, chapter 14A, 2009.
36. HKSE, chapter 14A, 2009, p. 10.
37. HKSE, chapter 13, 2009, p. 9.
38. CNOOC Ltd., SEC Form 6-K, June 23, 2005.
39. CNOOC Ltd., SEC Form 6-K, June 23, 2005.

Chapter 8

1. The discussion of Taiwan that follows, in addition to drawing on the author's personal experiences conducting research there, relies extensively on a number of excellent works that have been written about the island in recent years. I have found the following particularly insightful and provocative: Denny Roy, *Taiwan: A Political History* (Ithaca, N.Y.: Cornell University Press, 2003); Alan M. Wachman, *Taiwan: National Identity and Democratization* (Armonk, N.Y.: M. E. Sharpe, 1997); Shelley Rigger, *Politics in Taiwan* (New York: Routledge, 1999); Murray A. Rubinstein, ed., *Taiwan: A New History* (Armonk, N.Y.: M. E. Sharpe, 1999); David Shambaugh, ed., *Contemporary Taiwan* (New York: Oxford University Press, 1998); Jonathan Manthorpe, *Forbidden Nation: A History of Taiwan* (New York: Palgrave Macmillan, 2008); Dafydd Fell, *Party Politics in Taiwan* (London: Routledge, 2005).

2. Council for Cultural Affairs, "Green Island Human Rights Memorial Park," Explanatory Guide, 2008.

3. For an excellent summary of this incident, see Roy, 2003, pp. 167–170.

4. Roy, 2003, p. 169.

5. For a discussion of personnel flows between Silicon Valley and Taiwan, see AnnaLee Saxenian, *The New Argonauts: Regional Advantage in a Global Economy* (Cambridge, Mass.: Harvard University Press, 2007).

6. The per capita income statistic is taken from the CIA's online *World Factbook*, https://www.cia.gov/library/publications/the-world-factbook/geos/tw.html. In terms of its diplomatic status, Taiwan (the Republic of China) is officially recognized today by twenty-three nations, among them Palau, Haiti, Panama, Burkina Faso, St. Kitts and Nevis, and Tuvalu. No major global power recognizes the Republic of China on Taiwan as either an independent sovereign entity or the legitimate government of all of China.

7. The per capita income statistic here is based on the *World Bank's Atlas* methodology. The World Bank's calculation of Chinese per capita income in purchasing power parity terms is US$6,020, roughly the same level the CIA's *World Factbook* cites for Chinese per capita income. See World Bank, *World Development Indicators Database*, July 2009, www.worldbank.org; Central Intelligence Agency, *World Factbook*, 2009, https://www.cia.gov/library/publications/the-world-factbook/geos/ch.html.

8. For interesting perspectives on the democratization of Leninist parties, see Edward Friedman and Joseph Wong, eds., *Political Transitions in Dominant Party Systems: Learning to Lose* (London: Routledge, 2008); Bruce J. Dickson, *Democratization in China and Taiwan: The Adaptability of Leninist Parties* (New York: Oxford University Press, 1998).

9. The term "rightful" resistance is taken from Kevin O'Brien and Liangjiang Li, *Rightful Resistance in Rural China* (Cambridge: Cambridge University Press, 2006).

10. On the notion of flexible authoritarianism, extremely interesting perspectives— speculative but based on extensive empirical investigation—can be found in David Shambaugh, *China's Communist Party: Atrophy and Adaptation* (Berkeley: University of California Press, 2009); Andrew J. Nathan, "Present at the Stagnation," *Foreign Affairs*, 85, no. 4 (July/August 2006), p. 177.

11. For example, see Jonathan Ansfield, "China Web Sites Seeking Users' Names," *The New York Times*, September 5, 2009.

12. The term is taken from Francis Fukuyama, *The End of History and the Last Man* (New York: Free Press, 1992).

Index

Note: Page numbers followed by *f* denote figures.

United States, 8–9, 15, 18–19, 30, 39, 75, 113, 149, 231–32
University of California, Irvine, 86
Unocal, 176–77, 254n1 (*see also* China National Offshore Oil Corporation (CNOOC))
upward commodification, of firms, 104–10
urban Chinese society, 4
urban citizens, of China, 2
U.S. auto industry, 83
U.S. based software developers, 118
U.S. Securities and Exchange Commission, 35
U.S. Steel, 84
U.S.–China Economic and Security Review Commission (USCC), 143
U.S Federal Reserve System, 131

Verizon, 154
Vietnam, 97, 99

Wal-Mart, 93, 96
Washington consensus, 54
Wen Jiabao, 14, 38, 51
Western Europe, 19
Western political tradition, 38–39
wholly foreign-owned firms, 7
Woolsey, R. James, 178
World Trade Organization (WTO), 29, 58
WTO accession agreement, 29

xiaokang, 11–12

Y-10, 84
Yamaha, 106
Yan Fu, 65
Yi Gang, 136, 238n13
Yiwu City, 96

Zhu Rongji, 29, 32, 38, 51, 56, 58
ZTE, 84